Religious Studies, Theology, and the University

Religious Studies, Theology, and the University

Conflicting Maps, Changing Terrain

Edited by
Linell E. Cady
and
Delwin Brown

State University of New York Press

Published by
State University of New York Press, Albany

For information, address State University of New York Press,
90 State Street, Suite 700, Albany, NY 12207

Production by Judith Block
Marketing by Anne Valentine

Library of Congress Cataloging-in-Publication Data

Religious studies, theology, and the university : conflicting maps, changing terrain /
edited by Linell E. Cady and Delwin Brown.
   p. cm.
  Includes bibliographical references and index.
  ISBN 0-7914-5521-1 (alk. paper) — ISBN 0-7914-5522-X (pbk. : alk. paper)
   1. Theology—Study and teaching. I. Cady, Linell Elizabeth, 1952– II. Brown, Delwin,
1935–

BV4020 .R38 2002
200'.71'1—dc21

2002021088

10 9 8 7 6 5 4 3 2 1

To our colleagues, past and present,
in the Department of Religious Studies
at Arizona State University,
whose challenges prompted us to think
about the issues addressed in this book.

Contents

Preface

Our interest in the relationship between religious studies and theology goes back many years, as does our intention to coedit a volume of essays on the topic. The issues discussed in these essays are not merely academic or theoretical for either of us. They became very central, even urgent, issues as a result of a shared history. We were both trained in theology, and we both took a position in the Department of Religious Studies at Arizona State University. Delwin Brown was there from 1975–1983, and Linell Cady was hired to replace him when he left to teach at Iliff School of Theology. Our dual experience in the world of theological studies and in the world of religious studies proved to be illuminating for the light it shed on their mutual identities, and troubling for the tensions it generated. The intellectual and existential challenges involved in negotiating these disciplinary traditions has been a shared interest ever since. This project stems from our conviction that the issues generated by our personal situations have much broader import for religious studies and theology.

Although the relationship between religious studies and theology has been explored in the past, the changing intellectual and social context has posed this issue anew and with considerable urgency. The current debate has generated new takes on the disciplinary landscape. Although the focus of this collection is on the border between religious studies and theology, the implications for the evolving shape of each field are considerably more extensive. Far from speaking with one voice, this volume reflects a broad range of positions on the appropriate place of theology, if any, in secular institutions of American higher education. We want to express our thanks first and foremost to the authors of these essays for their interest and patience in bringing this project to completion. We also want to thank Deborah Creamer, a doctoral candidate in the Joint Ph.D. Program at Iliff School of Theology and the University of Denver, for her research assistance in completing the Bibliography and to Roxana Martin for her gracious help in preparing the manuscript for production.

The essays in this volume are published here for the first time, with the exception of Paula Cooey's contribution, "The Place of Academic Theology in the

Study of Religion from the Perspective of Liberal Education." This was previously published as "Fiddling While Rome Burns: The Place of Academic Theology in the Study of Religion" in *Harvard Theological Review* 92:4 (1999). (Copyright 1999 by the President and Fellows of Harvard College. Reprinted by permission.)

1

Introduction

LINELL E. CADY AND DELWIN BROWN

The North American debate over the relationship between theology and religious studies, and their appropriate institutional location, sometimes feels interminable. It flares up periodically, generating much heat and caricatured polemics. But no one seems to change positions, institutions appear unaffected, and there is little sense of progress, let alone closure. Why bother, one might ask, if a stalemate is the most that can be reasonably expected?

Although understandable, even tempting, such a conclusion fails to recognize the sense in which this episodic conversation is a ritual enactment of disciplinary identity and boundaries. It serves as an occasion for thinking through the nature and aims of forms of inquiry with close, even overlapping, historical lineages. Indeed, it is their tangled histories that make it all the more pressing to reflect on their similarities and their differences. Moreover, the apparent stalemate is the product of a lens with too low a magnification, one unable to detect the changes in the conversation, the shifting assumptions, contextual pressures, and anxieties that fuel its resumption. Although the most recent interchange shows few signs of resolving the argument, its permutations are revealing. They indicate shifting intellectual and social currents that have reinvigorated the conversation, destabilizing the borders that have defined the mutually articulated identities of religious studies and theology.[1]

There are a number of signs that point toward a reeruption of hostilities along the borders of religious studies and theology. Consider, for example, the cover article in a 1996 issue of *Lingua Franca* suggesting that a new movement is forming within religious studies, one that aims to sweep out the theologians whose presence continues—allegedly—to pollute departments of religious studies, decades after their post World War II emergence. Summarizing the article entitled "Is Nothing Sacred? Casting Out the Gods from Religious Studies," the editors write: "For years, religious studies departments have offered an awkward mix of social science and spiritual instruction. Now, a renegade group of scholars seeks to drive the theologians from the classroom."[2] This article is revealing, but not because it alerts us to a newly emerging battle between religious studies and theology. Quite

1

the contrary. The "renegade scholars" to whom *Lingua Franca* alludes, far from representing a newly formed vanguard, actually stand squarely under the modernist
banner. The modernist perspective has dominated the intellectual and institutional
landscape in this century, and its characteristic accents are clearly discernible in the
way the renegade scholars construct the respective identities and borders of religious studies and theology. Religious studies, sharply differentiated from theology,
is construed as a social science that belongs within the university. Theology, on the
other hand, is viewed as a form of spiritual instruction that belongs within an ecclesiastical or religious community concerned with personal formation. The presumption is that religious studies is (or more accurately, perhaps, should exclusively
be) an objective, empirical form of study, and theology a subjective, religious activity. This mutually defining dialectic, or close variants, has provided the basis for the
self-understanding and justification of religious studies within the modern university; legitimated the displacement or marginalization of theology from the university to the seminary or divinity school; and, in consequence, heavily influenced the
character and conversation partners of theology in the modern period. The *Lingua
Franca* article does not capture a novel development along the embattled frontiers
of theology and religious studies, but directs our attention to renewed efforts to for-
tify the identities and borders between these long-standing antagonists.

Although part of a much older story, the timing and tenor of this recent chapter are revealing. The waning of the modernist paradigm that has dominated intellectual and institutional life throughout the twentieth century has proved very
unsettling to the established identities, aims, and presumed publics of the academic
disciplines. This may be especially the case with the fields of religious studies and
theology, given the central role that the mutually reinforcing constructions of
"modernity" and "religion" have played in determining the contours and location
of these intellectual traditions. This can most readily be seen by considering, if only
briefly, the historical trajectories of theology and the much younger academic
study of religion.

A Historical Overview

The multiple strands that constitute the discipline of theology, and that account
for its contemporary diffuseness, are a product of its long, variegated history. In its
earliest period, Christian theology was primarily construed as a form of wisdom,
as salvific knowledge of God associated with the faithful orientation of the self. It
typically assumed the form of biblical commentary, an exercise that was governed
by certain assumptions regarding the revelatory character of the Scriptures. It was
conducted in the service of the church and reflection was deeply integrated with
individual and communal piety. Although there were antecedents in the first mil-
lennia, the sense of theology as a discipline gradually emerged with the rise of the
medieval universities in the twelfth and thirteenth centuries. Relying on methods

of dialectical reasoning, this theological genre privileged the systematic, logical study of religious doctrines and beliefs. Although harboring significant critical potential, this form of theology was rooted in a fundamental confidence in the ultimate congruence of reason and revelation. So long as Christendom reigned, then, both senses of theology persisted in close alliance, despite periodic skirmishes over the relative priority of each sense, and the most appropriate institutional location—university or monastery—for its cultivation. Theology's status as "queen of the sciences" of the medieval university was attributable to the mix of elements that constituted it: a discipline with a distinctive method; the revelatory status of its principles; and its governing purpose in providing salvific knowledge.[3]

The dethronement of theology was directly correlated with the erosion of Christendom and the rise of the modern university rooted in Enlightenment ideals. These developments fundamentally undermined the sources and norms operative in theological reflection. Classical Christian theology operated, as Edward Farley puts it, within a "framework of authority," evident in the fact that "what settled the disputes and grounded the judgments were not so much evidence-gathering inquiries as appeals to some entity, place, or person which was regarded as authoritative."[4] This mode of intellectual reflection appeared less and less legitimate as the authorities were increasingly contested, and, even more fundamentally, new intellectual ideals gained ascendancy. In Van Harvey's classic account of this transformation, the transition to modernity is marked by "a new morality of critical judgment that has seized the imagination of the scholar in the Western world" and it stands in marked contrast to the "ethic of belief that dominated Christendom for centuries."[5] The new intellectual ideals included a commitment to the autonomy of the scholar, open inquiry, and, under the increasing influence of the sciences, empirical studies. With this revolutionary shift, theology not only lost its position of privilege, but was increasingly attacked for its lack of intellectual legitimacy. Theology's identification with a particular tradition, its appeal to ecclesiastical and/or scriptural authorities, and its apparent lack of empirical warrants precluded its status as an academic inquiry within the Enlightenment ethos.

Immanuel Kant was particularly influential in exposing the fatal deficiencies of theology as an academic discipline within this shifting intellectual paradigm. His revolutionary call daring scholars to think independently, combined with his epistemological critique of metaphysics, challenged the very presence of theology within the intellectual core of the university. Kant proved equally influential in determining the new location of theology within this intellectual milieu as he entered the debate over the appropriate missions of the various faculties within the university. In *The Conflict of the Faculties*, Kant essentially distinguished the philosophical, or what we would call the liberal arts, faculty from the professional faculties of law, medicine, and theology.[6] The former constituted the heart of the modern university, epitomizing its fundamental commitment to autonomous, open inquiry, whereas the latter professional faculties were appropriately constrained by different missions. The theological faculty was defended within the university, not for its independent engagement in the pursuit of knowledge, but for the professional training of ministers, for which the state had a legitimate need. Although this provided a rationale for the continued presence of the theological faculty within the German university, the cost was exceedingly high. Moreover, in the United States, with its sharp separation of church and state, it led to the exclusion of theology from public and other secular colleges and universities, and its establishment within seminaries and divinity schools that were understood to have an explicitly religious and professional agenda.

The exclusion of theology from the liberal arts and sciences and its relocation within an institutional context that is governed by ecclesiastical and professional interests have profoundly shaped the discipline in its modern trajectory, a point several of the essays explore. Given this history, it should not be surprising that the academic study of religion sought to secure its scholarly credentials largely through constructing itself in opposition to theology. Intense effort has been made to distinguish carefully between the study of religion and the profession of religion or, in the words of the decisive 1963 Supreme Court ruling, "teaching about religion" and the "teaching of religion," a watershed mark in the institutionalization of religious studies within public universities. Disciplinary histories have been written to buttress this oppositional construction of the academic study of religion and theology, exemplified most powerfully in J. Samuel Preus's *Explaining Religion: Criticism and Theory from Bodin to Freud.*[7]

The sharp distinction between the study of religion and the profession of religion has been exceedingly effective in legitimating religious studies in the modern secular university context, and it still enjoys considerable political currency among the wider public. Significantly, however, the theoretical cogency of this distinction has become increasingly suspect, appearing more and more, as Jonathan Z. Smith bluntly puts it, a "ploy."[8] Its dethronement from axiomatic principle to political ploy—at least among (some) scholars—is a reflection of the erosion of the modernist framework within which it is rooted. He writes: "Not only is the putative distinction naïve and political, it is also anachronistic. It speaks out of a period when the norms of theological inquiry (as experienced in the West) were largely governed by an intact canon, when the ideology of the human sciences were chiefly governed by the goal of achieving "objectivity" or "value-free" knowledge."[9] Smith's comment is instructive not only because it calls attention to the increasing untenability of the conventional take on the identity of and relationship between theology and religious studies, but also because it does so by pointing to the misleading "modernist" interpretations of both of these forms of inquiry.

REDESIGNING THE LANDSCAPE

But if the conventional approach is diminishing in cogency and influence, what is a more appropriate interpretation of their respective identities and relationship? The fundamental question is whether the movement past modernism, which weakens the reigning boundary demarcation between religious studies and theology, warrants their reintegration, calls for new modes of distinguishing them, or suggests a more jagged boundary. The exploration of this question is highly charged, primarily because the academic integrity of each side is on the line. Many theologians, excluded from the intellectual core of the modern university, seek legitimacy through reintegration with religious studies in the liberal arts and sciences; arguments to the contrary implicitly, if not explicitly, challenge the scholarly merits of their discipline. Most scholars of religion, on the other hand, are threatened by the rapprochement of the fields, recognizing that the intellectual legitimacy of the modern academic study of religion has been secured through its oppositional contrast to theology. Diminishing the opposition is experienced as endangering the academic status of the field within the context of the liberal arts and sciences. The motives and stakes of the debate foster polemics that reflect caricatures of the various camps. Theologians are prone to offer a highly selective, charitable rendition of their own discipline in an effort to underscore its similarities to the human sciences; scholars of religion, on the other hand, also tend toward selective portraits of theology, albeit ones that—far less charitably—accentuate the differences between theology and the human sciences. Both sides capture something important, although recognition does not lead toward any simple solutions. This is largely because our current situation is shaped by multiple vectors—including intellectual, political, legal, and institutional traditions—that may preclude a theoretically coherent resolution to this impasse. But we can gain a better sense of the complexity and determine how best to proceed through a consideration of the conflicting vectors that need to be negotiated.

The essays in this volume explore the respective identities of religious studies and theology, paying particular attention to their borders. The contributors include theologians and scholars of religion, in roughly equal numbers. Just as importantly, they reflect a wide range of institutional affiliations, including seminaries, divinity schools, private universities, private liberal arts colleges, and large public universities. Bringing their contributions together in this volume enables us to see just how important institutional location is in reflecting on the shape and future direction of these forms of inquiry. Insofar as scholars of religion and theologians stand under the same professional umbrella institution, the American Academy of Religion (AAR), the differences that mark their pursuits—differences of assumptions, audiences, and aims—are obscured, if not tempered, as the leadership seeks to broker the tensions and conflicts. In a 1999 AAR presidential address, for example, Margaret Miles insists that "theological studies" and the "study of religion" are now distinctions "without a difference." According to Miles, they are misleading because both "must integrate critical and passionately engaged scholarship." Hence she concludes, "I use, then, the providentially ambiguous term 'religious studies' to integrate the falsely polarized terms, 'theological studies' and 'the study of religion'."[10] But this polarization is foregrounded in these essays as scholars explicitly reflect upon their field in relation to its most salient "other."

The essays in this volume reflect a wide range of positions regarding the boundary between religious studies and theology, and their appropriate institutional locations. Although there are multiple axes along which the essays could be compared, the widest fault line runs between those who take contrasting positions regarding the presence of theology within religious studies and the modern secular university.

Standing at one end of this continuum, Russell McCutcheon and Ivan Strenski argue that a clear line of demarcation separates religious studies and theology, in theory if not in practice, and the intellectual credibility of religious studies depends upon protecting the viability of this line. For McCutcheon, theology constitutes part of the "data" that scholars of religion seek to theorize, and any perceived overlap simply reflects a failure to distinguish the markedly different order of questions each addresses. Significantly, the wall separating theology from the academic study of religion in McCutcheon's conceptual landscape also functions to separate the humanist interpreter of religion, who, in his view, essentially reinscribes the emic perspective, from a more anthropological variant of the academic study of religion. McCutcheon calls for scholars of religion to abandon their role as "caretaker" of religion and pursue the naturalistic redescription of this form of cultural discourse and practice. Similarly committed to maintaining the boundary between religious studies and theology, Ivan Strenski defends this position by taking on two challenges to it that have recently been mounted from different ends of the theological spectrum. One he dismisses as a sophisticated form of confessionalism, cloaked in fashionable postmodern garb, and the other he considers a form of hermeneutics, perfectly appropriate within religious studies but not distinctively theological. Reflecting on the various senses of the term "theology" and the motivations for seeking to retain it, he concludes that it is "too late" to nuance the term, given its deep theistic and confessional ties.

For other scholars of religion, postmodern shifts have exposed the limitations, if not untenability, of the conventional demarcation between religious studies and theology, and prevented the question of including or excluding theology from the university from being a simple one. In quite different ways, the essays by Christopher Chesnek, Richard Martin, Sam Gill, Linell Cady, and William Hart seek to disclose and explore the ambiguous relationship between theology and religious studies. Christopher Chesnek challenges the sharp distinction that has been drawn between religion and theology on the one side, and the academic study of religion on the other. Although grounded in legitimate intellectual and political concerns, the debate over their relationship, Chesnek argues, has been governed by politically motivated stereotypes that rely upon and reinforce a narrow conception of religion and obscure the religious dimensions of the academic study of religion. To support his argument, he explores the history of religious studies and considers the discipline's impact on the religious lives of its students. Reflecting on the debate over reductionism, Chesnek argues that the vast, theoretical resources of the academic study of religion have both theological and antitheological dimensions, either of which are eradicated only to the detriment of the discipline. Although arguing that religiosity and theology cannot be fully bracketed, Chesnek concludes that they must remain incidental to the aims of the scholar of religion, neither explicitly cultivated nor assiduously policed.

Richard Martin reaches a similar conclusion in his essay that focuses on the tangled relations between theology and the history of religion during the latter's development in the past century and a half. Martin explicitly rejects the model in which the history of religions is subsumed under the umbrella of theology, its location within much twentieth-century scholarship. However, he also admits his increasing doubts about a model that denies the presence or the legitimacy of personal commitments in the study of religion. For Martin, the issues have become much more complicated as scholars of religion find themselves "analyzing, critiquing, and sometimes defending other people's theologies in a changing intellectual environment that includes the other."

In a similar vein, Sam Gill seeks to expose the deeply rooted beliefs that inform religious studies, as well as the wider academy. From a distance, Gill argues, the differences between theologians and scholars of religion are less salient than the deep similarities that reflect their common roots in the Western tradition. Gill develops this argument by exploring contrasting attitudes toward the body in Western and Australian aboriginal cultures. Like Chesnek and Martin, Gill does not want to abandon the distinction between explicitly religious and academic scholarship, but the blurring of the boundary poses new questions and problems for the field. In this emerging situation, Gill concludes that the question is "how theology can be reconstructed and reimagined beyond explicit religious theologies," in a manner that will facilitate engagement with the world's diverse cultures and critically illuminate the root beliefs that inform the academy itself.

Linell Cady's essay also explores the limitations of the conventional mapping of religious studies and theology, and the implications of recent scholarship that has exposed the jagged boundary between religion and its study. These developments, she argues, can help facilitate the further evolution of religious studies by making greater room for both naturalistic theorizing and existential normative reflection on religion, pursuits that the reigning liberal phenomenological model of the field has sidelined, if not precluded. Although the normative strand of this disciplinary evolution has clear parallels to theology, Cady considers this label misleading and inappropriate given its theistic and confessional associations. But she concludes that normative engagement with the diversity of worldviews, spanning the religious/secular divide, is increasingly important within the university context in our emerging global environment.

William Hart reflects upon the widespread feeling that theology is a polluting presence within religious studies and the wider university, an attitude he admittedly shares to some degree. He takes the emergence of religious studies at Princeton University as a case study to show the early and continuing traces of theology in shaping the field. Rejecting the cogency of the standard argument for the exclusion of theology, Hart concludes that it is necessary to distinguish between confessional and academic theology, the latter an open, revisable form of inquiry. He concludes with some surprise and reluctance that the latter cannot be excluded from religious studies or the university on epistemological grounds. However, insofar as he connects theology with theism, he raises some concerns about its pragmatic value in terms of relevance and interest. He concludes that academic theology is a "legitimate mode of inquiry within the methodological plurality of religious studies," but he nonetheless wishes for the day when "God-talk in its hallowed and explanatory senses is as quaint as ether-talk."

The next set of essays share the view that the model of the university and religious studies that has excluded all forms of theology is no longer compelling, making possible—even essential—the incorporation of a form of academic theology as a subset of religious studies. However, recognizing the variety and lingering confessional imprint on the discipline of theology, Delwin Brown, Sheila Davaney, and Darrel Fasching focus directly on how to envision a theology that would be appropriately at home within a university context. Delwin Brown traces the historical antecedents for academic theology and argues that a contemporary version properly belongs within religious studies. His case does not depend on construing the university as an open forum housing all forms of inquiry, but in identifying a form of theology that embraces the norms and values of the academic tradition. Although there are some contemporary practitioners of this form of theology, they remain largely scattered and overshadowed by religious theologians, with primary loyalties to religious communities or traditions. Failure to include an academically credible form of theology within the university—which has emerged as the most "influential arbiter of knowledge" in the modern West—precludes analysis and critique of one of the most powerful and important dimensions of human culture. Arguing that the term "theology" remains an honorific one within the culture, Brown suggests that it be retained in order to take advantage of this sensibility and to secure its place as a "counter" to less academic theologies circulating within the culture at large.

Concerned about the growing animosity to theology in religious studies, Sheila Greeve Davaney situates the conflict historically, tracing the dominant narrative that has tied the maturation of religious studies to its divorce from theology. She challenges the portraits of theology generated by this narrative, in particular questioning the rights of all academic disciplines, except theology, to evolve. She analyzes four major ways of rethinking the relationship of theology to the university that have emerged in response to recent developments in cultural theory. Seeking to contribute to the further evolution of the discipline of theology, Davaney concludes by identifying the salient features of an explicitly academic theology, one in which audience and allegiance are unambiguously framed in terms of the academy, not the church or tradition.

Rejecting essentialist interpretations of theology frozen in premodernity, Darrell Fasching also explores the appropriate shape of a theology within a university context. He suggests that we take "the sacred," interpreted as "that which matters most" to people, as the central organizing concept within the study of religion and theology. The academic theologian, Fasching argues, is not a confessional or church theologian, but a "free-agent" who pursues the "study and critique of human religious experience (i.e., of the sacred) in all its diversity." Far from defending the superiority of one's own tradition, Fasching proposes the model of the "alienated theologian" who desacralizes all traditions, including one's own, in an effort to gain through comparative study the "wisdom to live more humanely," the overarching goal of the humanities.

The remaining three contributor—Paula Cooey, Frederick Ware, and Kathryn Tanner—seem less convinced that radical revisioning of theology is required if it is to be a university discipline. They hold that theology as a normative, constructive effort to extend particular religious traditions belongs in the secular academy. They make the case for this view, however, in significantly different ways. Paula Cooey offers two related lines of argument. One is that the humanistic inquiries provided by the liberal arts remain an element, perhaps even the central element, of a beneficial university education. The critical study of the religious aspect of cultures, and of religions and religious beliefs—especially their central symbols such as "God"—is a valuable part of a liberal arts education. But the critical study of religion need not be solely analytical or descriptive. Just as literature departments include authors and poets as well as linguists and theorists, so also religious studies departments may include "those who actively seek to deconstruct and intentionally reconstruct [particular] religious symbol systems." Cooey argues, further, that all scholarly disciplines, not simply the humanistic ones, are constitutive and constructive. To exclude theology from the university because it is constructive is therefore untenable.

Frederick Ware assumes something like Cooey's kind of argument as the basis for his further contention that Black theology should be undertaken as an academic inquiry located in the university. Ware acknowledges that there is a place for the more common forms of Black theological reflection answerable to the norms of the African American religious tradition, but he adds that, if Black theology wishes to be taken seriously beyond its own community, it must also subject its claims to the kind of public scrutiny characteristic of the university. In the academy, Black theological claims are to be tested in the same way that any other critical religious reflection is examined.

Ware and Cooey take some care to distinguish what they term academic theology from theologies that are governed by the norms of particular religious traditions. Kathryn Tanner, however, argues for the equitable inclusion of all forms of disciplined religious reflection, including Christian theology, in the university. Tanner rejects attempts to reconceptualize theology in order to make it palatable to the academy. Such efforts, she says, seek "to meet a strict methodological bar that no longer exists" with the advent of postmodernism. What she proposes instead is a reconceptualization of the university itself, or rather a return to its earlier aim "to serve society . . . through the formation of a citizenry educated to make good decisions" about their life together. In her view, the university should become the site for the contest of all "socially significant . . . visions of the world and our place in it" including those of the sciences, humanities, and religions. This would include, too, efforts to create and advocate a Christian theological outlook designed to meet today's pressing challenges.

A number of recurring themes crisscross throughout these essays. Perhaps the most prominent, if most diffuse, is a recognition that the postmodern shift has destabilized the university, reopening questions about the nature of knowledge, open inquiry, forms of evidence, and appropriate norms. The boundary between scholar and data has become fuzzier. This is a particularly troubling development for a field such as religious studies, whose "myth of origins" builds upon the disjunction between religion and its study. A number of the essays challenge the sharp demarcation between religion and its study, undermining the purported objectivity of the scholar in his or her pursuits. Discontent with the reigning narrative, however, does not necessarily lead to arguments for including theology as a subfield within religious studies. Although some argue thusly, others prefer to see theology as an incidental by-product of the study of religion; some question the appropriateness of the label; and others take evidence of a jagged boundary as motivation and justification for making the separation sharper and neater.

Despite the prominence of the theme in this collection that the weakening of modernism and its pretensions to objectivity and neutrality make room within the university for a form of academic theology, it is important to note that other grounds for its exclusion remain salient. As Hart expresses this point, although epistemological barriers against theology may have eroded, pragmatic ones may have not. Indeed, for Hart, the subject matter of theology, what he calls God-talk, is simply not interesting or compelling, and hence perhaps should go the way of alchemy and astrology. It is significant that many of the essays advocating the inclusion of theology within the university operate with a more expansive understanding of the term. Rather than limit theology to God-talk, theology is located within a global arena and identified more generally with intellectual reflection in relationship to broadly encompassing religious/cultural traditions.

A number of the essays express discontent with the constraints of the reigning conceptual landscape, with its sharp distinction between the religious and the secular, and the corollaries that work to sustain this division. Some point to the way this bifurcation blinds us to the "religiosity" of the secular, whereas others point to the way it hinders the evolution of religion in more naturalistic idioms. Globalizing developments that have accelerated encounters with multiple "worlds," both traditionally religious and secular, have contributed to this uneasiness with the fundamental categories through which we have engaged our fields, and distinguished the academic study of religion and theology.

The essays also make apparent the importance of institutional location in addressing these issues. Disciplines and fields do not float free from their institutional embodiment in actual colleges, universities, seminaries, and divinity schools, including public and private, secular and religious, liberal and conservative. Constraints on intellectual inquiry will be experienced differently across these varying sites. Given the strong church-state separation in the United States, it is not surprising that scholars of religion at public institutions appear most concerned about sustaining the objectivity of the scholar of religion. Nor is it surprising that private institutions seem to provide a more hospitable context for including the study of religion within the mission of a traditional liberal arts education. But the importance of considering this issue in relationship to secular and public institutions—the focus of this volume—is particularly pressing given the demographic trends. Almost 80 percent of students attending institutions of higher education in the United States now attend public institutions.[11]

Another theme that recurs in this collection is the importance of envisioning a form of theology that is appropriate within a university context. A number of the essays acknowledge that the discipline of theology remains deeply shaped by its historic roots, which have located it within particular religious communities and traditions. However, they argue that history is not necessarily destiny, that theology has as much right as any other discipline to self-transformation. Hence they focus attention on delineating the character of a specifically academic theology, one located unambiguously within the academy, not a hybrid standing betwixt and between church and university. Although there is consensus among a number of essays about the critical importance of forging such an intellectual enterprise, the arguments in support of this consensus differ, and there is a difference of opinion about how this enterprise should be named. Some argue for keeping the label of theology, primarily on pragmatic grounds, and others argue the opposite, also on pragmatic grounds. The varied connotations of the term "theology," both positive and negative, are strikingly evident in this collection, making clear that the question of name is not a minor semantic consideration.

Finally, the essays collectively point to the transitional character of our disciplinary traditions. There is a significant recurring refrain that recent trends in scholarship have opened new questions about the nature of our pursuits and the intellectual and moral ideals that govern them. These questions have been accentuated and multiplied by the global context into which Western education, including the study of religion, is now moving. It is clear that the ability to understand and to engage, both sympathetically and critically, this multiplicity of "worlds" will become even more indispensable as this future unfolds. The further evolution of religious studies and theology, to say nothing of the academy itself, will almost certainly be guided in part by the need to meet this vital cultural demand.

NOTES

1. Reflecting the dominance of Christianity in the West, the discipline of theology in the North American context has been largely Christian theology. Hence, religious studies

has primarily emerged to some extent within, and to some extent over against, Christian theological inquiry. Although "theology" sometimes presupposes the Christian modifier, reflecting the historic roots of the discipline, it has increasingly been appropriated to identify a form of intellectual reflection within other world religions, such as Islam, Judaism, and Buddhism, and more amorphous religious/cultural traditions, such as post-Christian and New Age. There are problems with the global extension of the term "theology" analogous to the problems identified in the extension of the term "religion" beyond its Western roots. Nevertheless, the migration of the term "theology" beyond its Christian prototype does have interesting implications for the issue of its relationship to religious studies and the university in an increasingly global environment.

2. Charlotte Allen, "Is Nothing Sacred? Casting Out the Gods from Religious Studies," *Lingua Franca* 6,7 (1996): 30–40.

3. Edward Farley, *Theologia: The Fragmentation and Unity of Theological Education* (Philadelphia: Fortress Press, 1983), see especially 29–48.

4. Edward Farley, *Ecclesial Reflection: An Anatomy of Theological Method* (Philadelphia: Fortress Press, 1982), 27.

5. Van Harvey, *The Historian and the Believer* (New York: Macmillan Publishing, 1966), 38.

6. Immanuel Kant, *The Conflict of the Faculties*, trans. Mary J. Gregor (New York: Abaris Books, 1979).

7. J. Samuel Preus, *Explaining Religion: Criticism and Theory from Bodin to Freud* (New Haven: Yale University Press, 1987).

8. Jonathan Z. Smith, "'Religion' and 'Religious Studies': No Difference at All," *Soundings* 71 (1988): 231.

9. Ibid., 233.

10. Margaret R. Miles, "Becoming Answerable for What We See," *Journal of the American Academy of Religion* 68, no. 3 (2000): 472.

11. This estimate, from the U.S. Department of Education, is cited in Samuel F. Barbett and Roslyn A. Korb, *Enrollment in Higher Education: Fall 1995*, National Center for Education Statistics, Department of Education (Washington, DC, 1997).

2

The Study of Religion as an Anthropology of Credibility

RUSSELL T. MCCUTCHEON

> Know then thyself, presume not God to scan
> The proper study of Mankind is Man
> —Alexander Pope, *Essay on Man* (Epistle II)

DÉJÀ VU ALL OVER AGAIN

Thinking about the question of the relationship (or lack thereof) between the academic study of religion and theological studies of religion, I must admit that I had a difficult time coming up with anything new or interesting to say. Staring at the blank computer screen, I recalled Jonathan Z. Smith's words from a recent essay on the same question: "One might have the initial sense," Smith wrote, "on reading the question we are here called together to discuss, of 'here we go again'. . . ."[1] For a number of us working in the field today, there is a weariness in tackling this question yet again because we happen to think that it was settled to our satisfaction quite some time ago—possibly as early as David Hume's theory of religion in the eighteenth-century, or at least with F. Max Müller's and Cornelius P. Tiele's apologies for a *science* of religion in the late nineteenth century. However, it seems that with the arrival of every new generation of scholars, we find a renewed assault on the distinction between scholarship on the enduring meaning and value of religion, scholarship aimed at promoting one or another form of the object under study, on the one hand, and, on the other, scholarship on the origins and functions of religion, where religion is conceived as but one among a species of ordinary cultural practices. Over the past two decades, one of my doctoral supervisors at the University of Toronto, Donald Wiebe, has been among the most vocal apologists for a nontheological science of religion; now, I find myself adding my voice to this long-standing debate. It almost seems inevitable that every new generation of academics intent on studying religion as nothing more or less than human behavior will have to keep reinventing the wheel so as to retain a space in the public university for their brand of scholarship.[2]

THEOLOGY AS DATA

As others before me have said, I see these two practices—theology and the study of religion—as being *intimately related* yet *utterly different.* They are related much as any particular social group, on the one hand, is related to scholars intent on *explaining* the workings of social groups per se, on the other. I am therefore part of a scholarly tradition that sees theology and its practitioners as nothing more or less than native informants;[3] they are but one more group whose reports and actions need study and theorization. For instance, I recall that the Protestant process theologian and liberal advocate of religious pluralism, John Cobb, once spoke at a university where I was teaching; I found it rather odd attending his talk for I did not see myself there either as Cobb's colleague or his dialogue partner. Rather, I attended the lecture much as an anthropologist might attend a ritual ceremony—as a participant-observer gathering descriptive data for later theoretical reworking.

Scholars of religion, such as myself, therefore conceive of and study theologians as elite religious practitioners, as generally privileged, influential mythmakers.[4] Although not all of the scholar of religion's data will come from the ranks of theologians (after all, not all of the people and groups we study are involved in the articulate, systematic reflection and rational expression on the meaning, context, or implications of "the faith"), *all theologians are fair game as data.* It is for this reason that I decided to open a collection of my essays with an epigraph taken from David Lodge's novel, *The British Museum is Falling Down*: "I don't have any myself, but I believe in other people having religion";[5] I believe in other people having religion for the simple reason that, without such people, their claims, and the institutions they establish and reproduce, scholars of religion would have nothing to study.

ANSWERING THE *HOW* AND *WHY* QUESTIONS

But what is it about theologians or other so-called religious people that scholars of religion study? To make a complex answer simple, I can say that we study *how* it is that they believe and behave and, having gathered this descriptive information, we go on to theorize as to just *why* it is that they believe and behave as they do. To accomplish this, we draw on descriptive and comparative skills followed by explanatory theories concerning such things as the workings of human brains, bodies, and social formations to study why it is that people, from all over the globe and for countless generations, invest such tremendous amounts of intellectual creativity and social energy talking about invisible beings or the origins, purpose, and fate of the universe. Although some scholars—known variously as phenomenologists, historians of religions, or simply liberal humanists—are equally interested in investigating the descriptive where, when, what, who, and how of religious traditions (i.e., they pursue detailed descriptivist information and are generally concerned with what religion *means*, either to the participant or for humanity in general), the scholar of religion I am describing draws on the descriptive 'how' of religion as data in need of theorizing. Unlike theologians, assorted other religious practitioners, and even liberal humanists—all of whom take the existence of religious beliefs as given, inevitable, necessary, or self-evidently meaningful and good (though they differ dramatically as to what this meaning may be)—scholars of religion go beyond mere description and comparison to inquire as to *why* people find such beliefs, behaviors, and institutions attractive, compelling, effective, and worthy of reproducing. Of course, not everyone studies religion in this way but, when studying religion in a publicly funded context—a "public" comprised not just of members of assorted complementary and contradictory religious traditions but also agnostics and atheists who equally pay taxes to support the education system—it strikes me that this is the only viable option for our field. Despite their intimate relation, then, there is a tremendous gulf between public scholars of religion, on the one hand, and theologians, on the other.

To phrase it as I do in my own introductory classes, whereas theologians (if we can use this term for not just Christians or theists in general, but for all forms of elite, systematic participant reflection on the meaning of their participation in those social movements we commonly name as religions) study the gods, scriptures, and origins (as opposed to historic beginnings), then scholars of religion study groups of historically embedded people who talk about the gods, scriptures, origins, etc. Because I draw this distinction, the above epigraph from Alexander Pope's poem, *Essay on Man* (1733–1734), is very useful to me (but, I must add, it is useful only to a point).[6] As I have said elsewhere, scholars of religion do not study religion or the gods whatsoever—as counterintuitive as that may sound, I think it worth stating. Instead, they use a tool (the category "religion" itself is one such tool, the comparative method is another, as are the explanatory theories they bring to their work) to demarcate, name, and study a relatively small range of the complex collection of observable, cross-cultural human doings that are available to us through such human artifacts as written and oral texts, architecture, archeological sites, ritual behavior, social institutions, etc. Whereas religion may have something to do with salvation or damnation for a theologian, for the scholar of religion, "religion" (which I now purposefully place in quotation marks) is a tool with a specific history and possible analytic utility for scholars studying but one aspect of the complex range of human behaviors.[7] Other than human reports we can hear, the human systems of classification used to convey information, the human texts we can read, the human actions we can observe, and the social institutions that make these reports, taxonomies, texts, and actions possible, what else is there for scholars in the human sciences to study? Thus, updating Pope's language and jettisoning his own theological agenda, I can simply say: "The only study of Humankind is Human Beings."

What should be clear is that the theologian and the scholar of religion I am describing have two completely different starting points; whereas the former presumes religion to contain a world of meaning and value somehow apart from, and therefore impinging on, the world of human doings, the latter presumes all meaning and value (including the social practice named theology) to be a thoroughly human, historical concoction. This presumption makes the latter approach thoroughly anthropological.

Given this way of distinguishing between these two groups, I must now refine my terms; it should be clear that I find it misleading to talk about the study of religion vs. theology. After all, as already suggested, phenomenologists and other liberal humanists intent on studying the various manifestations of the enduring Human Spirit or *Geist* (notably as manifested in the so-called Great Works of Literature) have much in common with so-called theologians: all are equally invested in studying what the scholar of ancient Greek religion, Walter Burkert, simply terms "non-obvious beings" (i.e., "things" you don't bump into).[8] Although I would be the last to suggest that such things as "society" or the "nation-state" were real in the same way that my laptop, or the chair I'm now sitting in, are real, unlike the humanist or theologian, I see "society" "economy," and "the nation-state"— not to mention "God," "sin," or "heaven"—as *analytically or heuristically useful fictions* that people in certain groups use to organize and live in the complex world around them. Others before me have made this same observation about our tool "religion" (most notably Jonathan Z. Smith). This term, "religion," and the set of ideas and social arrangements that we are able to name and identify when using it (e.g., the presumption that "faith" is somehow a private, privileged insight into reality), is a way that certain socio-linguistic families (those traceable to Latin— from which we get our term "religion"[9]—or those influenced by the European world) name, divide up, and act out their world. Whereas for the theologian, religion or faith have something to do with salvation, human shortcomings, or communication with an unseen world, the scholar of religion understands the term "religion," or such rhetorical pairs as sacred/profane, as one way that certain human communities concoct cognitively and socially habitable "worlds."[10] Although not all human communities concoct their worlds by means of interrelated discourses on nonobvious beings, absolute origins, and final end times, etc., some of us do just that. But why?

If you are not curious about this specific why question, then perhaps you should not be a scholar of the academic study of religion. If all you are curious about is where and when and by whom Hindu death rituals are enacted (description) or whether Buddhist rituals are similar to Christian rituals (comparison), then perhaps the academic study of religion is not your home, for it is precisely this question, "Why?" that sets the anthropologically based study of religion apart from both its theological and humanistic counterparts.[11] Whereas both of these are concerned with the never-ending hermeneutic quest for meaning and significance, the study of religion, as I practice it, is concerned with what the late Michel de Certeau termed an anthropology of credibility[12]—with examining and explaining the conditions and sociorhetorics that enable a group to portray a piece of social data as meaningful, significant, and credible in the first place. This different focus—a metafocus when compared with quests to determine stable meanings—raises a host of questions and opportunities peculiar to the public study of religion.

FOUR ASSUMPTIONS

To summarize, then, I provide the following assumptions that drive the anthropological study of religion as I understand it.[13]

1. World and the Natural World

The backdrop for all human doings is the natural world (i.e., the world we bump into when we try to cross either a street or the hotel lobby at the annual American Academy of Religion meeting); because I presume the natural world to be a complex place, I also presume that no human community knows what is *really* going on in it (i.e., metaphysical reductionism simply makes no sense to me as an explanatory option; following Don Wiebe, I advocate methodological reductionism). Instead, whether we're relying on individual hunches or socially authorized traditions that began long before we came on the scene, we all recall just this or that past event, and anticipate this or that possible future event, all in an effort to narrativize a meaningful "world" that is never quite in perfect step with the natural world.[14] I borrow the term "world" from William Paden, who notes that, unlike the more philosophically idealist terms worldview, philosophy, or viewpoint, "world" connotes "the operating environment of linguistic and behavioural options which persons or communities presuppose, posit and inhabit at any given point in time and from which they choose courses of action."[15] I place this "world" in quotation marks when using it so as to draw attention to the fact that this is the contestible, ad hoc social lens or template by which we plot ourselves in relation to a select few aspects of what I referred to above as the natural world, a world whose many aspects are constantly competing for our attention.[16] As an aside, given this presumption, one of the goals of a liberal arts education is to persuade students that the natural world is far more complex than suggested by their inherited "worlds."

2. Pluralistic Methodological Reductionism

Because of this presumed complexity of social "worlds," a variety of methods and theories will be necessary to start talking about them in an academic manner—

which means, first, describing them, but then situating them within their contexts, explaining their attraction to people, accounting for both their endurance and their change over time, etc.[17] I therefore support pluralistic methodological reductionism. I would be quite mistaken to think that, once the work of studying social formations is exhausted (as if it could ever be exhausted), *either* there would be nothing left for colleagues using other scales of analysis to study *or* that there would remain some refined distillate called experience, consciousness, belief, the sacred, or Human Nature that we could only study by means of some special methodology from outside the human sciences.[18]

3. Mythmaking vs. Theorization

Any system of thought and practice that fails to presume 1 and 2 is a candidate for the status of data. Reflection on the deeper truth or meaning of religion (whether that reflection is theological *or* humanistic) attempts to bypass the historically grounded nature of all human attempts to know the world around us, making them instances of mythmaking in need of theorization. It is for this reason that I think it sensible to exclude certain approaches from the pluralistic methodologically reductionist study of religion as carried out in the public university. Those approaches to be excluded (i.e., those approaches that are themselves instances of data) are those that (i) presume the natural world to be the tip of an unperceivable, supernatural, or ahistoric world and (ii) presume that the underlying principle, workings, meaning, or purposes of both this natural world and the supernatural world can be known by those possessing special, gifted, intuitive, or privileged knowledge/wisdom.

4. Totalizing Discourses Are Data

Finally, there are no final explanations; explanations, like all cognitive endeavors, are products of specific social contexts and concerns, although when correctly understood in their technical sense, theories and explanations are a part of a specific, academic (as opposed to folk) discourse about the natural world. Having said this, however, we must never fail to recognize that scholars are just as deeply involved in the art of rhetoric, contestation, and social formation as anyone else. It is just that scholars do not draw on the same rhetorics to accomplish their acts of social formation. As Bruce Lincoln has most recently phrased it, "scholarship is myth with footnotes."[19] Therefore, it is a useful rule of thumb to say that it is the people we study who typically propose final, universal, total, metaphysical explanations (e.g., "At the end of time . . . ," "God's will is that . . . ," "The meaning of life is . . . ," etc.).[20] Because scholars in the study of religion are methodological reductionists, their explanations are purely a function of their interests and the theories they propose and apply ("Given my theory of social formation, rituals function to . . . ," etc.). This means that scholars of religion must own up to their own curiosities, instead of misportraying them as eternally interesting and obviously relevant questions. *Nothing is self-evidently compelling or interesting.* Things are compelling, interesting, or boring only in light of systems, grids, and lenses of meaning, value, and significance—in a word, "worlds"—that are produced and reproduced in social groups. That not just every "world" counts as a participant in the institution we call "academe" should go without saying.

CASE IN POINT: THE PROBLEM OF "EVIL"

As a way to demonstrate what can be accomplished in the study of human doings by agreeing that the university operates by means of just these assumptions, I would like to examine a specific piece of human data. Rather than ask questions concerning what it means to the actors, how it works within their context, or whether this sort of behavior is good or bad, I would like to suggest that the metafocus of the anthropologically based study of religion allows us to formulate general theories to investigate the historic precedents and effects of cross-culturally observable human behavior. The general theories of human minds, behaviors, and institutions that we employ in this activity thus enable us to interact with our colleagues throughout the human sciences. As opposed to being what I—following Mack—have termed caretakers for the behavior under study,[21] I would like to provide the following as a case study in applying a different sort of scholarship to the study of religion, an approach that makes scholars active and public culture critics. I would therefore like to turn our attention to the genre of theological writing traditionally known as "theodicy" to demonstrate what is to be gained by the anthropological approach to the study of religion.

THEODICY DESCRIBED

The term "theodicy" is generally credited to the German philosopher Gottfried Leibniz (1646–1716); it is a compound derived from combining two ancient Greek words, one referring to a divine being or god (*theos*) and the other referring to justice (*dike*): a theodicy is therefore a discourse on the justice of god. Although when strictly used, the term applies only to those belief systems that posit some sort of moral, supernatural being who controls the universe (i.e., ethical monotheism), it is nevertheless widely used to denote any human attempt to deal with the fact that events in the natural world do not always unfold according to our plan or anticipation. An example of this wider usage of the term can be found in the work of the early sociologist Max Weber, who used the term to name any attempt to grapple with the problem of human suffering. For instance, although many Buddhist systems hardly posit a loving God ruling the universe (although countless, compassionate *bodhisattvas* are central to many Mahayana groups), philosophers of religion have no difficulty speaking of a "Buddhist theodicy"; after all, as is made clear from the origins tale concerning Prince Siddhartha's disillusionment and subsequent awakening, the problem of human suffering and disquiet (Pali, *dukkha*) is one of the central topics in Buddhist thought. Also, even though a "Hindu theodicy" may strike some as an awkward choice of terms, others will undoubtedly answer that the interrelated notions of karma, caste, and dharma provide a powerful way of explaining why events in the world happen as they do. In fact, Weber called the law of karma "the most radical solution of the problem of theodicy."[22] However, despite this wider usage for the term "theodicy," even a quick glance at the world's religions makes it clear that Muslim, Hindu, and Buddhist writers, for example, have not been nearly as concerned with this issue as have been Christian writers.

Within the history of Christian theodicy writing, the problem of evil comes down to what many others before me have named as a trilemma: three related premises, any two of which can be held, but to the exclusion of the third: (i) God is all-good; (ii) God is all-powerful; and (iii) Evil exists. For example, holding (i) and (ii) excludes (iii); in this case the observable evil in the world (whether natural evils such as rock slides or moral evils such as genocides) is explained away as merely the result of our inevitably limited, human viewpoint. Emic reports from this perspective would likely take the form of, "Yes, but in God's eyes . . . ," "The time will come when we will see . . . ," or "These seemingly evil events are actually tests. . . ." Holding (ii) and (iii) would exclude (i); in this case a malevolent but powerful God would be responsible for evil events. Holding (i) and (iii) would posit a well-intentioned God who was incapable of preventing certain harmful events—events caused by Fate, human freewill, or possibly the actions of some other God. It should be apparent that, in the history of Christianity at least, all three of these combinations have struck various participants as appealing explanations for evil, since evil events have been variously attributed to the inscrutable will of God; as tests for human worthiness, as the corrupt, rogue actions of Satan, or as the prideful acts of human freewill traceable to Adam and Eve's rebellion. Actually, despite the seeming logic of the trilemma, often mutually exclusive options arise in the same theodicy; reporting on why he was bitten by a rattlesnake during a Pentecostal ritual ceremony, a snake handler in the Appalachian region of the U.S. informed the documentary filmmaker that "It was God's will but the devil's work"—a theodicy that effectively frees God from responsibility for capricious events *while simultaneously* attributing to this same God absolute power and control.[23] Although this partial list hardly exhausts the many different solutions that Christian writers have offered for the problem of evil, it nonetheless provides a descriptive starting point for our redescriptive efforts.

THEODICY REDESCRIBED

Prior to embarking on a redescription of "theodicy," it is important to state explicitly that "theodicy" is part of an emic, insider vocabulary that etic scholars of religion freely accept as part of their first-level, descriptive lexicon, a term used to demarcate a specific discursive domain of interest to them. Sadly, virtually all treatments of theodicy—from textbook and encyclopedia entries to the work of contemporary philosophers and, of course, theologians—are concerned simply with grappling with the emic problem of evil and offering solutions to it *rather than* engaging in etic theorizing as to just *why* human beings even bother to grapple with this thing they call "the problem of evil." Where we *do* find attempts to explain the existence, attraction, or function of theodicies, they usually follow along the lines of Ronald M. Green's thoughts as found in his entry on theodicy in the *Encyclopedia of Religion*: there is, Green asserts, "essentially a moral motivation" behind formulating theodicies, for they "draw upon and deepen our moral self-understanding."[24] As evidenced by Green's comments, there are few, if any, attempts to talk about the problem of evil that are not themselves instances of mythmaking. Relying on the presumed existence of a nonempirical "essential moral impulse," Green's explanation only mystifies our topic, for what we as anthropologically based scholars of religion are trying to account for is not *how* independently existing moral impulses are expressed and deepened but *why* human communities presume the existence of such "things" as inner or immutable moral impulses and how such rhetorics are employed for very specific, tactical, sociopolitical gains. Green does not help us in this endeavor because he presumes the existence of that which we as scholars of religion are trying to explain. The tremendous difference between solving and studying why people attempt to solve the problem of evil will hopefully become evident as we proceed with our redescription.[25]

To begin a redescription of theodicy, we need to recall that, as suggested by the epigraph from Pope—as I am using it—the study of religion is not concerned with discourses on the gods but with studying groups of people who engage in discourses on the gods. To provide an example of this latter sort of scholarship, let me suggest that, when redescribed, the problem of evil is both a problem in cognitive intelligibility and a problem in political justification. I will deal with each in turn.

First of all, a theodicy is an attempt to come to terms with the divergence between a *belief* in a rational, coherent, meaningful natural world, on the one hand, and those daily *observations* of the empirical, natural world (once again, everything from rock slides to genocides) that contravene that belief. Redescribed in this way, theodicies are one of the ways in which human beings address anomalies in their expectations for how the natural world works. To appeal to a biological metaphor, theodicies are symptomatic of cognitive nausea; according to most recent studies, motion sickness "occurs when there is a conflict between the motion we experience and the motion we expect to experience. . . . Nausea arises when the brain receives unanticipated sensory inputs—for someone new to boats, say, feeling the ground beneath him pitch up and down, or, for someone in a virtual-reality helmet, seeing oneself move through the world while one's body knows it is standing still."[26] Moving from the biological to the cognitive, we can say that this is also the case with theodicies.

Given that a belief system that provides a context for our expectations is part of a larger social "world," then theodicies mediate between our "world" (i.e., our systems of socially reproduced knowledges and expectations) and the nagging observation that the natural world does not always conform to our expectations; because theodicies work much as shoehorns once did, to make the natural world fit our "world" (or vice versa), we can conclude that they are part of a totalizing discourse and are evidence of "worlds" conflicting with the world. Where we find a theodicy, we thus find an attempt to make an ambiguous, natural world totally intelligible, knowable, and controllable.

Given our presumption of the utter complexity of the natural world, it is inevitable that all human communities will develop mechanisms to explain the lack of fit between their "worlds" and the world. An important point arises here: although scholars using the scientific method are equally engaged in constructing a "world" and actively constructing theories to mediate the lack of fit between their "worlds" and the natural world, their classification systems do not authorize themselves by appealing to destiny or the gods. Although such scholars are deeply engaged in making the world intelligible and knowable, they presume that their master narrative (a narrative that has something to do with objectivity, neutrality, evidence, verification, falsification, progress, theory building, testing, etc.) is a thorough historical product. To appeal to Daniel Dennett's imagery, they see their methods and theories as heuristically useful cranes that are firmly grounded in human history and contestable social interests, rather than understanding them to be free-floating skyhooks originating from nothing in the historical world.[27] The former are tactical, ad hoc, and open to being discarded when their practical utility fails. The latter, however, are totalized, all-inclusive, and are understood as necessary and beyond falsification and testing. So, although the British literary critic Terry Eagelton is correct to observe that theories of all sorts are "just a practice forced into a new form of self-reflectiveness on account of certain grievous problems it has encountered [i.e., anomalies in expectations]," we must be careful to distinguish the differing ways humans grapple with these anomalies: we can develop naturalistic theories, as in the technical practices of the human and natural sciences, or we can develop theologies and, more specifically, theodicies. "Like small lumps on the neck," then, both theories and theodicies are "a symptom that all is not well."[28]

The efficiency of theodicies in particular in addressing anomalies lies in their ability to smoothly posit two contradictory premises: (i) the natural world is rational and (ii) this rationale is a mystery beyond comprehension. Take for example, the following quotation from the *New York Times*:

> "All those people died for a reason [said a sixteen-year-old sophomore at Columbine High School outside Denver, CO, site of the April 20, 1999, shootings]. God was with them every step of the way," she went on to say. "He chose them for some special reason."[29]

As the student makes clear in this attempt to understand what I would certainly agree to be a tragic event, *there was a reason* for the many student deaths at Columbine High School in Colorado, but it's just that it was "some special reason" known, it seems, only in the mind of God. The presumption of "unknowable rationality" functions because "God" or "mystery" here plays the role of an empty signifier, which is, by strictest definition, devoid of content because it is, after all, "special" or, to us, "unknowable." "Mystery" thus provides a place that acts, as Robert Sharf recently commented on the related concept "experience," as "a mere placeholder that entails a substantive if indeterminate terminus for the relentless deferral of meaning. And this is precisely what makes the term experience [and I would add, theodices] so amenable to ideological appropriation."[30] In the words of Gary Lease, religions—most notably, we can now add, by means of their theodicies—attempt "to be totally *inclusive* of all paradoxes by establishing *exclusive* meanings." Because, as we have assumed, historical life is rather more complex than any totalized model, Lease predicts that, despite theologians' best attempts to completely rationalize the natural world, the dissonances and conflicts that inevitably arise will eventually cause "the societal system to *breakdown* (emphasis added) and the 'structures' [i.e., 'worlds'] which allowed such a paradoxical mutuality to dissolve."[31] One set of such structures are, I suggest, theodicies. Lease goes on to suggest that embarking on writing a history of the rise and decline of a social formation requires one to "catalog [the] strategies [i.e., structures] for *maintaining* paradoxes, *fighting* over dissonances, and *surviving* breakdowns."[32] Such a catalog would amount to a map of the many social sites where such devices as theodicies are developed, deployed, and contested.

As should by now be quite evident, theodicies are not only cognitive interfaces but are also an exercise in overt political justification and the exercise of power. Both of these two redescriptions are related, for, insomuch as a theodicy can be understood as mediating between the natural world and social "worlds"—thereby allowing participants to gloss over anomalous experiences and observations—then theodicies are also the mechanisms whereby this or that "world" is authorized as being satisfactory and in a one-to-one fit with the natural world. Intelligibility is therefore intimately linked to social legitimacy (this is nothing other than the old knowledge/power equation). *Theodicies therefore rationalize, in both senses of the term ("to make rational" and "to legitimize").* Because "worlds" are neither innocent nor disconnected from their builders, theodicies are political insomuch as they enable participants to actively portray any one particular "world"—along with the interests that shape this world—as being just or unjust, changeable or inevitable, bearable or unbearable, necessary or contingent, or simply—to borrow the infamous words from Voltaire's character, the metaphysico-theologico-cosmolo-boobologist, Dr. Pangloss—"the best of all possible worlds."[33] Even a casual reader of Voltaire's biting satire, *Candide* (1759) easily sees the sadly comic lack of fit between Pangloss's "world" and the incredibly tragic situations in which he and his young student, Candide, repeatedly find themselves.[34] Even the naive Candide has sufficient ironic sense to appreciate the lack of fit; early on in their travels, after they have been arrested—"one for talking and the other for listening with an air of approval"—Candide is flogged and Pangloss hung, all as part of an elaborate *auto-da-fé*—a public ceremony of repentance designed to protect the city from further earthquakes (a ritual, it turns out, that does not work).[35] Candide, stunned by the whole affair, simply remarks, "If this is the best of all possible worlds, then what are the others like?"[36]

Although it is only a short novel, *Candide* nicely demonstrates how people (such as its author, Voltaire) with different interests and political commitments actively contest the status of competing social "worlds" by means of differing theodicies (cosmogonies and apocalyptic tales can be redescribed in precisely this way as well). For, when read in his historical context, Voltaire's Pangloss is clearly a critique of Pope's (1688–1744), and, before him, Leibniz's, well known "philosophical optimism." Voltaire correctly understood the wider implications of their brand of complacent optimism: it is not only naive but it also amounts to little more than a politically conservative apologia for the status quo. After all, active social change of any sort is not really encouraged when, in the last lines from Epistle I of Pope's *Essay on Man*, we read those often cited lines:

> All Nature is but Art, unknown to thee;
> All Chance, Direction, which thou canst not see;
> All Discord, Harmony, not understood;
> All partial Evil, universal Good:
> And, spite of Pride, in erring Reason's spite,
> One truth is clear, "Whatever is, is RIGHT."

Although not all theodicies are politically regressive (obviously, Voltaire's parody was clearly oppositional to the conservatism of both Pope and Leibniz), *all theodicies are at their root political.* Insomuch as they portray one possible "world" as *the* World (whether that "world" is conservative or liberal, dominant or oppositional), they are by definition ideological, for their function is to portray the part as the Whole. As evidence of this, we need look no further than the lines from Pope's poem already quoted; they provide an example of the very totalizing of which Lease spoke earlier—all viewpoints, we are persuaded, are partial, limited, and subsumed under one harmonious, coherent, universal totality—a totality that, upon closer examination, is none other than yet another part dressed up as the Whole. This is the ideology of liberalism at its best; it is a profoundly political stance that seeks nonempirical, essential unity amidst empirical difference.[37]

So, when redescribed, *theodicies* become *sociodicies* (discourses on the status and legitimacy of this or that "world") and the problem of evil then becomes the problem of "evil." By this, I mean that, for the scholar of religion, the *presumption* that evil exists (and must therefore be addressed somehow) is itself the datum under study. So, instead of asking, along with Harold Kushner's popular book on the problem of evil, "Why do bad things happen to good people?" the scholar of religion asks two very different questions: "Why do people presume that the world *ought* to be coherent, sensible, intelligible, meaningful, or good in the first place?" and "What ends are served by this or that application of the good/bad pairing, or the rhetoric of 'evil'?" The assumption that drives this sort of redescriptive work is that value judgments, such as identifying this or that event as "evil," always take place within ambiguous, ever-changing historical, social "worlds." This means that we must seriously entertain that the designation "evil" tells us far more about a particular social "world" and the interests of the classifiers than it tells us about the act being classified.

Once again, the academic study of religion—when religion is conceived as but one more cultural practice—turns out to be an exercise in (i) determining the limits of what social groups understand as credible and (ii) identifying the mechanisms used to police and contest those limits. It is a conclusion seemingly related to Green's own conclusion: "theodicy's deepest impulse," he writes, "is not to report the bitter facts of life but to overcome and transform them."[38] But upon a closer look, Green is still engaged in *mythmaking* rather than *explanation*, for the "facts of life" (i.e., events in the natural world) in themselves are neither bitter nor sweet—they just are. Theodicies are the means by which communities plot and process the generic stuff of experience as either bitter or sweet. Also, Green's sense of "overcoming and transforming"—something that sounds suprisingly close to my notion of making "world" fit the natural world—arises from a view of theodicies as expressions of private, essentially moral impulses and motivations, rather than seeing theodicies as structural mechanisms that enable communities to posit and act out this thing we come to know as morality.

CONCLUSION

Public scholars of religion study the way people such as theologians artfully deploy and manipulate such classifications and social focusing devices as discourses on evil, origins, end times, and nonobvious beings. Or, to put it another way, because not all events in the natural world equally attract our attention (remember, the world's a busy place and I've only got so much attention to focus), such things as doctrines, creeds, traditions, myths, and rituals constitute the mechanisms whereby groups concoct and reproduce their "world" by exercising and managing what Jonathan Z. Smith terms an "economy of signification." It is an economy efficiently managed by cognitive and social classifications that delineate this from that, important from unimportant, saved from damned, good from evil, and, finally, us from them. As public scholars of religion, we therefore examine a rather specific group of narrative, behavioral, and institutional devices employed by people like, but not just, theologians—devices that represent and contest differing conceptions of who gets to count as part of the social "we."

What should be clear is that public scholars of religion are not in the business of nurturing, enhancing, or—despite the caricatures of those who wish to make the academic study of religion essentially a theological pursuit—criticizing the communities they study; this is the business of the various groups' members, theologians included. Neither are we in the business of proposing final, definitive, totalized theories; our work presumes the ambiguous, ad hoc nature of all social activity—scholarship included—making the academic study of religion tactical, problem oriented, and ironic. As a cultural critic, the anthropologically based scholar of religion's contribution is therefore made as a scholar of classification and social rhetoric—both of which are all too human, historic activities with discernible beginnings and discernible consequences.[39]

Given this conclusion, I repeat something that I suggested earlier in this essay: unlike the theologian, for the scholar of religion *qua* anthropologist of credibility, there is nothing religious about religion. Religion is simply the classification some of us give to various collections of artful but all-too-human devices that help to portray any given "world" as the "world without end. Amen."[40]

NOTES

1. Jonathan Z. Smith, "Are Theological and Religious Studies Compatible?" *Bulletin of the Council of Societies for the Study of Religion* 26, no. 3 (1997): 60.

2. Before spinning my wheels, however, I refer the interested reader to the various essays written over the past few decades by such figures as Sam Gill, "The Academic Study of Religion," *Journal of the American Academy of Religion* 62 (1994): 965–975; Hans Penner, "Criticism and the Development of a Science of Religion," *Studies in Religion* 15 (1986): 165–175, *Impasse and Resolution: A Critique of the Study of Religion* (New York: Peter Lang, 1989); Hans Penner and Edward Yonan, "Is a Science of Religion Possible?" *Journal of Religion* 52 (1972): 107–133; J. Samuel Preus, *Explaining Religion: Criticism and Theory from Bodin to Freud* (New Haven: Yale University Press, 1987); Robert Segal, "In Defense of Reductionism," *Journal of the American Academy of Religion* 51 (1983): 97–124, *Religion and the Social Sciences: Essays on the Confrontation* (Atlanta: Scholars Press, 1989), "How Historical is the History of Religions?" *Method & Theory in the Study of Religion* 1 (1989): 2–19, *Explaining and Interpreting Religion: Essays on the Issue* (New York: Peter Lang, 1992); Robert Segal and Donald Wiebe, "Axioms and Dogmas in the Study of Religion," *Journal of the American Academy of Religion* 57 (1989): 591–605; Jonathan Z. Smith, "'Religion' and 'Religious Studies': No Difference At All," *Soundings* 71 (1988): 231–244, "Are Theological and Religious Studies Compatible?" *Bulletin of the Council of Societies for the Study of Religion* 26, no. 3 (1997): 60–61; Ivan Strenski, "Reductionism Without Tears," in *Religion and Reductionism: Essays on Eliade, Segal, and the Challenge of the Social Sciences for the Study of Religion*, ed. Thomas Idinopulos and Edward Yonan (Leiden: E. J. Brill, 1993), 97–107; and Donald Wiebe "Beyond the Sceptic and the Devotee: Reductionism in the Scientific Study of Religion," *Journal of the American Academy of Religion* 52 (1984): 157–165, "The Failure of Nerve in the Academic Study of Religion," *Studies in Religion* 13 (1984): 401–422, "The Academic Naturalization of Religious Studies: Intent or Pretence?" *Studies in Religion* 15 (1986): 197–203,

The Politics of Religious Studies (New York: St. Martin's Press, 1999), notably the spirited exchange between Wiebe, Charles Davis (see Davis's "The Reconvergence of Theology and Religious Studies," *Studies in Religion* 4 [1974]: 205–221, "Wherein There is No Ecstasy," *Studies in Religion* 13 [1984]: 393–400), and several others that took place over a period of time in the Canadian journal *Studies in Religion*. Any informed conversation on this topic cannot take place without being familiar with the arguments of such writers.

3. I rely here on Jonathan Z. Smith: "From the perspective of the academic study of religion, theology is a datum, the theologian is a native informant" ("Are Theological and Religious Studies Compatible?" 60). Smith elaborates: "In the same spirit in which I welcome the study of the totalizing mythic endeavors, the *univers imaginaires*, of an Ogotemmêli [Marcel Griaule, *Conversations with Ogotemmêli* (Oxford: Oxford University Press, 1965)] or an Antonio Guzmàn [Gerardo Reichel-Dolmatoff, *Amazonian Cosmos* (Chicago: University of Chicago Press, 1971)], I would hope, some day, to read a consonant treatment of the analogous enterprise of Karl Barth's *Church Dogmatics*."

4. Mythmaking is a term I derive from Burton Mack; by "mythmaking" I simply mean those discourses that dehistoricize and decontextualize. On this alternative use of the term "myth," see Russell T. McCutcheon, "Myth," in *Guide to the Study of Religion*, ed. Willi Braun and Russell T. McCutcheon (London: Cassell Academic Press, 2000), 190–208; on the relations between mythmaking and the Althusserian term "social formation," see Burton Mack, "Social Formation," in *Guide to the Study of Religion*, and McCutcheon, "Redescribing 'Religion' as Social Formation: Toward a Social Theory of Religion," in *What is Religion? Origins, Definitions, and Explanations*, ed. Thomas A. Idinopulos and Brian C. Wilson (Leiden: E. J. Brill, 1998), 51–71.

5. *Critics Not Caretakers: Redescribing the Public Study of Religion* (Albany: State University of New York Press, 2001).

6. Given the approach to the study of religion I advocate in this essay, Pope's epigraph has limited use. When we take into account the rest of the *Essay on Man* (ed. Maynard Mack [London: Meuthen, 1950]), Pope's other writings, and his historic context (1688–1744), it is obvious that he is not advising against metaphysical speculation and theology but, rather, warning against using human reason to pry into the mysterious ways of God. For instance, compare Pope's counsel to that found in Milton's *Paradise Lost* (VIII: 72–75):

> . . . the great Architect
> Did wisely to conceal, and not divulge
> His secrets to be scann'd by them who ought
> Rather admire.

It should be clear that, despite my use of the epigraph, I follow neither Pope nor Milton in their counsel against the use of human reason when it comes to the study of religion.

7. For an example of a scholar who argues that "religion" has little analytic utility, see Tim Fitzgerald, "A Critique of the Concept of Religion," *Method & Theory in the Study of Religion* 9, no. 2 (1997): 91–110, *The Ideology of Religious Studies* (New York: Oxford University Press, 2000), "Experience," in *Guide to the Study of Religion*. For the geopolitics of the category "religion," notably during the cold war period, see my own *Manufacturing Religion: The Discourse on Sui Generis Religion and the Politics of Nostalgia* (New York: Oxford University Press, 1997).

8. Although I found the 1996 cover story on the field published by *Lingua Franca* helpful in many ways (Charlotte Allen, "Is Nothing Sacred? Casting Out the Gods from Religious Studies," *Lingua Franca* 6, no. 7 [1996]: 30–40; see also Allen's "Response to *Bulletin* 26, no. 4," *Bulletin of the Council of Societies for the Study of Religion* 27, no. 2 [1998]: 45–46, which comprises her rejoinder to replies to her *Lingua Franca* article that were published in the *Bulletin of the Council of Societies for the Study of Religion* 26, no. 4 [1997]), the way it was framed by pitting so-called religious members of the American Academy of Religion (AAR) against so-called nonreligious members of the North American Association for the Study of Religion (NAASR) only clouded the issue; the very social rhetoric of most interest to study, the sacred/secular and private/public distinctions, was presupposed and therefore left intact.

9. Despite my disagreement with Wilfred Cantwell Smith's well-known criticism of the category "religion" for its misplaced emphasis on the external, cumulative tradition at the expense of what he understands as the prior, inner, personalistic faith (a rhetorically loaded distinction), his survey of the history of "religion" is still one of the most widely read (*The Meaning and End of Religion* [Minneapolis: Fortress Press, 1963]). For a more useful survey, see Jonathan Smith, "Religion, Religions, Religious," in *Critical Terms for Religious Studies*, ed. Mark C. Taylor, (Chicago: University of Chicago Press, 1998), 269–284.

10. This really is the old insider/outsider problem; see Russell T. McCutcheon, *The Insider/Outsider Problem in the Study of Religion: A Reader* (London: Cassell Academic Press, 1998).

11. I think here of Delwin Brown's recent attempt to define academic theology as an analytic, comparative endeavor, as "the analysis of religious beliefs" per se ("Academic Theology and Religious Studies," *Bulletin of the Council for the Study of Religion* 26, no. 3 [1997]: 64–66). "The academic theologian," writes Brown,

> attempts to understand a community's religious beliefs in their context, including how they are related to and interact with other discursive and non-discursive practices, and what these beliefs actually do in that context. The academic theologian asks how these beliefs can be evaluated in relation to various normative horizons, including the diverse norms within the community, the norms of adjacent communities and, if relevant, the scholarly community as well. Finally, the academic theologian explores the various alternatives to the beliefs in question, whether they are options implicit in the tradition itself or possible adaptations from the outside.

Because his concern with purely emic description (i.e., analysis of beliefs "in their context") is then joined to normative judgment and a search for alternatives, Brown's "academic theology" is clearly far removed from the naturalistic theorizing that goes on in the academic study of religion. In fact, his purely descriptive, comparative, normative "academic theology" is little different from the kind of work still carried out by phenomenologists and liberal humanists in general, providing support for my contention that all three sorts of scholarship are not just related, but are all fundamentally *religious* studies. As an aside, because the vast majority of scholars of religion produce descriptive/comparative studies that do not entertain naturalistic theories to answer the why question, it may make sense to distinguish the more common name for the field, "religious studies," from what I am calling either the study of religion or the academic study of religion.

12. Luce Giard, introduction to *Culture in the Plural*, by Michel de Certeau, trans. Tom Conley (Minneapolis: University of Minnesota Press, 1997), viii.

13. The following four presumptions are derived from my brief rejoinder to Bryan S. Rennie, author of *Reconstructing Eliade* (Albany: State University of New York Press, 1996). The rejoinder was published as "Of Strawmen and Humanists: A Reply to Bryan Rennie," *Religion* 29, no. 1 (1999): 91–92.

14. To establish this point with students, I tell them a story about a dinner party one summer evening at my brother-in-law's home in Niagara Falls. Several times throughout the course of the evening, guests moving from the house to the patio, and vice versa, unknowingly walked straight into the patio door, knocking the screen out. Although each time was funnier than the last, and each guest more embarrassed than the last, each instance was an example of how the guests' expectations for how the external world functioned were not quite in step with the natural world.

15. William Paden, "World," in *Guide to the Study of Religion*. We must be careful to distinguish "world" from ideology (when ideology is taken in its weaker sense as meaning "a system of ideas"); ideologies (when understood in the more critical sense) are the devices that actors employ to represent some "world" as the World. I will elaborate more on this below.

16. On the roles selection and archiving play in the production of "history," see Willi Braun, "Amnesia in the Production of (Christian) History," *Bulletin of the Council of Societies for the Study of Religion* 28, no. 1 (1999): 3–8.

17. Perhaps this is why I would argue that scholars intent simply on studying the "meaning worlds" of a novel are engaged in a rather different pursuit from the one I recommend here; they are engaged in a philosophically idealist study that sees the "meaning world" as an end in itself and not the tip of a sociopolitical iceberg.

18. On the social (and hence political) nature of "experience" see Robert H. Sharf, "Experience," in *Critical Terms in Religious Studies*, 94–115, and Joan Wallach Scott, "The Evidence of Experience," *Critical Inquiry* 17 (1991): 773–797.

19. Bruce Lincoln, *Theorizing Myth: Narrative, Ideology, and Scholarship* (Chicago: University of Chicago Press, 1999), 209. The full quotation reads: "If myth is ideology in narrative form, then scholarship is myth with footnotes." By this, I believe Lincoln means to suggest that differing discursive communities concoct themselves by means of differing rhetorical techniques; connecting one's ideas and arguments to a historical tradition of scholarship by means of footnotes is a technique that authorizes one's own work by weaving it within an already recognized body of work (something this very citation of Lincoln has already accomplished for my own essay). Myth without footnotes—in other words, narratives that actively contest their own historicity by appeals to, for example, the time of origins—is what Lincoln labels ideology.

20. Speaking of the "meaning of life," Monty Python's film by the same name comes to mind. What makes the film particularly comic is that it takes a topic of seemingly universal import and provides a number of clearly skewed, partial, and even biased takes on it, thereby effectively disarming the totalizing rhetoric of all "meaning of life" discourses.

21. See my own *Critics Not Caretakers: Redescribing the Public Study of Religion* (Albany: State University of New York Press, 2001).

22. Max Weber, "Theodicy, Salvation, Rebirth," in *The Sociology of Religion*, trans. Ephraim Fischoff (Boston: Beacon Press, 1993), 147.

23. This quotation comes from the anthropological film on U.S. Pentecostal snake-handling churches in the Appalachian region, *Jolo Serpent Handlers*, Karen Kramer, director. New York: Image Conversions Systems, 1977. 16mm.

24. Ronald M Green, "Theodicy," in *Encyclopedia of Religion*, general ed. Mircea Eliade (New York: Macmillan Press, 1987), 14: 441.

25. "Redescription" is a term derived from Jonathan Z. Smith; see in particular his essay "Sacred Persistence: Toward a Redescription of Canon," in *Imagining Religion: From Babylon to Jonestown* (Chicago: University of Chicago Press, 1982).

26. Atul Gawande, "A Queasy Feeling: Why Can't We Cure Nausea?" *The New Yorker*, 5 July 1999, 36–37.

27. Daniel Dennett, *Darwin's Dangerous Idea: Evolution and the Meanings of Life* (New York: Simon and Schuster, 1995), 73–80.

28. Terry Eagleton, *The Significance of Theory* (Oxford, UK: Blackwell, 1992), 26.

29. Sara Rimer, "Columbine Students Seek Answers in Their Faith," *New York Times*, Sunday, 6 June 1999, sec. 1, p. 22.

30. Sharf, "Experience," 113.

31. Gary Lease, "The History of 'Religious' Consciousness and the Diffusion of Culture: Strategies for Surviving Dissolution," *Historical Reflections/Reflexions Historiques* 20, no. 3 (1994): 475.

32. Ibid., 475.

33. In the French original, Pangloss is described as a teacher of "*métaphysico-théologo-cosmolonigologie*"; the French *nigaud*, whose phonetic equivalent "nigo" appears in this comical compound, translates as "boob."

34. Voltaire, *Candide, or Optimism*, ed. and trans. Robert M. Adams (New York: W. W. Norton, 1966).

35. Readers must keep in mind that *Candide* was written in the wake of the great Lisbon earthquake of 1755, where it was first thought that more than 100,000 people had perished.

36. Voltaire, *Candide*, 12.

37. It is my contention that the methodologically reductive stance adopted in this paper avoids the kind of totalizing identified here.

38. Green, "Theodicy," 440.

39. I can do no better than cite as examples some of Bruce Lincoln's work, especially, *Discourse and the Construction of Society: Comparative Studies of Myth, Ritual, and Classification* (New York: Oxford University Press, 1989), *Authority: Construction and Corrosion* (Chicago: University of Chicago Press, 1994), and his most recent, *Theorizing Myth*, 1999.

40. An earlier version of this paper was presented to the Faculty of Theology at Georgetown University, November 1999. My thanks to Professor Francisca Cho for kindly arranging my visit.

3

Why "Theology" Won't Work

Ivan Strenski

Some of My Best Friends. . . .

What makes entering this discussion worthwhile is my great respect and admiration for those whose opinions I have generally not shared in the past. In general, the folk I know on the opposite side of the religious studies-theology debate are some of the finest people I can think of. They have always in general struck me as well-meaning and attractive individuals. Here, it is perhaps worth a moment to salute the late Walter Capps. Walter was a person with whom I had serious differences over the relation of religious studies to theology both in print and in heated face-to-face debate at the University of California, Santa Barbara. These differences ran deep and, even though we tried, I do not think we succeeded in understanding each other as much as we would have liked. Perhaps we were both insufficiently clear about what we advocated, and insufficiently clear about how best to join the issues at stake. Certainly, I think we were surprised by the intensity of our exchange of over ten years ago. In any case, this fine man's untimely and tragic death aborted further workings through of our differences, something I regret, and which, I like to think, Walter does as well. My regard for Del Brown, the main target of my remarks, is equally high. Brown and I have also been at it for some time, and with considerable vigor.

The main reason I raise these personal matters in a public forum is that they turn out to bear fundamentally on the issues between religious studies and theology and upon which I wish to focus. Over the years, I have become persuaded that much of the debate between religious studies and theology—and to be sure much of the rancor attaching to it—is bound up in considerations about the personal motives and intentions of our partners in debate. To wit, I am convinced that the main motive of those on the side of theology is an extraordinary high-mindedness and desire to do good. I believe their reason for insisting on the place of what seems to me a perhaps unwittingly sectarian enterprise—so-called "theology"—in places where I believe it does not belong arises out of motives I can only admire. But there's the rub. For although I salute in all sincerity the motives (and it goes without saying, the intellect) of my colleagues across the table, I think they may be misdirecting their energies to projects that are finally not worthy of their efforts. Instead of trying to carve out a place for something called "theology," within the public university, I wish these superb people would throw their lot in with religious studies. As I shall argue, and in light of recent developments in the thought of such colleagues as Del Brown, we are close to intellectual reconciliation. To my mind, a most urgent priority of those who care about the academic study of religion is to throw their full and unqualified support to what has come to be known as religious studies. Brown, as I shall discuss, seems to me already to have done this. I want to urge all those of similar mind to rally to the cause. As I shall show in my discussion, this does not, I think, necessarily mean that most if not all of what Brown wants to do in doing theology might not also be done within religious studies in a public university. But, this is far from certain, as I shall explain in due course.

I risk escalating the emotional level of this discussion by writing of a "cause" in behalf of religious studies for a number of reasons. For one, the world today seems to be making it impossible and undesirable for us to ignore *religion* any longer. Who else but students of religion should take up the challenge of understanding *religion* and its place in explaining the way the world is? Yet, I fear we have once more failed the world in its time of need. As I write this, hundreds of thousands of refugees from Kosovo are being ruthlessly driven from their homes, primarily for being Muslims. And these are the "lucky" ones. Thousands already have been murdered and otherwise violated, as they had been just a short time ago in Bosnia for having chosen their religious ancestry "badly." Although the secularists among the punditocracy will go on interminably about "aged-old enmities," "ethnicity" and such, we know that, in very large part, *religious* differences have shaped affairs in the Balkans, especially as religious identity has shaped national identity in this and in many other parts of the world. We in the study of religion broadly speaking—theologians and religious studies types together—must share in the lack of understanding and explanation of how religion has played in these matters. Except for a few voices, such as Mark Juergensmeyer, Stanley Tambiah, Michael Sells, and others, we have not made the case that we have anything useful to say in cases where religion is a major factor in today's politics.[1] We have only just begun to show both how and that taking *religion* seriously makes a difference. Theology and religious studies need to speak with a single voice about the importance of religion in the world if we are to speak with voices loud enough to make a difference.

Now, my concern about promoting the understanding and explaining of religion—religious studies—concerns "theology," because this common effort cannot realistically be made under the rubric of "theology," no matter how scholars like Brown try to nuance the term. It is too late for that. Consider the centripetal flight of such subspecialities of religious studies as Buddhist, Jewish, and Islamic studies from the center onto the outer orbits of Area Studies. In my experience, this results directly from fears that religious studies conceals a theological, and worse yet, confessional theological program. As we will see in considering Garrett Green's proposals about Karl Barth's concept of religion, these fears are well justified. But let me be more precise; the common effort of which I speak requires a common united institutional base. In this day and age, as Del Brown himself cogently argues, that institutional base can only be "religious studies."[2] In the university, primarily for cultural, but also for intellectual, reasons, "theology" can never be the banner under which students of religion might unite because, rightly or wrongly, the term raises too many suspicions. In Brown's case, I think these suspicions appear to be unjustified. But, as I shall show in my discussion of Barthian strategies to transform religious studies, the suspicions of a neo-Orthodox Christian infiltration would be more than justified. Were they adopted, this would in turn guarantee the exclusion of both "theology" and religious studies from the university entirely. Were we to accept Green's proposals, we would deserve exclusion.

RELIGION AND BARTH ON "RELIGION"

Tossed about on unfriendly seas, today's Barthians have learned to tack into the winds of cultural fashion.[3] Instead of resisting the relativism of values that made Barthians heroes in the midst of the abject accommodation of theological liberals to the Nazis, some of today's Barthians now take cover under the flaccid relativism served up by postmodernism. In a recent attempt to present Barth's theology as "challenging the religious studies canon," Christian theologian Garrett Green has argued that, given the postmodern moment, we should admit Karl Barth's neo-Orthodox theology as an equal alongside other "secular" theories of religion.[4] Got up in his latest postmodern duds, Green says that, since postmodernists agree that all theories and inquiry are value laden, we might as well be open to theories with Christian assumptions— even in the public university. After all, did not Durkheim, Freud, Eliade, and others argue from value positions, some even pseudoreligious? If so, how can we exclude taking the Barthian theory of religion seriously alongside the others? Thus he asserts in his conclusion that "religious studies would do better to attend to those representatives of a tradition who speak with consistency from its central sources of truth."[5]

The short answer to this is that Barth's Christianity is too narrow and sectarian a starting point for the study of religion in our religiously diverse nation and universities. Christianity, as well as Judaism, Islam, and such, are simply nonstarters when it comes to the foundations of the study of religion. As I shall show, Barth's concept of religion is, for one thing, theologically "loaded" in a way that ipso facto disqualifies it and Barthian theology from any foundational role in a study of religion proper to a university. Green may or may not know this, but he is not to be deterred. Instead, he treats us to a lengthy interpretation of Barth's thought about "religion," calculated to guarantee a place for Barthian theology in the same epistemological class as the religious naturalists such as Freud, Durkheim, and the rest. But does this really work?

I want to argue that even Barth's negative interpretation of religion is so compromised by his Christian theological commitments that it scarcely makes things
better. His entire position requires commitments that exclude entire populations
from the serious study of religion. The classic, but woefully unexamined, Barthian
critique of "religion" thus constitutes one of the main seats of resistance to further
progress of religious studies. In another place, I sketched out an argument why
Barthian dominance in Christian theology, along with its inhospitality to the religious history and experience of non-Christians, may even be a principal factor in
the current dismal state of Christian theology.[6] Those guided by Barth's view that
"religion" is man's [sic] attempt to grasp the ungraspable, while the Word (*mutatis
mutandis*, "Christianity") is radically different—literally, not a "religion"—will
never be persuaded that they have anything much of value to learn from the study
of religion. So to Barth's conception of religion.

Barth's discussion is now classic. Green's attempt to rehabilitate it bears repeating and analysis to reveal the sophistry that I believe disqualifies Barthian
approaches to religious studies.[7] I have called Barth's notion of religion "loaded"
because it incorporates within it a piece of neo-Orthodox Protestant doctrine. For
Barth, religion is a kind of sin: it is humanity's attempt to grasp the (ungraspable
for Barth) divine. For Barth, the religions are "attempts by man to justify and sanc-
tify himself before a willfully and arbitrarily constructed image of God."[8] Further:
"Religion is unbelief. Religion is a concern—the concern, one must say straight-
away—of the Godless human being."[9] Accordingly, Barth decries the emergence
of religion as "an independent known quantity alongside revelation" until at last
"religion is not to be understood in terms of revelation but rather revelation in
terms of religion."[10]

Now, how could such a notion of religion possibly serve as a foundational concept upon which to ground the study of religion in a university? Can Barth's
notion of religion, for example, even pass a simple "says-who?" test? Do the other
religions think they are trying to grasp what to Barth's mind they are incapable of
grasping? Do they think of themselves as "religions" in the Barthian sense? And, if
not, what gives Barth the right to say that they are? Many of the great religions,
such as Theravada Buddhism or the many schools of Vedanta, have sophisticated
accounts of the limits of ordinary knowledge and human abilities—often long in
advance of anything developed by Christian theologians. They do not feel that their
religions are products of human construction in Barth's sense. People these days
should surely know that Muslims are abundantly clear as to the divine origins of
the Koran; Hindus see the Vedas as originating from beyond the human realm; the
Buddhist dharma is likewise something transcending humankind and its history. Do
they too not feel that revelation favors them rather than the Christ? Does the question even need to be asked? Do they even accept the ideal of revelation assumed
by Barth as the measure of the ultimate worth of a religion? They do not—at least
while remaining what they are. The entire Barthian discourse on religion is simply
a piece of question-begging neo-Orthodox Protestant apologetics.

In its parochialism and abject ignorance, the Barthian position is not only embarrassing for its coarse ignorance of the religions, but also offensive to the dignity of the spiritual and religious lives of literally billions of fellow human beings. At the beginning of his article, Green asks why the "religious studies canon . . . includes some theologians while excluding others."[11] Although I cannot answer for all, the answer, as far as Barth is concerned, is that his position, especially on the notion of religion itself, as I have argued, is a piece of neo-Orthodox Protestant apologetic. Thus, Barthian theology cannot challenge any sort of intellectual paradigm—whether of religious studies or not—because its position on religion is hopelessly sectarian and dogmatic. Compare, for instance, however theory-laden Durkheim's thought may be, how his notion of the sacred has generated several generations of fruitful research on religion—everyone from Marcel Mauss and Henri Hubert, to Robert Bellah, E. E. Evans Pritchard, and Mary Douglas. At best, Barthian theology provides an object lesson in how religious studies ought *not* be done. (This is in fact how I use Barth in my theory course at the University of California.) Barth's approach to religion is certifiably sterile, having produced no studies of religion outside a narrow circle of confessional mission-minded theologians exemplified by such a notorious partisan as Hendrik Kraemer.

Am I being too hard on Barth and Green? Citing other parts of the *Church Dogmatics*, Green seeks to redeem (or seems to redeem) the notion of religion, but at the cost of a paradoxical dogmatism. Says Barth, "the Christian religion is the true religion."[12] Forgetting for the moment the affront to understanding among the religions that this seems to be, the Barthians have—or think they have—more to say to mollify critics. Green tells us that when Barth asserts that Christianity is the "true" religion, he does not really mean it. He is only speaking in a paradoxical sense about such a would-be "true" religion. Thus, Barth immediately adds that Christianity is only the "true religion" in the sense that humans are "justified sinners." That is to say, not at all. As Barth would have it, this is at best to say that if Christianity is the "true" religion, it has nothing to do with the qualities of Christians or the institution called Christianity, but depends solely on divine election and grace. Christianity is subject to divine judgment just like any other religion, and in this sense is not in principle special.[13] As if to reassure us that Barth is not just another apologist for a kind of Christian faith, Green says of Barth that "one is hard pressed to find a non-theological interpretation that makes as negative a value judgment about religion as does Barth."[14] So Barth seems to escape charges of preferring Christian "religion" above all other "religions," because Christian "religion," like all others, is simply the futile and sinful attempt by creatures to put themselves in the place of the creator. All "religions" once more stand in judgment before divine supremacy.

This attempt by Green to rehabilitate Barth, however, is profoundly dishonest and/or self-contradictory. Thus, when Barth is challenged by being presented with religions as equally devoted to an ideal of grace and divine transcendence, such as the several forms of Japanese Pure Land Buddhism, Jodo, and Jodo Shinshu, he flatly declines to admit them. They cannot be "true religions," says Barth—even in the paradoxical sense that Christianity can. And why is that, Barth asks? Not because all religions are flawed and under the judgment of revelation as he claimed earlier. But because they fail to be religions identified with the name of Jesus—simply because they are not Christian:

> Through the grace of God there are human beings who live by his grace. Or, stated concretely: through the name Jesus Christ there are human beings who believe in this name. To the extent that this is the self-understanding of Christians and of the Christian religion, it can and must be said of it that it and it alone is the true religion.[15]

Thus (surprise, surprise), since Christian religion is the only religion "'bound to God's revelation'"[16] in Jesus, it alone can be truly true, so to speak.

Thus, after pages and pages of Green's labored exegesis of Barth, and after all the wriggling over Barth's paradoxical dialectics, we are back where we started with Barth's original dogmatic Christian triumphalism, with his vulgar apologetics. Religion is unbelief, and Christianity is exempt. The whole Barthian effort seems shot through with deviousness and bad faith.

What the Debate between "Theology" and Religious Studies Is Not About

Aside from Green's maneuvering to read Barth as someone who studies religion, rather than creating and propagating a confessional form of it, few members of the academy today would argue for doing confessional theology within a department of religious studies. I know of no one who would seriously consider engaging the study of religion with as loaded a notion of religion as Barth's. Other attempts to articulate a theologically friendly study of religion stand out in recent years. The members of the St. Louis Project, which I severely took to task some years ago, for example, represent a conceptually muddled but nonetheless goodwill attempt to make room for a kind of theology within the university—here adding further confusion to the issue because their plan was proposed for a Roman Catholic university.[17] Equally confused are the attempts by Richard B. Miller to criticize the so-called "purity" of religious studies by admitting theology in some undisclosed way into the religious studies curriculum. One is even tempted to question Miller's good faith in this debate, in light of the way his arguments amount to dragging one red herring through this discussion after another. Sincere or not, Miller makes the amazing claim that the quarrels between theology and religious studies are about whether the theologies ought to be studied in a religious studies curriculum! Thus, Miller makes the totally absurd and unsupported complaint that religious studies wants to "exile theology altogether from the study of religion."[18] Can anyone name *any* program in religious studies where theologies are *not* studied—indeed almost exclusively Christian ones? The issue has *never* been the red herring of the *study* of theology, but its practice, its "doing" as I argued a decade before Miller's book appeared, and as Miller knows well, given his citations of this same article.[19] Typical of Miller is his asking of such vacuous questions such as this while hiding his real intent to justify what he calls "normative theological inquiry."[20] Thus, Miller leads with the innocent-appearing question: "Could a student of Western culture claim basic literacy without having studied Augustine's *Confessions?*" only to follow with an appeal for "normative theological inquiry."[21] Does Miller really think this question raises an issue pertinent to the relation of theology to religious studies? The issue is and has always been the "doing" of theology within an institutional setting in which this may be inappropriate—as Miller eventually admits.[22]

The Debate between "Theology" and Religious Studies Is Partly Semantic

In another class entirely, therefore, are the cogent and rigorous proposals of real integrity by Del Brown. It is Brown's program that in many ways, I believe, offers the most honest and considered approach to the issues dividing religious studies and theology to date. And, since as I read him, Brown's position seems in part informed by the issues raised in my critique of the St. Louis Project and in its defense, let me briefly review some of that earlier discussion.

In general, I see Brown's arguments at once to be more viable than anything produced by the St. Louis Project. But, at the same time, some of his key proposals seem snagged in a sticky web of semantics that in effect rather immobilizes them. First, the good news. By contrast with the St. Louis Project Report, Brown never says religious studies should become the basis for a new religion formed round the classroom.[23] Unlike the members of the St. Louis Project, he knows the difference between "studying" theology and "doing" it.[24] He also offers an interesting historical narrative about how a "non-religious theology" came to be with the rise of individualism in the West, thus turning out many of the interesting characters of Western intellectual history possessed by the theological muse, but unable to abide their home religious communities. He alludes to how this quirky "personal theology" set the terms for much of the rambunctious style of American discourse about religion as it emerged out of the early Christian and medieval world of a "religious theology" governed firmly by the collective will of the church and dedicated to expressing it.[25] Despite Brown's appreciation of the possibilities and great influence of these "personal theologies," he believes that intellectual activities like theology cannot forsake the reality of collective life. Theologies arise in concrete historical and social contexts; they have a salience and life in relation to their social bases. Today, where the churches would not provide the social bases of Brown's theology, the university could and, he argues, should.

Thus, Brown advocates what he calls an "academic theology"—not to be confused with my sarcastic use of the same term.[26] Brown's theology is thus "academic" in that he believes it unambiguously conforms to the ideals of the university,[27] even praising present-day religious studies for its leadership in many areas in which he seeks to see theology thrive.[28] Thus, Brown feels his "academic theology" needs to adhere to canons of self-criticism that are rigorous and all the rest. This is not to say that Brown has no qualms about the present state of the university (don't we all?), but this does not stop him from embracing the university's values, if reserving the right to reform and criticize them. For Brown, theology is about *studying* religion, studying it in historical and social contexts, even, as Brown advocates, "empirically" and with added doses of field work to boot. Even Brown's belief that beyond *studying* religion, we should also be interpreting and thus constructing religion may in the end not turn out to be that much of a departure from the practices prevailing in many other secular disciplines.[29] All Brown's talk of the constructive activity of "academic theology" seems to entail is a recognition of the value-laden character of inquiry—something he believes all academic disciplines share. We are constantly "evaluating" what facts are important enough to be the focus of our attention, which interpretive lens to apply to a particular subject and so on. Hermeneutics is inescapable.[30] From the viewpoint of religious studies, what is there not to like about what Brown has conceived and so cogently argued now for some years?

In a way, the first source of my criticism is the very inoffensiveness to religious studies of Brown's "academic theology." What escapes me is why we should not call this "academic theology" by its real name—"religious studies"? (Come home, Del Brown!) Thus, like religious studies, Brown's "academic theology" is analytic in exploring the interrelations among religious ideas, empirical in exposing the articulations of ideas and their concrete contexts, and interpretive in recognizing the choices made all along the way. All well and good. But, more to the point of my objections, what is gained, what is at stake, in persisting to use the term "theology" at all? Brown generously and sincerely celebrates the many achievements of religious studies, holding them up as ideals for what his "academic theology" might do—granted to an audience of more traditional theologians, one imagines. So, why, one is driven to ask, not just opt for doing religious studies? Why persist with the term "theology"? Brown's engagement of religious studies with theology seems to come down to a semantic quibble.

Having said that semantics may be part of the issues dividing "theologians" and religious studies types, let me say that I do not think semantics a trivial matter. In my experience of self-identified theologians and others, there is an affection for the venerable term "theology," transcending most arguments and evidence one might bring to bear against it. Loyalty to the term "theology" in a case where not many good reasons can be found for distinguishing it from religious studies is a strange and mysterious thing. There's a magic in the word "theology" that still casts its spell. In my experience, such reverence is about the way calling something a "theological" inquiry grants it a measure of seriousness and sobriety in a way it might otherwise not have. We all know how calling activities "scientific" performs a similar trick. To test this at least anecdotally, imagine a course proposed on popular culture. Left unadorned in the course catalogue, the term "popular culture" might evoke some sneers and jeers. But if this "popular culture" course were actually advertised as "popular culture: a theological inquiry" a hush would fall over the faculty sitting in committee to consider it worthy of inclusion in the roster of courses offered for the degree. A "theological inquiry" must be a weighty thing, a matter of considerable seriousness. So, let the course pass. I wonder how much of the persistence of Del Brown and others in pressing on with talk of "theology" is really about lending gravity—no doubt well deserved—to their endeavors?

"ACADEMIC THEOLOGY," RELIGIOUS STUDIES, AND HERMENEUTICS

But at least three problems arise with this attachment to the term, "theology." They are serious. First, outside of Brown's attempts to ground such a term, it is unclear whether there is such a thing as "theology" in the generic sense in which Brown and others use it. Christians, whether Catholic, Orthodox, or Protestant, are not alone in the world, as I know Brown knows. I would agree that one could fairly speak of Advaita, Dvaita, and Vishishtadvaita Vedantin "theologies" and also Aryasamaji, Shaiva, or Vaishnava Hindu "theologies," as well as Reform, Reconstructionist, Conservative or Orthodox Jewish "theologies," not to mention various Sunni or Shi'i Muslim "theologies." But besides these, we must admit other very different religious systems, such as the atheistic or nontheistic religious systems of much of the Buddhist world, as well as Jainism, Taoism, Yoga, and such. For them, the term "theology" is deeply offensive. Likewise, there are religious traditions in which the very idea of a "theology" is so weakly developed as to be virtually nonexistent. What Confucian theologians come to mind? Some other term for the activity that Brown describes must step in to reduce this offense. If one wants to maintain a kind of semantic parallelism with "theology," perhaps we need to get accustomed to speaking of the "nibbanologies," "mokshologies" or "atheologies" of nontheistic or atheistic systems of religions in their moments of constructive endeavor?

Second, while Del Brown recognizes the importance of theology having a social base, I think the analogy Brown would have us accept between confessional theology and the church, on the one side, and "academic theology" and the university, on the other, is inapt—unless certain precautions are taken. "Academic theology" still needs to inhere in religion for it to be recognizable as theology. The same follows for religious studies as well. It is not enough for "academic theology" to abide by the values of the university—in its values, rituals, and such—to guarantee that "academic theology" would be both "academic" and "theology." Such adherence only guarantees the "academic" part of the dyad. Brown needs to say how the "theological" part comes in without undoing the "academic" part. By the same token, we could speak of an academic place for political ideology along parallel lines with what Brown advocates for "theology." If the term "academic politics" were not already so badly tarnished by its conjuring up images of the pettiness of faculty squabbles, perhaps the term "academic politics" would serve as a fitting parallel term to "academic theology." But this is really not possible, anymore than the term "theology" can escape its home generative context in real religious discourse. The *doing* of political ideology, like the *doing* of "theology," cannot but help inhering in real extra-academic political life even while they are taught at the university. What would be the difference between James Carville promoting his political ideology in a classroom from Swami Vivekananda advancing theosophical "mokshology" in the same venue? None really in terms of their lack of fit in the public university. Political ideology taught at the university for the purpose of political advocacy is as problematic as "theology" *done* in the same way. The university should not be in the business of providing captive audiences for the preaching of belief systems—other than its own belief system of universal open inquiry. In Brown's own terms, "academic theology" would have to have the same relation to religion as political science, say, had to political life. I think this means that it would have to be global and comparative in reference, all the while ascribing to the norms of good citizenship in the university. That our political "scientists," like our economists, philosophers, sociologists, and such, practice their crafts in the public university from a position as narrowly "confessional" or ideologically compromised as I accuse our theologians of being, does not excuse so-called "academic theology." It will only make matters worse for open inquiry in the university if now "academic theology" were to join in deepening the corruption of the university. What we need is not more ideologizing of the university, but a great deal less. We need economists to put aside their commitments to right wing political economy and open their discipline to serious alternatives to market forms of economic life; we need philosophers to get out of the business of being "theologians" of secular humanism without lapsing back into formalism; we need sociologists to leave off advocacy of the latest bleeding-heart social agenda, hiding under a cloud of statistics and masquerading behind the mask of the "scientific" study of society. The university needs to get off the "needle" of ideology (or theology), not to make excuses for more of it.

This leads me to a third point: whether this empirical and contextual "academic theology" would be anything recognizable as a theology, rather than, say, just religious studies? If theologians like Brown want to use "theology" to stake out a term, and activity, of their own, I would argue that hermeneutics might ably serve this role without causing the scandal that "theology" does.[31] Let me recapitulate a proposal I made along these lines in 1986, and bring it up to date with Brown's arguments.

In my reply to the St. Louis Project Report of 1986,[32] I tried to make a case for what I took to be a possible distinctive role for a properly rehabilitated theology within the university. Unlike what I think Brown actually proposes, I did not try to reshape theology into religious studies. Instead, I sought to get at what theologies had contributed to the religious traditions in which they had a part. To me, this was not the academic activity of *studying* religion—analytically, empirically, etc.—that Brown has laid out. That is, and always properly will be, religious studies. To me, the theologies were rather notable for their hermeneutic genius, their *making* and *constructing* religion in a self-conscious way. In this sense, their practice of the interpretive art was more robust than that which Brown assigns at least to some portion of the performance of his "academic theology." Accordingly, Brown believes that "academic theology" "evaluates" and thus constructs in at least two ways.

One may evaluate deliberately, in which case one performs a "critical examination and reconstruction of religious ideas."[33] In this sense, one is constructing in the full sense of the term. As theologian, Aquinas was not just an excellent student of Aristotle, nor was he just adept at analyzing the myriad relations among an equally large set of conceptions, even with implications for the Christian life and church order. He created an immense and original theological edifice permitting Christians for centuries thereafter to imagine a Christian life in durable and meaningful ways. So also my conception of what theologians should do—stripped of their academic role of doing *"studies"*—is that they are imaginative creators of religious conceptions like those an Aquinas exemplifies.

But Brown also believes we cannot avoid construction and evaluation. One does so by default, so to speak, when one assumes certain values in exploring the inner relations among religious ideas or the relations between those ideas and the various empirical life-forms with which they may be related. Thus, using my example of Aquinas, when the great Dominican friar did his analyses of ideas, and then when he thought about them in terms of their related forms of life, he also selected things in these investigations that pointed back to his own values. Thus, he presupposed some sort of constructed world of values, however incomplete and fragmentary it might have been.

Now several questions need to be raised in terms of this vision of inadvertent or unconscious interpretations or evaluations. First, what could the "academic theology" equivalent of the confessional creativity of Aquinas be? Upon what set of common values could such a creative edifice be built? It is easy to imagine such creative efforts within various religious traditions. But, when those restrictions are removed, the "academic theology" that Brown recommends seems a little like the proverbial playing of tennis with the nets down. What norms would guide and give shape to such an "academic theology"? How would one know when and if one did it well? The same doubts would adhere to a university political "scientist" who would seek to be creative and constructive about political ideology and such, yet who would want, indeed need, to do so free of any partisan commitments. I know what it would be to have James Carville or Billy Kristol in a political science department as distinguished, say, visiting, creative constructive political ideologists. And I think it would be good to have such occasional or part-time appointments in political science departments as living examples of what such activity is. Equally well, I understand what it might be to have Karl Barth or Joseph de Maistre in a religious studies department as distinguished, say visiting, creative constructive theologians. Buddhist thinker K. N. Jayatilleke would find the term offensive, but one could (and should) adopt a term to cover the same sort of full-blown constructive efforts in extending a nontheistic religion's self-understanding as used for theists—terms (barbaric though they may be) such as "nibbanology" or "mokshology." But, I do not know what an "academic theologian" constructing religion out of *no particular tradition at all* would look like. I find this hard to imagine, again, because outside a particular religious tradition—outside a particular community's history, enduring values, and present-day consensus—how would one know whether the construction counted as a good or bad one? In this sense, I suppose this means I do not believe there is such a thing as a universally human *religious* community—at least at this stage of the human project. Lacking such a universal human religious community, I cannot see how a "theology" or for that matter a "nibbanology" or "mokshology" could be constructed. What would be the rules of this academic religious "tennis match with the nets down"? This leads me to doubt the fruitfulness of the effort Brown outlines for "academic theology," as well intentioned and rigorously argued as it might be.

What then might an "academic theology" do? What could it contribute to the study of religion in the university? To answer my own question, I would make another play for the suggestion I made in my article on the St. Louis Project Report. To wit: what the university needs from those literate in theological discourse is some understanding of exactly how a "theology," "nibbanology," "mokshology," or "atheology" might work. We would learn an immense amount about the human religious condition if we would learn how "theologies," "nibbanologies" and the rest happen—even including showing students how one might create a "theology," "nibbanology," or an "atheology" within the laboratory context of the classroom. In order to begin understanding what such systems are, we need demonstrations and analytic understanding of the various styles of religious construction, evaluation, or hermeneutics, if you will—both theistic and nontheistic. How has human imagination performed in the arena of religious hermeneutics?

Now doing so will be better done, I believe, within the real-world context of the real religious traditions. After all, it is in the real, historical world of religious communities that the overwhelming bulk of the stuff we call "religion" is created. The study of religious hermeneutics must, in a word, be cross-culturally comparative. Do Muslim or Hindu theologians operate the same way as Jewish or Christian ones? Are there systematic similarities and/or differences between and among the way different religious traditions generate new intellectual visions? This job is tailor-made for the university and our diverse religious world. Returning to my reference to the recent Balkan wars and other occasions of religion active in today's politics, "academic theologians" like Brown could help us all understand many confounding puzzles. How have theologians of the Serbian Orthodox church contributed to the anti-Muslim political culture of today's Yugoslavia? In another context, how have Theravada Buddhist "nibbanologists" managed to reconcile—interpret—political violence in Sri Lanka against Hindu Tamils with Buddhist values? Here I mean to ask our "academic theologians" not just to report what they say, but to help us understand how religious people think—especially those charged with representing and developing the intellectual resources of their traditions. How do they square their traditions with today's bloody politics? How do we? Similarly, what are Kosovo Albanian Muslim "theologians" saying in the same context? How do they justify saying what they say? On what grounds and in what ways are they reading local events in the light of their Muslim traditions? How are they doing theology? For our "academic theologians" to perform here only requires a reasonable degree of knowledge and imagination. Such qualities are not in short supply, although they need to be awakened and focused. I hope, at least, that in writing this article I have done my small part to rouse my theologian colleagues and friends to assume the place in religious studies that many of us wait for them to occupy.

Notes

1. Michael A. Sells, *The Bridge Betrayed: Religion and Genocide in Bosnia* (Los Angeles: University of California Press, 1996); Mark Juergensmeyer, *The New Cold War: Religious Nationalism Confronts the Secular State* (Los Angeles: University of California Press, 1992); Stanley J. Tambiah, *Levelling Crowd: Ethno-nationalist Conflict and Collective Violence in South Asia* (Los Angeles: University of California Press, 1991).

2. Delwin Brown, "Believing Traditions and the Task of the Academic Theologian," *Journal of the American Academy of Religion* 62, no. 4 (1994): 1170.

3. Despite my deep reservations about Richard B. Miller's arguments, I am gratified that even a retheologizer such as he substantially agrees with my criticism of Green's neo-Barthian scheme for retheologizing religious studies. See Richard B. Miller, *Casuistry and Modern Ethics* (Chicago: University of Chicago Press, 1996), 285–6 n. 28.

4. Garrett Green, "Challenging the Religious Studies Canon: Karl Barth's Theory of Religion," *The Journal of Religion* 75 (1995): 473.

5. Ibid., 486.

6. Ivan Strenski, "Comparative Study of Religions: A Theological Necessity," *Christian Century*, 13 February 1985, 126–9.

7. Green, "Challenging the Religious Studies Canon," 473–86.

8. Karl Barth, *Church Dogmatics*, vol. 1–2, ed. G. W. Bromiley and T. F. Torrance, trans. G. T. Thomson and Harold Knight (Edinburgh: T. & T. Clark, 1956), 280.

9. Green, "Challenging the Religious Studies Canon," 480.

10. Ibid., 291.

11. Ibid., 474.

12. Karl Barth, *Church Dogmatics*, 280, cited in Green, "Challenging the Religious Studies Canon," 477.

13. Green, ibid., 482, citing Barth, *Church Dogmatics,* vol 1–2, 326, 329.

14. Ibid., 485.

15. Barth, *Church Dogmatics*, vol. 1–2, 346, Cited in Green, "Challenging the Religious Studies Canon," 482.

16. Green, ibid., 482, citing Barth, *Church Dogmatics,* 329 (emphasis original).

17. Ivan Strenski, "Our Very Own 'Contras': A Reply to the St. Louis Project Report, *Journal of the American Academy of Religion,* 65 (Summer 1986): 323–35.

18. Richard B. Miller, *Casuistry and Modern Ethics*, 199.

19. Ivan Strenski, "Our Very Own 'Contras': A Reply to the St. Louis Project Report," 330–2. Richard B. Miller, *Casuistry and Modern Ethics*, 199–200 and 287 n. 40.

20. Richard B. Miller, *Casuistry and Modern Ethics*, 200.

21. Ibid.

22. Ibid.

23. "Thus, religious studies has come to the place in its own development when it no longer need restrict itself to studying fundamentally already-happened phenomena. . . . [R]eligious studies is in a position to be more constructive and creative with the phenomena it studies. It can lend new formation in seemingly countless ways because of the immense body of materials at its disposal." Walter H. Capps, "The Interpenetration of New Religion and Religious Studies," in *Understanding the New Religions*, ed. Jacob Needleman and George Baker (New York City: Seabury Press, 1978), 105.

24. Ivan Strenski, "Our Very Own 'Contras': A Reply to the St. Louis Project Report," 330–32.

25. Delwin Brown, "Believing Traditions and the Task of the Academic Theologian," 1168–9.

26. Ibid., 1175–8. Ivan Strenski, "Our Very Own 'Contras': A Reply to the St. Louis Project Report," 329f.

27. Delwin Brown, "Believing Traditions and the Task of the Academic Theologian," 1170.

28. Ibid., 1175f.

29. Ibid., 1172–5.

30. Ibid., 1174f.

31. Ivan Strenski, "Our Very Own 'Contras': A Reply to the St. Louis Project Report," 332f.

32. Ivan Strenski, "Our Very Own 'Contras': A Reply to the St. Louis Project Report," 323–35.

33. Delwin Brown, "Refashioning Self and Other: Theology, Academy and the New Ethnography," in *Converging on Culture: Theologians in Dialogue with Cultural Analysis and Criticism*, ed. Delwin Brown, Sheila Greeve Davaney, and Kathryn Tanner (New York: Oxford University Press, 2001), 50.

4

Our Subject "Over There"?
Scrutinizing the Distance
Between Religion and Its Study

CHRISTOPHER CHESNEK

> The argument in this book has moved strictly within the frame of reference of sociological theory. No theological or, for that matter, antitheological implications are to be sought anywhere in the argument—if anyone should believe such implications to be present *sub rosa,* I can only assure him that he is mistaken.
>
> —Peter Berger, *The Sacred Canopy*

Thus Peter Berger expressed a foundational and now widely invoked argument regarding the intention, scope, and limitations of the academic study of religion. In what is most aptly described as his searching bid for both the theological innocence and purely scientific standing of his sociological theory of religion, Berger argued that it is possible to conduct scholarship on religion—unearth new information about it, describe it, critically engage it, and theorize about it—without doing theology or antitheology, even "*sub rosa.*" As he so unequivocally put it, the academic study of religion "and theological assertions take place in *discrepant, mutually immune* (emphasis added) frames of reference."[1] Despite the apparent conclusiveness of this statement, in the same appendix Berger gradually developed another, quite contrary line of argument that not only eroded his earlier claims to theological innocence, but generally raised doubts about the mutual immunity of the academic study of religion and theology. What could have been a very short appendix, had their relationship been as simple as that of mutual exclusivity, developed into a rather long and densely argued appendix that outlined the various challenges that the human sciences, and his theory in particular, posed to theologians. In light of Berger's ambiguous and even self-contradictory position, what are we to make of his earlier, unequivocal claims to theological innocence, and the relationship between the academic study of religion and theology?

Berger's vacillation over the theological dimensions of his scholarship reflects a broader truth about the academic study of religion, one that is often denied because of the intellectual, political, and legal exigencies of appearing nontheological and scientific, or rendered invisible because the crass, categorical oppositions typically employed to differentiate these disciplines (e.g., naturalistic vs. supernaturalistic, empirical vs. normative) effectively obfuscate its presence. Borrowing a term from ritual studies, Berger's vacillation reveals the inherently interstitial or liminal nature of the academic study of religion (a term derived from *limen*, the Latin word for "threshold"). As Victor Turner defines them, "liminal entities are neither here nor there; they are betwixt and between the position assigned and arrayed by law, custom, convention, and ceremonial."[2] In defying classification into clear and distinct categories, liminal entities are difficult to conceptualize and frequently seen as polluting, compromised, and dangerous. Consequently, they are surrounded by taboos of avoidance, removed in space, or treated as dead or invisible. To read Berger's appendix is to read about a project haunted by issues of purity, danger, and liminality. It is the impurity of contact with theology—the threat of betweenness and hybridity—that forces Berger to assert the complete disjunction of his project with that of theology. At the same time, there is an ineradicable liminality at the heart of his project that undermines his claim of mutual immunity, explains his vacillation on the matter, and allows him to speculate on the theological consequences of his theory.[3]

This ineradicable if not always manifest liminality is not unique to Berger, but lies at the very heart of the academic study of religion. Its presence is especially evident in the history of religious studies, where issues of purity and danger have produced a long-standing debate over the discipline's identity. Since its emergence in the midnineteenth century, *Religionswissenschaft* has wrestled with the question of its relationship to the sacred,[4] and, concomitantly, its relationship to a thoroughgoing "science of religion," thanks in large measure to the liberal Protestant tradition out of which it emerged. Early on in its history, and by way of an instructive contrast with *Religionswissenschaft*, the sociology of religion did its best to eradicate the sacred by either reducing it to society and "social effervescence," as Émile Durkheim did in *The Elementary Forms of Religious Life*, or by recasting it as the purely human pursuit of meaning, as Max Weber did in his work. By virtue of its focus on "the primitive," the anthropology of religion disregarded the question of the sacred because the falsity of primitive religion was automatically assumed. In contrast to these disciplinary histories of the sacred—one an (attempted) eviction, the other a nonstarter—*Religionwissenschraft* was born of an elemental and ongoing tension within the liberal Protestant tradition. Both Friedrich Schleiermacher and G. W. F. Hegel, two of the earliest luminaries of this tradition, sought to use the insights of the burgeoning human sciences and yet retain the presence of the sacred in their theories of religion. In his *On Religion: Speeches to its Cultured*

Despisers, Schleiermacher sought to isolate a uniquely religious "feeling" that was common to all religions, and more fundamental than the religious diversity and strife that was dividing Europe at the time. Hegel pursued a similar reconciliation of human diversity (the human sciences) and divine unity (the sacred) through his concept of *Geist*, a self-unfolding and self-comprehending world-historical subject thought to not only animate but also unify the religions of the world. Rather than displacing the confrontation between the sacred and the human sciences outside of their borders—a displacement, I argue, that cannot be accomplished in an absolute sense—liberal Protestantism, *Religionswissenschaft*, and now their modern-day descendant, religious studies, place this confrontation within their borders. As the debate over reductionism illustrates, religious studies harbors impulses to both preserve and destroy the sacred—preserve it in the name of the sacred (even while reconciling it to the human sciences), and destroy it (reduce it) in the name of the human sciences.

Far from standing over and against its subject, then, as the often glibly delivered distinction between the "teaching of" and "teaching about" religion suggests, religious studies plays host to a battle between the sacred and the human sciences. Nearly one hundred fifty years after Max Müller's call for a "science of religion" (which he saw as being compatible with the truth of religion), the on-again off-again relationship between the sacred and the human sciences within religious studies has gone through its cycles, flaring up and subsiding, only to flare up once again. Their confrontation has continued to manifest itself in obvious and not-so-obvious ways: one, in the interminable debate between naturalists and religionists over reductionism and related attempts to articulate and promote a discipline-wide, theoretical orthodoxy; two, in the discipline's bid for a separate department within the university based on its unique subject matter, i.e., the sacred; three, in the discipline's heightened interest in defining and policing its boundaries, especially in contrast to theology for naturalists, and anthropology and sociology for religionists; and four, in the discipline's heightened interest in writing and rewriting its history, usually as a means of criticizing its crypto-theological identity, or conversely, for failing to take the sacred "seriously."

Since the early years of *Religionswissenschraft*, the sacred and the human sciences have increasingly been seen as mutually profaning, compromising, and destructive forces, with the consequence that a liminal space has opened up between them.[5] This is especially true for scientific purists or naturalists who consider any trace of the sacred within the human sciences—that can include excessive sympathy towards the sacred and even the insider's perspective—as a source of contamination, resulting in "crypto-theology" rather than science. Religionists, in contrast, welcome the copresence and collaboration of the sacred and the human sciences with the caveat that the human sciences must recognize and respect the nature of religion, or in the words of Mircea Eliade, approach it on its "own plane of reference."[6] Hence, the battle between the sacred and the human sciences has come to be driven by the twin ideals of creating a science of religion free from the sacred, and, conversely, a discipline that acts as a kind of safe harbor for religion and religious motivations, protecting them from the totalizing aspirations of the human sciences. Naturalists argue that religionists, by insisting on the primacy, authority, and irreducibility of the insider's perspective, limit the discipline to approaches that preserve the reality of the sacred. As a phenomenon that not only contaminates but also inhibits the full development of the "science of religion," the sacred and all of its clandestine stand-ins should be removed from the discipline. This can be accomplished, so the naturalists' argument continues, by making religious studies into a reductive/critical discipline. In practical terms, this means that the scholar's project should always be that of redescribing the insider's account in social scientific terms, while second-order abstractions referring to the sacred, the transcendent, the existential, and even the category of "religion"[7] should be stricken from the scholar's lexicon.

To this proposed orthodoxy, religionists like Lawrence Sullivan counter that reductionism "trivializes religion by recasting religious motivations as essentially non-religious ones, translating religious claims into languages of self-interest which are only political, economic, or psychological in nature."[8] Wendy Doniger, who is generally not known as a religionist per se, elaborates on this sentiment when she argues that reductive approaches are severely limited, missing what is most essential, interesting, and revealing about religion. In a statement that harkens back to Rudolf Otto's *The Idea of the Holy*, in which he recommends that the irreligious read no further, Doniger writes: "We might as well exclude from the start of our discussion the thoroughly unmythologized, the people who have never had, and never will have, any inclination to take religion seriously, the people who are tone deaf to religion; they will not be interested in myth, or religion, at all."[9] Programmatically, religionists propose that religious studies adopt an anti-reductive orthodoxy—comprising the phenomenology of religion, the history of religions, interpretive approaches, and symbolic interactionism—all of which are attuned to the depth, special character, and apparent music of religion.

For the remainder of the paper, I will develop two, interrelated arguments. First—and in contrast to the naturalists' attempt to articulate a science of religion free of the sacred—I argue that the academic study of religion is irreducibly religious, regardless of the shape it takes. The idea that religion is a discrete "other" that can be kept "over there" while scholars "teach about" it was instrumental in founding the discipline intellectually, legally, and politically. But gratitude aside, this distinction not only relies on and reinforces a limited conception of religion—often thought to be marked by a dogmatic belief in the supernatural—but encourages a kind of academic false consciousness in which scholars do not recognize the religious impact of their classes on students, or their larger role in shaping the religious landscape and future of the cultures in which they teach. Religiosity is simply too spontaneous, diffuse, and, frankly, often too mundane for us to be able to bracket it, wall it off, keep it at arm's length—pick your favorite metaphor for impermeability or distance.

Does this mean—as naturalists would have us believe—that religious studies is forever fallen from "scientific" and "critical" grace? No, because in this view religious thought is not in all cases some contaminating, stereotypical "other" that must be purged at all costs. Religious thought goes on imperceptibly, furtively, and in silence in even the most "scientific" classes, not only because it is beyond the control of the instructor, but even the control of the student.[10] In the slightly altered words of a popular bumper sticker, "Religious Thought Happens," for students and professors alike, despite our best (and most misguided) attempts to bracket or eradicate this dimension of the discipline. Does this mean that constructive religious thought as it is explicitly and self-consciously practiced by academic theologians should be pursued within religious studies? No, for despite its spontaneous and irrepressible nature, the religious dimensions of religious studies should remain *incidental* to its critical, theoretical, and historical projects.[11]

In arguing that religious studies is incidentally and ambiguously theological—rightfully containing, as it does, both theologically hostile (reductive-atheistic) and theologically sympathetic (nonreductive, vaguely theistic) approaches to religion—I am also arguing against attempts by naturalists and religionists to restrict and teach the discipline at this level. In the final section, I take up my second argument, which is that attempts to define religious studies in terms of its religious implications have resulted in lopsided and theoretically limited agendas, each ironically promoting itself as the most advanced and authoritative form the discipline can take. By framing the debate in religious rather than strictly social scientific terms, naturalists and religionists respectively limit our options to the false ideals of a thoroughgoing reductionism and antireductionism, leaving their relative strengths and weakness—and a more viable, middle ground—unexplored. A more productive approach will treat the religious dimensions of reductionism and antireductionism as incidental rather than primary, and conduct the debate on strictly social scientific grounds.[12]

OUR SUBJECT "OVER THERE?"

As an enterprise that regularly professes its inability to offer a precise definition of religion, it is curious that the academic study of religion can be so certain that it stands outside the boundaries of its subject, "looking in," so to speak, from what amounts to a privileged—because nonreligious—perspective. Given the rejection in recent years of essentialist definitions of religion in favor of family resemblance definitions, and the widening of our subject to include such quasi religions as humanism, communism, capitalism, and even science, the question arises: by what logic—by virtue of what qualities or absence of qualities—does the discipline escape its own inclusive definitions? Why are we not an instance of a subject that by our own admission is diverse at a fundamental level? And the more venturous the discipline becomes in analyzing heretofore "nonreligious" phenomena in religious terms, the more difficult it becomes to answer the question. In his article, "The Church of Baseball, the Fetish of Coca-Cola, and the Potlatch of Rock 'n' Roll: Theoretical Models for the Study of Religion in American Popular Culture," David Chidester puts religious categories to unconventional use by applying them to such "nonreligious" phenomena as baseball, Coca-Cola, and rock 'n' roll.[13] Now a question arises: if Chidester can tease out the religious dimensions of Coca-Cola, what might the same analytic aspiration find if it were to set its sights on the academic study of religion? Could it be, despite our inability to precisely define our subject and the ever-widening application of our discourse, that the academic study of religion is the only social phenomenon to which its own analytic agenda cannot fruitfully be applied? I think not. Unfortunately, outside of the instructive but overly passionate interrogation by naturalists, religious studies has been exempt from its own analytic powers for far too long. Such an inquiry, as I envision it, is not motivated by the desire to indict the discipline for being too theological or scientific, but by the same theoretical and historical curiosity that motivates the study of our traditional subjects. The academic study of religion should not be exempt from the larger project of "imagining religion," to borrow a phrase from Jonathan Z. Smith. In fact, I see it as being essential to it.

As a religious studies scholar, I have long been interested in this unthinkable, even heretical, line of inquiry, because it raises doubts about the widely asserted claim that the academic study of religion has no religious dimensions or consequences whatsoever, or at least ideally does not, and stands over-and-against its subject as some wholly, nonreligious other. Skeptical of the analytic value of the distinction between the "teaching of" and "teaching about" religion, Jonathan Z. Smith has argued that it is "preeminently [a] political contrast," one that serves "the old tactical ends of establishing legitimacy by lay, juridical language rather than theoretical discourse."[14] While to some degree understandable, it is nevertheless unfortunate that the legitimate concerns and distinctions that founded religious studies institutionally in the 1960s also gave rise to politically charged stereotypes that now distort and obscure this most interesting and promising of debates. And as important as these foundational concerns are *and continue to be*, it is also important not to confuse the exigencies and public cachet of appearing nonreligious with the analytic plausibility of the distinction, or the actual religious consequences of the discipline for students and professors alike. Certainly, traditional oppositions between natural and supernatural, empirical and normative, are useful *up to a point* and cannot, on all levels, simply be dismissed as politically motivated distinctions designed to purify and institutionalize religious studies at the cost of scapegoating theology. The question I am raising, however, is about the limitations of these oppositions—were only the world so neatly divided! Instances of scholarship and phenomena that are obviously different are not only uncontroversial and uninteresting, but unworthy of a volume dedicated to figuring out their relationship. As a religious studies scholar, the question as to whether some form of confessional theology belongs anywhere near the academic study of religion can resoundingly be answered in the negative. For me—as I suspect for most scholars contributing to this volume—the debate only becomes interesting and vexing with regard to scholarship that possesses qualities that cut across traditional oppositions and defy simplistic classification. It is this scholarship that: challenges our sense of categorical purity; prompts us to specify with greater accuracy the differences between theology and religious studies, in terms of substantive assumptions, goals, methods, and theories; and, most importantly, raises the question of whether an absolute distinction is a real possibility, or merely a rhetorical device that, *while "getting at" something*, can never be precisely located.

A familiar distinction that "gets at something" but is not exhaustive of the task is one already mentioned, that of "teaching of" and "teaching about" religion. The problem with this distinction is that it assumes that religious instruction is dogmatic and authoritarian, an assumption perhaps better explained by our own immersion in a particular religious culture—one of Biblical literalism, pulpits, and Sunday schools—rather than a judicious, empirical observation about the "nature" of religion. Once it is recognized that these qualities are not the *sine qua non* of all religious instruction and thought, and that both—particularly within our emerging, global culture—can be critical, religiously eclectic, historically and social scientifically informed, and even fundamentally marked by doubt and "seeking" rather than certainty and "faith," the difference between the academic study of religion and religion—at least this particular form of it—is considerably diminished. The distinction between "teaching of" and "teaching about" does not articulate the boundary between religion and its study, but the kind of intellectual temperament that is appropriate and inappropriate to the university. Religious studies does not stand equally over and against all forms of religion, but only some forms of religion—a point supported by the historical proximity and influence of liberal Protestantism on the discipline. The opposition between religion (theology) and religious studies begins to break down once the former becomes less of a classic example or politically motivated stereotype—easily locatable "over there"—and takes on the qualities of a critical, comparative, and historically informed discourse. The response to this line of argument, of course, is to counter that such a discourse has been secularized, and that any so-called "religious discourse" that emulates religious studies cannot also be religious. According to the logic of oppositional thinking, such a discourse has made the transition to the "over here," and in the process has lost its ability to speak to religious/existential questions of meaning, purpose, value, and practice.[15] But is this really the case? Are the academic and naturalistic idioms of religious studies incompatible with the articulation and expression of religiosity?

Perhaps the best approach to this question is to begin with the history of the discipline, which reveals the intimate and ongoing relationship between religion and the human sciences. Two centuries before Schleiermacher and Hegel, liberal and even ecumenical tendencies were present in the expanding definition and currency of the category of "religion." Due to exposure to the non-Western world and an acute sense of religious diversity at home, "religion"—once employed more narrowly to refer to monastic life—increasingly came to refer to a cross-cultural phenomenon of human origins, and, in some cases, divine-human origins. As David Pailin has shown, early modern theories of religion had it variously comprising human reason, empirical observation, imagination, and a distinct mode of human awareness, combined with various forms of divine etiology.[16] By the time of the Enlightenment, "natural religion" (e.g., deism) was seen as the universal core of all religions, making the human more divine—at least in terms of anthropological faculties, i.e., reason—and the divine more accommodating to the whole of humanity. With the Romantic movement in the nineteenth century, a greater appreciation for the historicity of human thought helped to legitimate the "other's" religious "otherness" (i.e., their differences, as opposed to the Enlightenment's ability to only legitimate their sameness) and transform a world of *religious error* or superfluity into a world of *human perspectives* on the divine. These developments not only laid the groundwork for what would later become the phenomenological distinction between *Religion in Essence and Manifestation*, the title of Gerardus van der Leeuw's classic work, but also helped to dismantle evolutionary hierarchies and establish greater parity among religions—at least in departments of religion.

While exposure to the non-Western world and the burgeoning human sciences fostered religious doubt and atheism, it also prompted religious liberalism and creativity in light of these new horizons. In her book *Fits, Trances, and Visions: Experiencing Religion and Explaining Experience from Wesley to James*, Ann Taves exposes the historical and conceptual blind spot of traditional oppositions between the natural and supernatural, insiders and outsiders, explainers and explained, by uncovering the history of those who sought to articulate an intermediate position between them. According to Taves, "a threefold typology . . . does more justice to the cultural legacy that has informed and in many ways continues to inform such quarrels within the academic study of religion than does a dualistic formulation."[17] Mirroring recent trends in the history of science and religion that expose the traditional emphasis on "conflict" as the ideology of scientism, Taves employs a "threefold typology" that unearths their historical relatedness and dialogue. Religion and the human sciences are not intrinsically antagonistic idioms, but historically dynamic idioms that are frequently and quite naturally found in dialogue and creative synthesis. Like many scholars within present-day religious studies, scholars of this intermediate tradition sought to avoid (or at least avoid exclusive emphasis upon) the tradition of dismissive reductionism *within* the larger naturalistic tradition, while making use of the insights of the human sciences.

The history of the academic study of religion is not uncontested, however, and it is instructive to contrast Taves' threefold typology with the dualistic typology of J. Samuel Preus. In his book *Explaining Religion: Criticism and Theory from Bodin to Freud*, Preus—a theologian turned naturalist—interprets history through the lens of the current debate over reductionism.[18] In contrast to Taves, Preus presents the history of the discipline as a distinct and critical offshoot of its subject, beginning with David Hume's thoroughgoing critique of natural theology, and continuing with such scholars as Auguste Comte, Emile Durkheim, and Sigmund Freud. By extending the arena of theoretical competition into the past, Preus not only constructs a history of conflict, gradual emancipation, and explanatory success for the naturalistic tradition (or more precisely and narrowly, the reductive tradition), but one that unequivocally casts theology as the discipline's eternal "other," located "over there." His history derives its rhetorical and political effectiveness as much from the logic of conceptual opposition as from its selective reading of history—an admittedly unavoidable problem, as Preus notes, but one that does not cancel out the ideological implications of the final product. In Preus's hands, the history of the study of religion is one of conflict between scientific sobriety and religious illusion. Religion is confessional, authoritarian, irrational—and always the product of socialization—while "scientific" ideas are discussed in the language of the mind, as instances of "seeing" new truths. In the words of Catherine Bell, "Preus nearly demonizes Christianity and theology . . . [making them] an improbably monolithic and negative force for suppressing such secular thinking."[19]

Without denying the theoretical and political import of Taves's account, her history falls squarely within the genre of history proper, while Preus offers more of a theoretical/political treatise written through the medium of history. Taves's threefold typology provides a broader, more historically detailed, more dynamic, and less ideological account of the relationship between religion and its study. Whereas Preus turns a blind eye towards religion after deism in the eighteenth century, suggesting its intellectual stagnation—the end of the road—Taves treats religion as a full, critical, and dynamic member of modernity by attending to its transformations throughout her account. Unlike the dualistic typology's limited narrative of conflict, the decline of religion and the ascendancy of science—the classic secularization thesis—Taves's threefold typology reveals the ongoing conversation between naturalism and religion, and allows her to construct a narrative in which they grow in sophistication together. Her account not only challenges caricatured views of religious thought as rigid, intolerant, and inherently incompatible with naturalism, but diminishes the difference between religion and its study. Overall, the tradition she reveals is so intimately and yet critically related to its subject that it is fair to say that it is an instance of its subject without thereby impugning its intellectual status. A classic example of this is William James's *The Varieties of Religious Experience*.[20]

For more contemporary examples of this same dynamic, one need only visit a Borders Bookstore to see the collusion—even identity—of religious motives and such naturalistic disciplines as history, anthropology, and the social sciences. Books on Native American spirituality based on anthropological fieldwork, for example, are not only plentiful but mixed in with the "real" scholarship on Native American religions. As scholars of religion we pride ourselves on being able to distinguish the "real stuff" from "scholarship" that has been idealized and sugarcoated for religious consumption. Such texts, admittedly, are often easily identifiable, particularly if they are in our area of specialization. Under the influence of postcolonial studies, however, recent research on the history of the study of non-Western religions (by westerners) has severely undermined the idea of scholarship as a disinterested enterprise untouched by political, ideological, and religious interests. At least since the Enlightenment, when alienation towards Christianity and openness towards alternative values first gained a foothold in the West, the academic study of non-Western religions has served as a vehicle for religious inquiry—a looking towards the "other" for self-critique and religious insight. Recent disciplinary histories attest to the tendency of "exotic" cultures to be interpreted through the romantic/religious spectacles of Western scholars and their reading publics. For centuries now, the romance and mystery of "other" religions has held out the promise of a greater understanding of human existence and a better way of life, particularly in times and contexts of Western self-doubt.

Nor is this mixing of "academic" and "religious" dimensions limited to scholarship of a bygone era or contemporary publications intended for religious consumption. Some of the most recent scholarship in the study of Native American religions, for example, has been criticized for blurring the boundary between "academic" and "religious" interests. According to Thomas Parkhill, the academic study of Native American religions has been beset by a *positive* stereotype of the Indian: a spiritual "savage," attuned to the divinity of nature (and the self), who knows his rightful place, responsibilities, and limits within it. While this stereotype has some basis in the ethnographic record, it also reflects the religious desire and imagination of modern Western scholars and culture.[21] In his conclusion, Parkhill offers advice that is applicable to the whole of religious studies. He encourages his colleagues to "admit [that their] sidelong glances at these religious traditions have always been rooted in religious needs."[22] His solution is not a reinvigorated pursuit of "scientific" ideals—a reductive-critical approach that would only produce *negative* stereotypes and further wound academic-Native American relations.[23] His solution is "to explore—overtly and honestly—those [religious] needs while we deepen our stereotypeless understanding of the religious traditions of Native American peoples."[24] Significantly, Parkhill does not allude to the possibility of a scholarship completely devoid of religious interests nor offer it up as an ideal worthy of pursuit; he only encourages his colleagues to become aware of their religious motivations, make them explicit, and take corrective action whenever necessary. Parkhill's assessment of scholarship on Native religions is reminiscent of Berger's vacillation over the theological dimensions of his own scholarship. Both suggest that the difference between an academic text and one that speaks to the religious/existential interests of its reader can be slight to even nonexistent. The difference, in other words, can merely be attitudinal—the difference between seeing a vase one moment (in that widely known optical illusion) and two faces facing each other the next.

Taken together, Taves and Parkhill reveal the complex and ambiguous relationship between religion and its study. They not only show us that the human sciences are compatible with the articulation and expression of religiosity, but they undermine the distancing function they are thought to have in keeping our subject at arm's length. And yet, despite the virtues of Taves's threefold typology, I would argue that it is vulnerable to criticism in that it preserves a feature of the dualistic typology, which is the tendency to conflate the opposition between the natural and the supernatural with the opposition between irreligiosity and religiosity. While the principal expressive and intellectual medium of religiosity is commonly thought to be the idiom of the supernatural, it can also be expressed—as Taves has persuasively shown—through the combined idiom of the supernatural-natural. What her model further suggests, however, is that religiosity cannot be expressed through the idiom of the natural alone, or that if it can, it is somehow a diminished or paler version of those idioms that fall towards the supernatural end of the spectrum. The supernatural, in either case, acts as the normative pole from which religiosity is measured. The question that needs to be raised, however, is whether the supernatural-natural opposition reliably maps the opposition between religiosity-irreligiosity. What of the possibility of a naturalistic religiosity, one that could—and perhaps does—comfortably inhabit religious studies departments?

As I discussed earlier, the possibility of being able to stand over-and-against our subject depends on one's definition of religion. Religion defined as belief in the supernatural makes it relatively easy for a naturalistic discipline to claim that its subject is "over there." But the identity of belief in the supernatural and religiosity is highly questionable—and I am hardly the first to raise doubts about their equation (consider the debates over whether the atheism of Theravada Buddhism disqualifies it as a religion). Religions are such complex and dynamic phenomena that basing their categorical difference from religious studies on the basis of one feature—particularly such a contested feature as belief in the supernatural—is highly suspect. In light of other definitions of religion, however, the distance between religion and its study is either diminished or completely eliminated. If, for example, we were to rewrite Preus's history using Paul Tillich's definition of religion as "ultimate concern," or Ninian Smart's "worldviews," it is unlikely that we would find a decisive, Hume-like figure in which the discipline suddenly becomes the "other" of religion. According to these definitions, in fact, Hume's philosophical and naturalistic critiques of religion are continuous with theology, insofar as they dethroned and assumed its role in defining the elemental features of human existence. By using multiple factors to assess historical continuity and discontinuity (and denying the singular importance of the supernatural), Hume can be seen to inaugurate a new kind of theology or reverse theology, one that redefines the religious/existential conditions of human existence and articulates a new "worldview"—a new baseline from which to think about issues of meaning, purpose, value, and practice. Rather than being the categorical opposite of theology, religious studies, according to these definitions, has significant continuities with it. Unfortunately, religious studies is generally so accepting of the idea that the supernatural is the exclusive idiom of the religious/existential that it has failed to attend to the ways in which these same issues continue under the guise of naturalism and now inhabit the discipline.

The opposite of religiosity (belief in the supernatural) is not irreligiosity (belief in the natural to the exclusion of the supernatural), but areligiosity, that is, *indifference* to questions of meaning, purpose, value, and practice—which no person can permanently sustain given the vicissitudes of life. To limit religiosity to those who believe in the supernatural not only stigmatizes and underestimates the much broader and enduring appeal of the protean impulses and questions that the supernatural traditionally addressed (and still does for many people), but overlooks those people, discourses, and forums that continue to engage them in naturalistic terms, if only fleetingly and indirectly.[25] What needs to occur is an expansion of our understanding of religiosity from the person who has "faith" in a particular tradition—often a world religion—to that of a "seeker" interested in the human sciences and open to religious/existential questions (as if the human sciences and the religious/existential could be separated to begin with). This definition extends religiosity beyond "belief in the supernatural" to include those people who retain an interest in questions of meaning and purpose after the death of God, or a God irretrievably bracketed into irrelevance by methodological atheism, i.e., a situation found in some religious studies courses.[26] Despite appearances this addendum is not a radical departure from religiosity defined as "belief in the supernatural." It is simply a more inclusive definition based on the analytic strategy of the naturalistic study of religion, which is to reduce belief in God to the constitution of the subject/society. Why limit religiosity to belief in God when naturalism tells us that it is our intrinsic interest in our own well-being—and not an intrinsic interest in God—that is the true subject of religion? If concern for the self is the irreducible "core" of religiosity, why limit religiosity to the epiphenomenal and historically parochial idiom of the supernatural, when it could be expanded to include those naturalistic idioms that address the same or similar concerns? In true Feuerbachian form, this definition of religiosity recognizes that the true subject of religion does not die with the death of God or the effective equivalent of the death of God, i.e., methodological atheism.[27] Both only expose the true subject of religion—the meaning-starved and meaning-creating subject/society—they do not remove the impulse of wanting to intellectually and emotionally address "the" human condition—with all the necessary concessions being given to the irreducible historicity of that condition.

If we were to drop the facade that we only teach about religion, we would discover that religious studies can have a significant impact on the religious beliefs and lives of its students. There is considerable irony in a discipline that claims to bracket questions of religious truth but through its methods and theories challenge students' religious beliefs in untold ways, and thereby fixes their attention more resolutely on religious/existential questions. Insofar as religious studies undermines the intellectual plausibility of religion, it is in the business of *making* religion a matter of faith. Nor is "bracketing" as innocent as it sounds, for bracketing followed by a naturalistic explanation makes the truth of religion redundant, incidental, and completely unnecessary. And contrary to what "bracketing" suggests, students' minds are not neatly compartmentalized, so that what goes into the non-religious section never seeps over into the religious section, nor do they wait until after class when they can unbracket the larger implications of religious studies. Religious studies fails and fails miserably in creating a religion-free zone not only because the subject of study and the object of study are ultimately one and the same (humans indirectly studying the ultimate, existential conditions of their own lives through other humans), but also because it offers students rival and/or complementary accounts to their incoming beliefs. Our claim to have eradicated religious thought from religious studies sounds as curious and implausible as art history claiming to have eradicated moments of aesthetic appreciation on the part of its students. Even in those most "scientific" of art history classes, where paintings, for example, are reduced to expressions of political and class interest, the professor is impotent with respect to preventing the aesthetic response of his students. The same holds true for religious studies. By the time we become seasoned scholars, we seem to have forgotten how these theories affected our own lives, or how revolutionary they were when they were first developed by Schleiermacher, Feuerbach, Nietzsche, and Freud. The idea that we could bring together in one enterprise the most sympathetic and hostile views on religion and pronounce it theologically innocent is truly astounding.

Insofar as we convince our students that God is dead or effectively dead, we clear the way for naturalistic, this-worldly discourses with which to continue thinking about religious/existential questions. Historically, religiosity has found its articulation in a wide variety of naturalistic idioms and worldviews, such as humanism, communism, existentialism, and radical environmentalism, all of which offer their own brand of this-worldly salvation. Religious studies does not offer a comparable, naturalistic vision of human purpose and fulfillment, nor do I think it should. Aside from legitimate concerns about the separation of church and state and proselytizing (admittedly imperfect distinctions but valuable nonetheless), it is difficult to imagine what religious vision could address our diverse student body. Besides, many students are just fine with their religion or irreligion—thank you very much. But just because we do not self-consciously and actively shape the religious dimensions of religious studies (with the exception of religionists and naturalists) does not mean that religious studies is without significant cultural and long-term consequences. One can imagine our academic descendents looking back upon the present-day discipline as being instrumental in altering their own religious subjects, perhaps even giving rise to the "first *conscious* believers [of religion], people who know that religion is just human but have come to see it as no less vital to us for that."[28] To presently play this world-historical role as our own subject and not even realize it is deeply ironic. To see this myopia as the curiosity that it is will take a future in which the zealous and categorical distinctions between science and religion, fact and value, outsiders and insiders, have loosened their grips.

REDUCTIONISM: MOVING BEYOND THE THEOLOGICAL

As a theoretical-theological debate, reductionism is thought to situate religious studies vis-à-vis the university and religion simultaneously. By embracing reductionism and the critique of religion as ideology, naturalists argue that the discipline aligns itself with science and the secular university while putting that all-important distance between religion and its study. Religionists operate according to the same logic, but with a sight difference. By embracing antireductionism and approaches sensitive to the music of religion, religionists see themselves as aligning the discipline with *both* religion and the secular university, while putting that all-important distance between religion and scientism. (In light of the argument above—and contrary to the logic of both camps—I hope it is clear that one's position on reductionism does not align or disalign one against the religious/existential dimensions of the discipline. Since questions of purpose, meaning, value, and practice have no exclusive or stable idiom, one cannot stand in opposition to them. At best, one disaligns himself with one idiom only to align himself with another.) While the issue of reductionism is not unique to religious studies, it is unique with regard to the virulence over which it is debated, arguably because it has been conducted as more of a theological than strictly social scientific debate. The naturalists' demand for a reductive discipline is so out of proportion to that found in sociology and especially anthropology that their motivation seems more antitheological than scientific—a misguided overcorrection to our theological past. Religionists, likewise, are so opposed to reducing religion to "profane" causes—although reducing it to the sacred seems to be acceptable—that it raises questions about what they are protecting.[29] In a discipline that publicly proclaims its theological innocence, how else is a scholar going to express his or her basic theological position except indirectly through theory? While naturalists assume that religion is uniquely susceptible to reduction, religionists assume that it is uniquely resistant to it. For naturalists, sympathetic approaches that give the final word to the religious insider are incompatible with the falsity of religion—such a "science" settles for the illusion that is religion. For religionists, reductive theories are incompatible with the truth of religion, captured most directly and intimately by the religious insider. Unfortunately, using reductionism to eradicate religion or antireductionism to protect it not only results in narrow theoretical programs but robs the discipline of a more productive debate.

While I am sympathetic with the naturalists' efforts to push religious studies in a more theoretical direction, their solution for eradicating theology is an instance of the cure being worse than the disease. It not only leaves us with a predictable and impoverished discipline—completely incapable of putting religion in a positive light—but one that is so overtly and effectively atheistic that the discipline becomes "anti-theological," to use Berger's terminology. Reductionism is a perennial issue in religious studies not only because, as naturalists argue, the discipline is haunted by its religious and more specifically liberal Protestant past, but because reductionism is an ongoing issue in all of the sciences—*as it should be.* The idea that religious studies is somehow "preparadigmatic" or ideologically compromised until it lays official claim to a reductive or antireductive identity is not only contrary to the open-endedness of academic inquiry, but underestimates the enduring complexity of this issue. Moreover, the value of reductionism and antireductionism cannot be answered acontextually, or without reference to the question: "What do you want to know?"

Despite the specter of crypto-theology, there are sound, *nontheological* reasons for not reducing the insider's perspective; two of them are: the *semi-irreducible complexity* of the human life-world; and the *intimate knowledge* our subjects acquire by living in that world. Speaking on the issue of complexity and reductionism generally, Thomas Nagel argues that "it should be clear that not everything in the world is governed by general principles sufficiently precise and substantive to be embodied in a theory."[30] While parsimony is a scientific virtue, it is only a virtue up to the point where it begins to offer a *simplistic* explanation, what religionists describe as "explaining away." Without claiming that the insider's perspective lays bare all significant causal factors and perspectives, in comparison to the naturalists' program, the religionists rightfully draw our attention to the richness, complexity, causal efficacy, and emergent quality of the human life-world. In his characteristically astute fashion, Clifford Geertz poses a challenge to those who would dismiss the analytic value of the insider's perspective by pointing to the importance of the subject's life-world. Geertz asks:

> Who knows the river better . . . the hydrologist or the swimmer? Put that way, it clearly depends on what you mean by "knows," and, as I have already said, what it is you hope to accomplish. Put as which sort of knowledge we most need, want, and might to some degree conceivably get, in the human sciences anyway, the local variety—the sort the swimmer has, or, [in] swimming, might develop—can at the very least hold its own against the general variety—the sort the hydrologist has, or claims method will one day provide.[31]

The pervasive conception of religion as a set of dogmatic beliefs accepted through faith and *imposed on* the world, rather than knowledge developed through *living in* the world, encourages the devaluation of the insider's perspective. In reducing religion to the human, theories of religion are extremely anthropocentric (i.e., often reduce it to a kind of indirect self-talk to the exclusion of the world) and consequently fail—or fail to take seriously enough—the ways in which religion is engaged in a creative dialogue with the world. Geertz's analogy suggests that our subjects "earn" valuable insights by *doing* their religious activities and *living* religious lives. Insiders bring to our discussion an intimate familiarity with a particular complex life-world that reductive theories overlook. Naturalists, in contrast, seem to underestimate the interpretive challenge of reconstructing social realities long since past, or simply remote from the social reality in which religious studies is taught. Much of our expertise comes in exposing our own historicity and imagining diverse social realities far away in time, space, and sensibilities, and doing so in a way that does not merely export our own social reality. While methodological atheism is the foundation of religious studies, it is not a mandate for reductionism or eradicating the mystery and powerful emotions felt by our subjects. Approaches that preserve and build on the personal, intimate, anecdotal, and generally more allusive observations of our subjects are not only justifiable on purely theoretical grounds, but on the grounds that it gives us the world as it exists *for them.*

Only in religious studies—where the subject lends itself to being cast as a potent threat to the integrity of the discipline—could the naturalists' narrow formulation of our analytic and explanatory options be sold as the valiant pursuit of science to the exclusion of theology. From outside religious studies—from the vantage point of anthropology, for example—it is clear that the bogeyman of the sacred is being used to diminish the value of interpretive approaches and the insider's perspective.[32] The naturalists' crude lens of "theology" and "science" simplifies and polarizes their assessment of the theoretical terrain. Since the 1960s—and certainly since the Enlightenment—the value-free and reductive ideal of the physical sciences has been severely challenged and chastened, especially as an ideal for the human sciences to emulate. Consequently, the human sciences have become more interpretive and contextually sensitive, giving more analytic power and ethical consideration to the people under study. For naturalists, however, the failure of the discipline to adopt a reductive-critical program is explained in terms of the continuing influence of theology. In their aggressive pursuit of a science of religion, they lump all nonreductive approaches into the pejorative category of "crypto-theology," not recognizing the diversity of analytic goals within naturalism, many of which are ethnographic, interpretive, even explanatory, and yet not theological in intent.

If the weakness of reductionism is that it underestimates the analytic value of the insider's perspective, the weakness of antireductionism is that it overestimates it. To be a subject is not to be omniscient about oneself or the workings of one's society. We are not self-transparent beings, or to paraphrase Sigmund Freud, masters in our own houses. The fundamental virtue of reductionism is that it looks beyond the self-conscious world of the subject to expose the world that is hidden, neglected, and offstage. By dividing the world into appearance and reality, conscious and unconscious, reductionism sets up a causal model of explanation and distances itself from what can be the descriptivism and tautological "explanations" of antireductive approaches. Reductionism makes the "what" and "why" of inquiry clear and distinct moments. It assigns analytic and explanatory priority to the latter, thereby emphasizing the development and application of theory, and the interests and autonomy of our disciplinary traditions. "Religion," Bruce Alton argues:

[I]s the phenomenon; philosophy, psychology, sociology, phenomenology, history, textual analysis, etc., are the methods. The idea of a religious study of *religious data* is not just circular; it is self-contradictory and self-defeating; it suggests an approach in which one has 'gone native' so to speak, and lost one's academic perspective on the *content* of the inquiry.[33]

Like the arguments offered by naturalists, Alton's wholesale devaluation of the insider's perspective reflects the desire to unequivocally separate the discipline from its subject, rather than a more nuanced assessment of the subject's knowledge. His argument would seem to contradict Geertz's analogy of the swimmer and my defense of the insider's perspective. But rather than being irreconcilable, Alton and Geertz's positions are mutually corrective, for Geertz's analogy cuts both ways. After years of studying the hard-won knowledge of generations of hydrologists, our hydrologist can "read" the river in ways that the swimmer cannot. The hydrologist has theoretical models, questions, and means of answering them that the swimmer does not.

Carrying this analogy over to religious studies results in a depressingly commonsense conclusion, perhaps as is typical of debates where ideological passions and stereotypes triumph over more evenhanded assessments of the issues involved. The scholar of religion must adopt two voices, those of the sympathetic insider and critical outsider, and make him- or herself the site of their dialogue, mutual critique, and, when circumstances allow, corroboration. Our art is that of being able to view religion honestly and critically from multiple social locations. This means that we must gather insights from where we can find them, and not resort to value-laden oppositions between religion and science (which cut both ways) to prejudge issues of authority, method, and theory. To invoke one more analogy, we must play the artist and the art critic, because for most of our audience a religion simply does not exist without our first "painting" it for them. And yet this constitutes only half of our responsibilities, for religious studies is about far more than religious appreciation.

NOTES

1. Peter L. Berger, *The Sacred Canopy: Elements of a Sociological Theory of Religion* (New York: Doubleday, 1967), 181.

2. Victor Turner, *The Ritual Process: Structure and Anti-Structure* (Ithaca: Cornell University Press, 1969), 95.

3. Liminality is a technical term tied to a rich theoretical universe, not all of which I would apply to the academic study of religion.

4. Throughout this essay I will use "theology," "religion" and its cognates, and "the sacred" somewhat interchangeably. Here I employ the sacred because scholars of *Religionswissenschaft* have generally contrasted their approach with theology, seen as sectarian and

confessional, while the sacred, for them, captures the nonsectarian essence common to all religions. There are two "distancing traditions," so to speak, within religious studies: *Religionswissenschaft*, which takes theology as its "other"; and naturalism, which takes *Religionswissenschaft* (and theology) as its "other(s)."

5. It is important to note that liminal spaces are *historical* developments born of an increasing sense of incompatibility between categories, in this case, the sacred and the human sciences; these are not inherently incompatible categories.

6. Mircea Eliade, *The Quest: History and Meaning in Religion*, (Chicago: University of Chicago Press, 1969), 6.

7. See Timothy Fitzgerald, *The Ideology of Religious Studies* (New York: Oxford University Press, 1999).

8. Lawrence Sullivan, "'No Longer the Messiah': U.S. Federal Law Enforcement Views of Religion in Connection with the 1993 Siege of Mount Carmel Near Waco, Texas," *Numen*, 43 (1996): 213–34, 231. While I am sympathetic with the spirit of Sullivan's argument, it is somewhat tautological in that it assumes that we know what it would mean to treat religion as religion. And unfortunately, treating religion as religion has often meant a Protestant-like emphasis on the individual's personal relationship to, and experience of, God.

9. Wendy Doniger, *Other Peoples' Myths* (New York: Macmillan, 1988): 120.

10. A good analogy to this dynamic is the unpredictability of humor in the classroom. We have all experienced the phenomenon of finding a statement humorous that was not intended as such, or not laughing at something that others find funny. The difficulty in giving a substantive face to the kind of religion that occurs in the classroom is due precisely to its unpredictable, silent, and evanescent qualities.

11. To be clear, I am not exempting religious studies from being a constructive enterprise—it is, only unconsciously, incidentally, and haphazardly so. Most, if not all, the distinctions that separate theology from religious studies are matters of degree rather than kind. This continuity does not give one grounds for calling them the "same thing," however, for the issue of degree is all-important. It is possible and intellectually fruitful to recognize continuities across categories without conflating them. A gorilla and an orangutan are both simians, but this does not mean that a gorilla *is* an orangutan, an orangutan *is* a gorilla, or that they should be housed in the same cage.

12. Whether a scholar can ever *fully* bracket his or her sympathy or antipathy towards religion and treat the theological implications of his or her scholarship as merely incidental is doubtful; this is another respect in which the academic study of religion is irreducibly religious. But the ineradicability of one's biases is a far cry from allowing them to overdetermine one's scholarship or vision of the discipline.

13. David Chidester, "The Church of Baseball, the Fetish of Coca-Cola, and the Potlatch of Rock 'n' Roll: Theoretical Models for the Study of Religion in American Popular Culture," *Journal of the American Academy of Religion* 64, no. 4 (1996): 743–65.

14. Jonathan Z. Smith, "'Religion' and 'Religious Studies': No Difference at All," *Soundings* 71 (1988): 231, 232.

15. Throughout this essay, I focus on the "religious/existential" dimensions of religion, i.e., meaning, value, purpose, etc., but do not thereby mean to suggest that religion is

reducible to these dimensions. Aligning religion solely with the "religious/existential" is problematic in that it reflects the modern migration of religion from questions of value *and* fact to questions of value primarily. The particularity of this modern migration is evident in myths and sacred scriptures where questions of "how?" "when?" and "where?" are as important as the question of "why?"—and in fact are inseparable. Fundamentalists—or anyone whose religious literalism disagrees with science—appear "dogmatic" because of their unwillingness to concede questions of fact to science, and, along with religious liberals, satisfy themselves primarily with questions of value. It is telling that, in the modern context, religious literalists are often the ones most readily described as "religious," and even seen as quintessentially religious. The distinction between "teaching of" and "teaching about" trades on the modern migration of religion to questions of value and accomplishes, apparently by fiat, the religious innocence of questions of "how?" "when?" and "where?"—at least as they get addressed in religious studies. We put ourselves in the enviable position of not only being able to analyze/attack religious traditions on these issues and call it nonreligious, but being able to dismiss those who might respond in kind as "religious." Religious studies has more in common with religion—especially in its premodern and literalistic forms—than the distinction between fact and value suggests.

16. David Pailin, "The Confused and Confusing Story of Natural Religion," *Religion* 24 (1994): 199–212.

17. Ann Taves, *Fits, Trances, and Visions: Experiencing Religion and Explaining Experience from Wesley to James* (Princeton: Princeton University Press, 1999), 6.

18. J. Samuel Preus, *Explaining Religion: Criticism and Theory from Bodin to Freud* (New Haven: Yale University Press, 1987).

19. Catherine Bell, "Modernism and Postmodernism in the Study of Religion," *Religious Studies Review* 22 (1996): 180.

20. James's *The Varieties of Religious Experience* is one of the clearest examples of what I call "vicarious religiosity." A strong undercurrent in the book is James's sympathy and attraction towards a form of experience he claims never to have had personally, but nevertheless seems to "experience" vicariously through the richly detailed accounts of his subjects. Insofar as religious studies encourages students to empathize with the insider's perspective, or see the world "from the native's point of view," it invites them to participate in a kind of vicarious religiosity. Significantly, James also saw enough continuity between religious and "nonreligious" experiences to include the latter in his study. William James, *The Varieties of Religious Experience* (New York: Collier Books, 1961).

21. Thomas C. Parkhill, *Weaving Ourselves into the Land: Charles Godfrey Leland, "Indians," and the Study of Native American Religions* (Albany: State University of New York Press, 1997).

22. Ibid., 148.

23. A weakness of the naturalists' program—and one shared by Jonathan Z. Smith and the Enlightenment tradition—is its silence on the ethics of theorizing about other people's religion, particularly people whose traditions have long been ransacked as fodder for theory. Naturalists rightly emphasize the autonomy of the discipline's theoretical pursuits, but these pursuits must be balanced against the legitimate concerns of our subjects.

24. Parkhill, *Weaving Ourselves into the Land*, 148.

25. It is interesting to consider how we unthinkingly assume that someone is "religious" if they "belong" to a world religion, or express—in a phone survey—a belief in God; and then contrast this with the high bar faced by scholars who argue that religiosity can be found outside traditional categories and confines. This just goes to show how much "thinking" our categories do for us.

26. A legitimate concern with more inclusive definitions of religion is that they are analytically vacuous. To this I would simply note that my definition does specify an "outside" or "not religion," that of indifference to questions of meaning, purpose, value, and practice. Being true to my views on the irreducible historicity of religion, however, I would likewise stop short of claiming that indifference to these questions is the *sine qua non* of areligion. Areligion and religion are simply too historically dynamic and complex to make the presence of one element their defining feature for all time. Indifference and, conversely, a passionate concern for religious/existential questions, are simply the *closest* candidates I can find for their respective *sine qua non*.

27. For a discussion of the death of God and nihilism in religious studies, see Thomas Altizer, "The Challenge of Nihilism," *Journal of the American Academy of Religion* 62 (1994): 1013–21.

28. Stephen Thornton, "Facing up to Feuerbach," *Philosophy of Religion* 39 (1996): 103–20.

29. More specifically, then, the perceived problem is not reductionism per se—reducing the complex to the simple—but reducing or translating the sacred into the profane.

30. Thomas Nagel, "The Sleep of Reason," *The New Republic*, 12 October 1998, 34.

31. Clifford Geertz, "'Local Knowledge' and Its Limits: Some Obiter Dicta," *The Yale Journal of Criticism* 5 (1992): 129.

32. Judging by the position of some hard-line naturalists, we could even go so far as to redescribe the "insider/outsider problem" as the "idiot/genius problem"—which, if this were the case, could hardly be called a problem.

33. Bruce Alton, "Method and Reduction in the Study of Religion," *Studies in Religion* 15 (1986): 156.

5

Other People's Theologies: The New Hubris of History of Religions

Richard C. Martin

"God lives, I can prove it by the history of religions."
—Nathan Söderblom

The Problem

One of the problems that scholars of religion like to fret about when they get together is the relationship of comparative history of religions to theology. In this paper, I raise this question once again as one who has studied theology within seminary walls, who now believes that theology is among the data that comparative religions must analyze, but who does not believe, as the previous generation of historians of religion generally did, that history of religions in the modern university should be construed either overtly or covertly as part of the theological enterprise. Nonetheless, I shall have to deconstruct this last claim slightly at the end of this paper—I shall have to give back a little of what I take from theologians up front. The purpose of this paper is to problematize my own long-held position that scholarship on religion should not be sullied by one's own personal commitments—theological or otherwise. I will launch the argument with an observation Clifford Geertz made nearly two decades ago.

In 1982, Clifford Geertz published an article in the *New York Review of Books* titled "Conjuring with Islam." In this review of recently published books on Islam, he remarked that, contrary to the anti-Orientalism mania which had begun four years prior with the publication of Edward Said's *Orientalism*, in fact "the more traditional Orientalists" are and were less "field agents of imperialism" than "mostly finicky textual scholars with the usual woods and trees problem of those who have read everything in sight."[1] As it happened, we had visited in his office at the Institute for Advanced Study in Princeton a couple of months before the article appeared. In our conversation, he proposed a different take on the Orientalism project, at least, the Orientalism of Protestant Christian scholars who wrote about Islamic religion. Far from consciously trying to do Islam in, what William Montgomery Watt, Wilfred Cantwell Smith, and other traditional Islamicists[2] were doing was presuming to help Islam out by giving friendly theological advice. In the article that appeared not long after our conversation, after reviewing quite different works by Ernest Gellner, Roy P. Mottahedeh, Wilfred Cantwell Smith, and Hamid Algar's translation of some of the Ayatollah Khomeini's writings, Geertz put it this way:

> The tendency has always been marked among Western Islamicists . . . to try to write Muslim theology from without, to provide the spiritual self-reflection they see either as somehow missing in it or as there but clouded over by routine for-mula-mongering. D. B. MacDonald made al-Ghazzali into a kind of Muslim St. Thomas. Ingaz Goldziher centered Islam in traditionalist legal debates, and Louis Massignon centered it in the Sufi martyrdom of al-Hallaj. Henri Laoust defended puritan fundamentalism from the charge of heresy. *A half-conscious desire not just to understand Islam but to have a hand in its destiny has animated most of the major schol-ars who have written on it as a form of faith* (emphasis added).[3]

In their invitation to the contributors to this volume of essays, Professors Brown and Cady have actually encouraged what Geertz said Islamicists were up to: "There is a clear sense," as they put it, ". . . that the academic study of religion must become more attentive to the intersections between the normative and the descriptive, to the inevitable ways in which the categories of scholarship function not just to mirror but to shape the phenomena under investigation." The aim of this paper is to explore some of those intersections of theology, phenomenology of religion, and Islamic studies. I am particularly concerned with historians of reli-gion who seek, however benignly, to have a hand in the destiny of a religious tra-dition that is not their own. I will argue that some scholars of this generation are indeed still so engaged. Most surprisingly, I have come to realize that I have been doing more than simply "describing" Islamic religion in my writing and teaching. To get at this problem will entail some discussion of what Brown, Cady, and oth-ers see as the postmodern softening of the boundaries between normative and descriptive practices in religious studies, theology, and history of religions, which are sometimes contiguous (as when theologians and scholars of religion are in the same department operating under a negotiated set of promotion and tenure crite-ria) and sometimes at greater geographical and intellectual distance (as when they are domiciled in different departments or in institutions serving quite different missions, e.g., seminaries and Bible colleges versus public universities). If the bor-ders between the two approaches really are more porous than they once were, the relations between some theologians and some scholars of religion nonetheless remain conflicted. I have interpreted Brown and Cady to be asking the parties to this conflict whether there are conditions under which it can be resolved, or at least managed, within the Academy. Is there a willingness to negotiate? Can interests be identified on both sides that would provide grounds for a successful negotiation? Or, when it comes to theology and history of religions, should we conclude with Robert Frost that fences make good neighbors?

Prior to the question of whether or not theology should be done in the modern university is whether or not historians of religion are themselves doing theology, as Gerardus van der Leeuw openly did in his phenomenology of religion. In this paper, it is more specifically the problem of doing someone else's theology that interests me. In some cases, those (mostly European and American) scholars who seek to mend spiritual and theological problems in Islam, or to rescue the Islamic religion from being seen by non-Muslims as the cause of terrorism and political violence, are not theologians in their own religious traditions. They do not see themselves as doing theology but rather as doing good deeds for a tradition that is misunderstood. Those who practice history of religions in this way are often quite suspicious of, if not hostile to, the mixing of religious motives with the academic study of religion, as I have been throughout my academic career. I will argue that Geertz's "excavation" of the motives behind the projects of Western scholars of Islamic religion applies to this generation as much as it did to the religion-friendly Orientalists of yore. Finally, and this is my reason for embarking on this discussion, I want to make the claim that an appropriate place for theology in the twenty-first century university curriculum would have to entail the comparative study of theologies. I am not speaking here of interfaith dialogue. I am speaking about university scholars who are trained in the appropriate languages, texts, and practices of particular religious traditions doing comparative studies of the theological problems and rationales that drive religious life and action in the world in the name of religion. I am suggesting to the reader that the comparative study of theologies is becoming more important than ever in the evolving marketplace of ideas enabled by the Internet and the globalization of religious traditions and movements.

The Argument

This paper is based on the well-known premise that scholarship in both theology and history of religions is deeply entangled historically and intellectually. The purpose of the paper is to try to sort out what is bad about that, and what might be good about it as well, in light of the mission of the modern university. From the outset, I cast my vote for rigorous and independent history of religions scholarship. That scholarship must include the religious ideas and the disputes they engendered (theologies) of all religious traditions. The foundational stage of this argument is that the university is the place where religion—any and all religions—can and will be studied vigorously and critically. Some will want to add other adverbs, such as "appreciatively" and "respectfully," and I have no quarrel with such courtesies as long as political correctness is not allowed to edge out rigorous critical analysis. Modern scholarship on religion should not confuse its mission with that of interfaith dialogue. Citizens of modern states in a pluralistic world have a right to expect the same high level of university scholarship on religion(s) that they expect in the fields of medicine, economics, the arts, and computer technology, among others.

My next point takes a turn and holds that historians of religion themselves have often pursued a theological agendum in their studies of religion. Let me put this a little more provocatively: Much of scholarship in the history of religions during the past century was in fact a part of the theological enterprise—studying other people's religions within a theological framework. When we reread the texts of our *Religionswissenschaftler* forebears, such as Gerardus van der Leeuw, we discover that the phenomenology of religion was construed as an integral branch of the liberal theological system. The theological enterprise is often just below the surface of the language of the "science of religion." There are good historical reasons for this. Nonetheless, I want to argue that, at the beginning of the twenty-first century, it is important to recognize that knowledge about religion is valuable in its own right. Accurate and analytical knowledge about other religions—even knowledge about one's own religion in other times, cultures, and minds—is foundational for self-understanding and for our continuing project of constructing a common humanity in a conflicted, pluralistic world.

The third stage of the argument is that the historical tendency of Western scholars, primarily Protestant theologians, to subordinate the study of other religions to the discipline of theology has invited attempts to correct such academic imperialism. One form of correction is coming from religious thinkers and intellectuals from other traditions who have challenged Western intellectual hegemony (both theological and phenomenological) in the study of religion and religions. Another development among historians of religion who specialize in Islam is the effort not so much to cast their analysis within a Protestant theological framework or mission, but rather to offer advice to Muslims on how to work out theological problems inherent within Islamic religious thought. This form of hubris among historians of religion studying theologies is more interesting than the more traditional hubris of theologians engaging religions. In place of interfaith dialogues, we find scholars from different traditions, who may or may not be practitioners within their own religious communities, trying to address problems in religious thought across confessional boundaries.

In launching this set of arguments, my own religious and educational background has some relevance. It is often said that history of religions is a child of the Enlightenment.[4] As one who combined graduate work in history of religions with doctoral training in Near Eastern Studies, I slept through the first crazes of postmodern deconstructionism under a double dose of post-Enlightenment modernism, namely *Religionswissenschaft* and Orientalism. My personal intellectual and curricular trajectory brought me through theological studies to history of religions, with primary scholarly interest in Islam rather than in the Protestant Christian tradition in which I had been raised and indeed trained in seminary, although the latter established the foundations for my own pursuit of comparative studies. Eventually I was brought back to theology—Islamic theology—as a field of comparative studies within history of religions. For me, as for the Academy as a whole, theology and history of religions are complexly intertwined. The rest of this essay is a meditation on that tangle of competing purposes and its consequences for the academic study of religion.

FREEDOM FROM PRIOR RESTRAINT

I return now to the first argument, which is based on a claim that I have held strongly throughout my career as a scholar of religion, namely: *The modern university, particularly in the West, is the one venue where citizens have a right to expect research on religion(s) that is held to rigorous standards of scholarship and unimpeded by prior restraint.* By prior restraint, I mean both confessional efforts to privilege and promote one "true" religion, as well the exclusion of scholarship on any religion by atheist ideologies, such as Marxism and Communism. In the past century, both confessionalism and Communism, for quite different reasons, sought to restrain severely the academic study of religion. However, they are not the only dangers to research on religion. Even with, and perhaps especially because of, a free press and an expanding and increasingly available information highway, bad information and disinformation about religions and their scholarly analysis have created a mutant strain of problems for historians of religion. Another important aspect of the global interactive effect of the World Wide Web (hereinafter Web) is that the doing of Islamic theology is no longer grounded in a specific communal context or subject to traditional religious authority. Now, theologically driven religious movements formerly thought to be subversive or heterodox can draw just as many hits on their Web pages as the University of al-Azhar in Cairo, especially if they have a good Web-page architect. In short, understanding the theology of other traditions will require a reconsideration of traditional notions of authority in religious studies.

In the United States, legal restraint and piety impeded the rise of religious studies as a separate discipline in public universities in particular until the 1960s. Nonetheless, as George M. Marsden has argued, there is a certain irony in this. For liberal Protestantism played a unique and effective role in creating a climate of opinion in major universities that would allow the study of any and all religious traditions on a nonsectarian basis. Although evangelical Protestantism inspired the building of many colleges in the nineteenth century, by the early twentieth century, many of these same colleges had determined that it was academically incorrect to promote evangelical Protestantism in the classroom. "In higher education," Marsden wrote, "Protestants insisted on a universal academic ideal, underwritten by Enlightenment assumptions concerning universal science and supported by optimism concerning human nature's ability to progress toward a universal moral

ideal."[5] Roman Catholics and others were moved to the periphery of the growing higher education establishment. By contrast to this "Protestant universality"
model of pluralism in American higher education, the religious denominations in
Europe had developed their own universities, teaching their own theologies. In
America for a time, Marsden went on,

> . . . liberal Protestantism also was still allowed to play a priestly role, signaled by
> the building of [college and university] chapels, blessing such academic arrange-
> ments. Eventually, however, the logic of the nonsectarian ideals which the Protes-
> tant establishment had successfully promoted in public life dictated that liberal
> Protestantism itself should be moved to the periphery to which other religious
> perspectives had been relegated for some time. The result was an "inclusive"
> higher education that resolved the problems of pluralism by virtually excluding
> all religious perspectives from the nation's highest academic life.[6]

As his title suggests (*The Soul of the American University: From Protestant Establishment to Established Unbelief*), Marsden laments this disestablishment of religion from
higher education. In his view, American higher education lost its soul when the
religious faith and practices of particular religious communities were no longer
privileged in denominational colleges and universities. One can argue, using Marsden's data on the history of religion in American higher education over the past
two centuries, that it was precisely the disestablishment of religion from higher
education that made possible the rapid increase of religious studies in public universities in the 1960s. This, however, Marsden dismisses curtly as an "increase in
the study *about* [religion(s)]," which is simply a further manifestation of the ban-
ishment of established religion that he so dolefully laments.

I simply disagree with Marsden on this point, although I find his book to be
informative and useful. I value the rise of the study *about* religion and religions in
the nation's colleges and universities, great and small. Knowing about other religions and societies, and their globalizing effects on American society, and the easy
export of America to the rest of the world, is a necessary component of modern
education. I submit that the broader liberal arts mission of the university normally
makes for a sounder academic environment for religious studies than the mission
of the divinity school (yeshiva, madrasa, etc.), which does not mean that colleges
run by religious communities cannot do religious studies well.

If the disestablishment of religion from higher education was an important
factor in the rise of religious studies broadly across American higher education,
another was the two world wars that, in the United States, brought the response
of federally funded area studies for training scholars in the languages, texts, histories, and cultures of non-Western religious civilizations. In Europe, the First World
War in particular had shattered the nineteenth century's faith in progress.[7] In the
United States, one could argue that an unintended consequence of Title VI in the
U.S. Department of Education (and the National Defense Education Act before
it), itself a government response to two world wars and the dangers of isolation-

ism, was the rapid development during the past four decades of the other half of the American Academy of Religion—the half that studies religions other than Christianity and Judaism. For this to happen, scholars could not find appropriate training in divinity schools such as existed in 1950. One had to seek training in languages and in the methods of the humanities and social sciences that made up area studies. Determining what a text or ritual act means on the thrashing floor of university scholarship depends on possessing the same kinds of training acquired by colleagues in history, anthropology, philosophy, linguistics, and other disciplines in the liberal arts. Those of us who were trained in graduate area studies programs found ourselves necessarily engaged in interdisciplinary scholarship, where faith-based theological arguments were not welcome.

For all that, many scholars of the past generation who migrated from area studies to comparative history of religions found themselves in need of methods and theories about religion as such, not just methods and theories about texts and practices as those were studied in the humanities and social sciences. This meant looking back in the direction of *Religionswissenschaft*, which itself had shouldered its way out of the divinity school a century ago, sustaining some bruises. Indeed, in North America, history of religions is still in many cases located in the divinity school (e.g., Chicago), or just adjacent to it and infused with divinity school faculty (e.g., Harvard, Duke, Emory). Let us take a closer look at history of religions scholarship and theology.

THE TRADITIONAL THEOLOGICAL AGENDUM
IN HISTORY OF RELIGIONS

History of religions scholarship, at least one phase of it, *Allgemeine Religions-geschichte*, arose on the Continent during the second half of the nineteenth century. Its stated goal was to remove the academic study of religion as far as possible from the confessional concerns of the church and of theological faculties.[8] The new concept of *Religionswissenschaft* took shape in roughly the same period when the medieval belief that theology was 'Queen of the Sciences' was falling prey to shifting scientific paradigms, such as Darwinian evolution. In the context of expanding curricula in the natural and social sciences, *Religionswissenschaft* was to open up the academic study of religion across many disciplines in the modern university. Historians, ethnographers, psychologists, sociologists, philosophers, and indeed philologists and scholars of religious texts, like the great Friedrich Max Müller, argued successfully that the *sacred* itself was a fit object of study, comparatively and scientifically. In no area was the new interest in religious studies more dramatic and conflicted than in biblical studies.[9] During the latter half of the nineteenth century, many new chairs in religious studies—separate from theological faculties—were established.[10] The notion of separation had begun already in the colonial and postcolonial periods a century earlier in the United States, when educators and statesmen like Thomas Jefferson and Thomas Cooper were sorely divided on whether or not to allow religious denominations to establish seminaries on the grounds of public universities.[11]

If in both Europe and the United States university scholars of religion sought to separate their studies of religion from the sectarian commitments of divinity schools, how successful were the new historians of religion in detheologizing their intellectual horizons? Was that even their goal? With respect to one branch of study, the phenomenology of religion, the separation of one's theological beliefs from the study of other religions was methodologically only temporary. The method of *epoché*, or "suspension of belief," did not claim that one's personal religious beliefs were irrelevant to the overall purpose of studying other religions. Rather, the scientific phase of scholarship on religion required the scholar to stand outside of his or her faith commitments for the time being to envision a datum of religion accurately. One's faith commitments were allowed to come back into play once one grasped the religious datum as an authentic phenomenon in the world of human experience.

Jacques Waardenburg's evaluation of the work of the phenomenologist of religion, Gerardus van der Leeuw (1890–1950), is instructive for the insight it gives into the theological framework and background of this great figure in history of religions scholarship. The title of Waardenburg's essay, "Gerardus van der Leeuw as a Theologian and Phenomenologist," and the order in which he arranged the predicate indicate why phenomenology of religion has not been particularly influential in religious studies in the United States. Under the influence of Friedrich Schleiermacher, Van der Leeuw, Rudolf Otto, and other European scholars in the late nineteenth and early twentieth centuries, scholars sought to understand religion and religions on the basis of experience, not textually embedded ideas. Waardenburg advises us that Van der Leeuw's "phenomenology should not be seen as an empirical, inductive and verifiable science, which it never claimed to be. It is rather, on the one hand, a method determined by theology and philosophy for describing human experience in general and religious experience in particular, and on the other an indirect expression of the personality and in particular the religious existence of the phenomenologist Van der Leeuw himself."[12] Methodologically, the post-Kantian discussion of *Verstehen* provided a way to grasp the religious experience of other persons. Van der Leeuw wrote about the "*verstehende* reconstruction,*" by which he meant that the scholar's subjective experience of the meaning of a revelatory experience (indeed, faith!) authorized him or her to intuit the meaning of that experience in another.[13]

The European legacy of *allgemeine Religionsgeschichte*, which demanded separating the academic study of religions from the divinity school, and the early twentieth-century movement in phenomenology of religion, which tended to identify itself as part of the theological enterprise, have left many historians of religions in North America with split personalities. There remain in most departments of religion, and among many scholars within them, both a theological agenda and a desire to adopt theories of religion and methods of investigation that will make the study of religion as untheologically biased as possible. In his brief but informative history of history of religions in America, Joseph M. Kitagawa documents the rise of the study of comparative religions in American colleges and universities. His essay introduces a small volume of papers, by eminent historians of religion belonging to the immediate past generation, on methodology in the history of religions.[14] For Kitagawa and many of his colleagues at Chicago, where history of religions was and is taught in the Divinity School, history of religions was considered a discipline separate from theology.[15] Kitagawa believed that if comparative history of religions was to survive in the university, both as an undergraduate curriculum of study and as a graduate training program, it must, in his words, clarify "the nature, scope, and method of the *discipline* of the history of religions itself."[16]

That being so, it is instructive to ask what the previous generation of historians of religion thought methodology consisted of. For these European and North American scholars who had lived through the brutalities of two world wars and all that implied about the failure of the nineteenth century's faith in human progress, the more burning issue of methodology was not *how* to study religious phenomena, but *why?* Indeed, there is a strong theological tone to most of the contributions. The lead chapter after Kitagawa's historical background on history of religions in America was Wilfred Cantwell Smith's "Comparative Religion: Whither—and Why?" Smith concluded that the initial phase of collecting data and editing texts, the phase of *Religionswissenschaft*, was now well under way and it was time to begin a new phase—one in which scholars from the "other" religions were no longer the object, but the subject of history of religions. Echoing Buber, Smith proposed that comparative religious studies was a personal form of scholarship, a study primarily of people, not artifacts. He saw a trend from dealing with the religious other as "it" to a contemporary (mid-twentieth century) "they," that is, other human beings, to "you" as a colleague from another faith, to a future discourse on religion where "we," that is, our common humanity would be the subject. To the distinctions made by the editors of this volume between normative and descriptive approaches, Smith adds still yet another mode, the "dialogic."[17]

Smith's lifelong project has been to guide history of religions toward the development of what he would call "world theology."[18] In his monograph by that title, he undertook to inquire into the possibility of a Christian theology of comparative religion, and what a Hindu, Muslim, or Buddhist theology of comparative history of religions might look like.[19] Smith reflected his optimism for modern humanity, and perhaps the optimism of others, through comparative history of religions *cum* a unifying world theology, despite the world wars, with the following prediction: "Future historians, it has been said, will look back upon the twentieth century not primarily for its scientific achievements but as the century of the coming-together of peoples, when all mankind for the first time became one community."[20] Humankind in general, and perhaps historians of religion in particular, have failed to achieve Wilfred Cantwell Smith's vision.

Elsewhere in the same volume, the German phenomenologist Friedrich Heiler contributed a chapter titled "The History of Religions as a Preparation for the Co-Operation of Religions," which began with these words from Malachi 2:10: "Have we not all *one* father? Has not *one* God created us? Why then are we faithless to one another?" (Emphasis added in Heiler's citation.) Heiler applauded Toynbee's condemnation of recent trends in Christian theological exclusivism, referring to without naming the neo-Orthodox theological movement led by Karl Barth. Like other phenomenologists, Heiler could read the Church Fathers, Stoics, and some Reformers as theologians who respected all manifestations of religion and the universal longing for one God.[21] Again, the intellectual history goes back through Rudolf Otto to Friedrich Schleiermacher, with the emphasis on religious experience as the authenticating criterion of the meaning of religion to one's self as well as to another. Why study other religions with an open mind? Heiler echoes others of his age in claiming that, in his words: "Non-Christian religions provide the student of religion with countless analogies to the central concepts of Christian faith and ethics."[22]

Let me bring my second argument to a close, that historians of religions have openly pursued a theological agendum. It seems to me that implicit in the envisioning of a world theology by Wilfred Cantwell Smith, or in the "all religions at base confirm the truth of Christianity" (and vice versa) of Friedrich Heiler, there is something quite important to be considered by those of us who are not theologians and who are not laboring in the service of establishing religious truths. In fact, our distinguished predecessors taught us very little about methodology that has inspired much of a following. They did what we are still having to do: learning from colleagues in languages, history, sociology, and other university disciplines. Their legacy is rather the insistence that knowing about and understanding the religions of humankind is vital in today's world. It is as much so, and perhaps more so, following the Gulf War, Ayodya, the Balkans, and above all, the globalizing effects of Internet religion, as it was following the Second World War, when Kitagawa, Smith, Heiler, and others wrote on what they preferred to call "methodology." Kitagawa worried whether or not history of religions had anything to contribute to undergraduate and graduate curricula that other disciplines that studied religions had not already established. To those who are habitually prepared to say "yes—history of religions has a theological method and framework for dealing with other religions that other university disciplines do not have or even allow," there is increasing resistance among historians of religion today. The modern university provides intellectual space for religious texts and performances to be studied with the same nonreligious, nontheological motivation and scholarly interest as society, culture, politics, and other human productions.

Does this mean that theological studies are irrelevant to religious studies in the liberal arts college of the modern university? I shall maintain in the next and final stage of the argument that theological studies, by which I mean the study of theological texts and the contexts in which they are produced, are in fact essential to the comparative study of religions. The strong bias of many contemporary historians of religions against any form of theological study is myopic and unhelpful. Theology functions to articulate religious identity over against the other by providing the means, among others, to apply received texts and symbols to changing situations. Theologies establish boundaries that define self as community and difference from the other. Theologies may some day break down those boundaries and unite all of humankind, as Smith and others have hoped, but that cannot be said of how theology has worked in the world thus far.

OTHER PEOPLE'S THEOLOGIES

In his keynote address at the 1994 annual meeting of the Middle East Studies Association in Phoenix, Arizona, the Tübingen Islamicist, Professor Josef van Ess, ended on a note of warning to the linguists, historians, social scientists, and public policy experts assembled.[23] In an age of media and scholarly concern about Islamic fundamentalism, Van Ess cautioned his audience that their ability to understand events in the Islamic world would depend on their willingness and ability to understand on their own terms the discourses generated by the Islamiyyin—the Islamic movements calling for a rejection of Western secularism and a return to the authority of the Qur'anic revelation and the Sunna of the Prophet Muhammad. This meant, he admonished those present, that Western scholars would have to learn the language of Islamic theology, the classical problems and issues in Islamic thought within which Islamist discourse about social and political issues was framed. It would not be enough, he argued, simply to reduce Islamist discourse to contemporary social, political, or psychological causes; there could be no communication with Islamist intellectuals if scholars resorted to reductionist methods to rid the conversation of theological premises. In this concluding section of the paper, I want to tease out some of the implications of Professor Van Ess's admonition that the language of Islamic theology must be taken seriously, against the background of Clifford Geertz's insight that those who undertake such studies are likely to want to have, consciously or subconsciously, a hand in Islam's destiny.

That history of religions scholarship is heavily laden with Christian theological overtones and rationales has not gone unnoticed among Muslim, Buddhist, Hindu, and other intellectuals in Africa, the Middle East, and Asia. Nonetheless, it is ironic that *Religionswissenschaft* in the nineteenth century and history of religions scholarship in the twentieth century have not come under the same critical eye that Orientalism has. Why is this so, or seemingly so? One reason is that nothing comparable to Edward W. Said's book *Orientalism* has investigated religious studies from outside the field in Western scholarship. Serious critiques of Western scholarship on religions, in fact, have existed for some time in the Muslim world. For example, in 1963, the Egyptian writer Anouar Abdel Malek published in a widely read Western journal a Marxist critique of Western Orientalism.[24] Other Muslim scholars criticized Western writing about Islam, but in languages such as Arabic that were not read by Western intellectuals. After the publication of Said's _Orientalism_ in 1978, many more Muslim scholars added their voices to the anti-Orientalism chorus that dominated Western scholarly venues during the 1980s and to a lesser extent the 1990s. One of the most interesting critiques of Western scholarship on Islam has been the work of Professor Hassan Hanafi, professor of philosophy at Cairo University. In a work titled _Introduction to Occidental Studies_ (in Arabic), Hanafi turned Orientalism on its head.[25] He argued that the post-Enlightenment Modernity project and Euro-American imperial control over the Muslim world and other Third World people are coming to an end. The new intellectual framework for constructing knowledge, including the study of the religions of humankind, will come from an Islamic _epistémé_, which derives from a classical heritage of incorporating and legitimizing non-Muslim religions within its theological, legal, and political order. The challenge to post-Enlightenment Modernity and to Orientalism coming from the Muslim world includes within its scope the academic study of religion in Western universities.

Among Euro-American historians of religion are several specialists in Islamic studies who are aware of this critique and are sympathetic to it. Some of them have sought to improve scholarly communication among Muslims and others by attempting to deconstruct the popular association of Islam and Muslims with terrorism, violence, and anti-Western attitudes. This genre of work seeks to present a more positive understanding of Muslim civilization in light of recent violent events linked to Muslim terrorists. The negative image came from many other directions as well that have been well documented by Esposito, as well as Edward Said, Bruce Lawrence, and others.[26] The negative image of Islam includes Western feminist critiques of gender relations and practices in the Muslim world, as well as the view that Islamic reform movements are striving to impose a medieval mentality on Muslim populations. A crucial event was the publication in 1992, almost one year after the Gulf War, of Samuel P. Huntington's now infamous article, "The Clash of Civilizations?"[27] Huntington postulated the view that the major fault lines of global conflict in the new world order would be the cultural boundaries of civilizations (world religions, roughly), not the political boundaries of states, and that the "Confucian-Islamic" connection would turn out to be the most problematic and dangerous for the West. During the next few years, at Islamic studies conferences I attended in the United States, South Africa, Egypt, Austria, and Indonesia, Muslim scholars were eager to express deep regret and anger that Huntington had published such a blatantly "West against the Rest" challenge to the Muslim world; it betrayed Western attitudes toward Islam that they saw as going back to the Crusades in the eleventh century.

On a certain level, then, it has been important for historians of religion to challenge misinformation and disinformation about Islam, as well as theories that conceive of Islam as the new Evil Empire, following the fall of the Soviet Union and the end of the Cold War. Esposito and others have retailed the notion that Huntingtonian attacks on Islam during the past decade are to be seen as "the new cold war." A mighty nation needs a worthy enemy, and Islam for many commentators and public policy intellectuals seems to fit the bill. That sad, grossly unfair, and indeed dangerous development is not what is at issue in this paper, however. I am asking, rather, whether or not the attempt by historians of religion to defend Islam against the clash of civilizations thesis is subject to Geertz's suspicion that many Western experts on Islam seek to have a hand in its destiny? That is a difficult judgment to make. One feels oneself to be too close to the action to discern properly the intentions of one's friends and colleagues when they undertake to adjust Western attitudes towards Islam. Ultimately, I am not innocent of that effort.

The point Geertz makes has a more personal bearing on my work as an historian of religions. I first had occasion to recall my 1982 conversation with Clifford Geertz not in relation to the work of other historians of religion but in relation to my own authorship, with Mark Woodward, of our recent book *Defenders of Reason in Islam*.[28] My research and writing on Islamic theology until then had dealt primarily with the Mu'tazili "rationalist" school of theology in the Middle Ages, and their disputes with non-Muslim and other Muslim schools of thought. Along the way, however, I had become deeply drawn, as an onlooker, into the disputes that many of my modernist Muslim colleagues were having with more traditionalist, and often less tolerant, theological points of view. Woodward and I both felt that part of the problem with endless Western writing and worrying about Islamic fundamentalism was that it concealed a whole history of lively disputation between what we may broadly call the rationalist and traditionalist movements in Islamic thought. What I came to realize after the publication of *Defenders of Reason in Islam* was that at a certain level I had written the book with Woodward in support of the theological struggle that many of our Muslim colleagues were facing in their own universities and intellectual environments. To be more blunt, somewhere toward the back of my consciousness was the belief that the reemergence of interest among Muslim intellectuals in Mu'tazili rationalism was a good thing for the development of modern Islamic societies. Had we sought to do more than "describe" a theological development in modern Islamic thought; were we trying to have a hand in Islam's destiny?

A problem we all face as history of religions becomes de-Westernized is related to the one Van Harvey discussed lucidly many years ago: What is our ethical responsibility in producing critical and historical knowledge about religious beliefs?[29] What would be our ethical responsibility as scholars and as historians of religion if a Muslim colleague wrote a critical book on the quest for the historical Jesus that a Christian leader or denominational authority or college president tried to ban from the classroom? How must we respond as scholars to the claim that the Qur'an and the prophet Muhammad are off limits to critical, non-Muslim scholarship?[30] These are not new problems, as Van Harvey showed us over thirty years ago, but these problems have a new dimension as we enter the new millennium. Now, we as Muslims, Christians, Jews, Buddhists, atheists, and agnostics (or can we now simply foreground our identity as scholars?) are critically examining *other people's texts and theologies*. We are crossing more boundaries than our predecessors in the nineteenth century generally had to. The Sacred Books of the East project of *Religionswissenschaft* was seen as an effort to reconstruct ancient texts, not the religions of living human beings. The new ethical dilemmas will arise from the problem I alluded to earlier—the easy manner in which encounters among ethnic, cultural, and religious communities devolve into demands for respect and accusations of harmful disrespect. Historians of religion, who by definition frequently operate on someone else's turf, will have to find ways to conduct research and analyze highly charged religious issues and deeply held theological commitments. Wilfred Cantwell Smith anticipated this problem forty years ago when he said, in his words, "that a situation has arisen wherein anyone who writes about a religion other than his own today does so, in effect, in the presence of those about whom he is speaking."[31] Smith's solution was to begin the study of religion with the proposition "that no statement about a religion is valid unless it can be acknowledged by that religion's believers."[32] Smith did not analyze the ethical dimension of this problem in the same way that Harvey unpacked the moral issues in the Western debate about biblical studies. Smith, as we have seen above, saw comparative history of religions as a necessary but insufficient stage of scholarly work along the way to the real point of it all, dialogue among all religious people as human beings. Like a booster rocket sending its payload into orbit, the history of religions could be jettisoned once it had accomplished its assigned task.

The comparative history of religions is an appropriate and, I would add, a necessary part of the mission of modern teaching and research universities. The religions of humankind, past and present, are too important in the world in which we live to entrust to any single religious community, authority, or cultural tradition the power to determine exclusively what shall be studied and how. The modern university of the twenty-first century should continue to provide intellectual environments where serious scholars of religions from many different backgrounds can create, debate, and solve problems.

As we have seen, the twentieth century produced a tradition of Western scholars, including phenomenologists and others, who ultimately wanted to construct theologies that could explain the fact that there were religions adhered to by humankind besides Christianity and Judaism. That Western-, post-Enlightenment-centeredness of trying to understand other religious persons and traditions is coming to an end as more and more scholars, religious or not, from Muslim, Buddhist, Hindu, and other societies contribute to research and understanding of religions. These rather dramatic changes in religious studies are presenting working scholars with new dimensions to old problems, such as "where are the moral boundaries of writing about other people's religions?" That this is a global and not just a "Western" problem has not yet been fully realized, but surely it is global and applies to Muslims and Buddhists as much as to Christian and agnostic scholars of religion.

Few scholars of religion these days would agree, perhaps, with Nathan Söderblom, that history of religions offers proof that God lives, or at least, that is not the purpose they attach to their scholarly work. There are other equally and, in light of the global revitalization of religions in recent times, more pressing things to know about them, including their theological discourses, and the claims they make against other religions and the nonreligious secular world. To have developed a curriculum that taught Europeans and North Americans that religions exist in the modern world, and not just in the past, in the eastern and southern, and not just the western, hemispheres, was perhaps the main achievement of history of religions in the past century. How religious groups and communities will construct their identities and press their claims against each other and work out their differences textually and performatively in the democratizing and globalizing world of information networks presents scholars in this century with a changing dialectical intellectual environment in which to work. New clusters of problems are emerging for scholars to explain, interpret, and resolve. As Cady and Brown have suggested, the boundaries have become so porous that, echoing W. C. Smith, scholars are now necessarily analyzing, critiquing, and sometimes defending other people's theologies in a changing intellectual environment that includes the other. Historians of religion from many (indeed global) religious and nonreligious backgrounds will have to develop methods and rules of discourse that will continue to entitle religious studies an honorable place in the arts and sciences of the modern university.

✦

NOTES

1. Clifford Geertz, "Conjuring with Islam," *New York Review of Books*, 27 May 1982, 25.

2. The term "Islamicist" is used in this paper to refer to scholars who study Islam. "Islamist" in more recent usage refers to the Arabic neologism *islamiyyin*, which denotes the supporters of Islamic reform movements, often referred to as fundamentalists.

3. Clifford Geertz, "Conjuring with Islam," 27 (emphasis added).

4. See, for example, Earle H. Waugh, "The Popular Muhammad: Models in the Interpretation of an Islamic Paradigm," in *Approaches to Islam in Religious Studies*, ed. Richard C. Martin (Tucson: University of Arizona Press, 1985), 41.

5. George M. Marsden, *The Soul of the American University: From Protestant Establishment to Established Nonbelief* (New York: Oxford University Press, 1994), 5.

6. George Marsden, *American University*, 5.

7. Richard Martin, "Introduction," in *Approaches to Islam*, 7.

8. Ibid., 6.

9. For a history of biblical criticism, see Martin J. Buss, *Biblical Form Criticism in its Context* (Sheffield: Sheffield Academic Press, 1999).

10. Particularly useful for the history of history of religions scholarship are the following: the older work by Louis Henry Jordan, *Comparative Religion* (1905; reprint, Atlanta: Scholars Press, 1986); Eric J. Sharpe, *Comparative Religion: A History* (New York: Charles Scribner's Sons, 1975); and Jean Jacques Waardenburg, *Reflections on the Study of Religion: Including an Essay on the Work of Gerardus van der Leeuw* (The Hague: Mouton, 1978).

11. George Marsden, *Soul of the American University*, 73–76.

12. Jean Jacques Waardenburg, *Reflections*, 224.

13. Ibid., 197f.

14. Joseph M. Kitagawa, "The History of Religions in America," in *The History of Religions: Essays in Methodology*, ed. Mircea Eliade and Joseph M. Kitagawa (Chicago: University of Chicago Press, 1959), 1–30.

15. I make a case for regarding religious studies as a discipline in my article, "Fazlur Rahman's Contribution to Religious Studies: A Historian of Religion's Appraisal," in *The Shaping of an American Islamic Discourse: A Memorial to Fazlur Rahman*, ed. Earle Waugh and Frederick M. Denny (Atlanta: Scholars Press, 1998).

16. Joseph Kitagawa, "The History of Religions in America," 11.

17. Wilfred Cantwell Smith, "Comparative Religion" in *The History of Religions*, ed. Eliade and Kitagawa, 47ff.

18. Twenty years later, Smith published a monograph titled *Towards a World Theology: Faith and the Comparative History of Religions* (Philadelphia: Westminster Press, 1981).

19. Ibid., especially chapters 6–9 in Part III, titled "The History of Religion: Theological."

20. Friedrich Heiler, "The History of Religions as a Preparation for the Co-Operation of Religions," in *The History of Religions*, ed. Eliade and Kitagawa, 133.

21. Ibid., especially 136–42.

22. Ibid., 140.

23. Josef van Ess, "Verbal Inspiration? Language and Revelation in Classical Islamic Theology" (keynote address at the meeting of the Middle East Studies Association, Phoenix, Arizona, November 1994).

24. Anouar Abdel Malek, "Orientalism in Crisis," *Diogenes* 44 (1963): 103–40.

25. Hasan Hanafi, *Muqaddima fi 'ilm al-istighrab* (Cairo: Madbouli, 1991).

26. See Edward W. Said, *Covering Islam: How the Media and the Experts Determine How We See the Rest of the World* (New York: Pantheon Books, 1981); and Bruce B. Lawrence, *Shattering the Myth: Islam Beyond Violence* (Princeton: Princeton University Press, 1998).

27. Samuel P. Huntington, "The Clash of Civilizations?" *Foreign Affairs* (Summer 1993): 22–49. The Fall 1993 edition of *Foreign Affairs* published responses by Fouad Ajami, Robert L. Bartley, Lui Binyan, Jean J. Kirkpatrick, Kishore Mahbubani, Gerald Piel, and Albert L. Weeks. Huntington answered his critics in *The Clash of Civilizations and the Remaking of World Order* (New York: Touchstone, 1997).

28. Richard C. Martin and Mark R. Woodward with Dwi S. Atmaja, *Defenders of Reason in Islam: Mu'tazilism from Medieval School to Modern Symbol* (Oxford: Oneworld, 1997).

29. Van A. Harvey, *The Historian and the Believer: The Morality of Historical Knowledge and Christian Belief* (New York: Macmillan, 1966).

30. See the remarks to this effect by Muhammad Abdul-Rauf, "Outsiders' Interpretations of Islam: A Muslim's Point of View," in *Approaches to Islam*, ed. Richard Martin, 179–88.

31. Wilfred Cantwell Smith, "Comparative Religion," 42.

32. Ibid., 42; cf 52.

6

Embodied Theology

Sam Gill

Human beings embody theology despite the Western intellectual penchant for associating theology with thought, not with body. Furthermore, the discourse on definitions of religion—endlessly tiring quarrels that ought to, but do not, establish the foundation for the academic study of religion—reflect embodied theology more than they shape academic discourse. Being bodied, rather than being simply minded, is why such discussions are often so emotionally charged and turn out to provide so little satisfaction. We embody our beliefs so naturally that we are scarcely even aware we are doing so and embodied beliefs are rarely propositional. We do not think our theologies so much as we "be" them. I am considering theology as similar to mythology in the sense of being the grounding for lived truth and reality.

Mind (spirit, soul, intellect) and body are in many ways inseparable despite the ease with which our Western religious and intellectual heritage has prepared us routinely to dualize and hierarchize them. Both theology and the academic study of religion, indeed the entire academy, tend to ignore the physical body while focusing on the mind, yet it must be seen that to focus on the mind remains no less a statement about the body and, even though explicitly ignored, our body practices and habits enact our theologies. The rituals of both church and secular academy effectively show how theology is embodied. In the high mass of the Christian church, we see bodies—principally adult, white, and male—covered with liturgical vestments to such an extent as to render the body inarticulate. These processions of floating heads demonstrate the devaluation and suspicion of the gross body, the body from the mouth down, with the focus directed toward the head, the face. The high ritual occasion of the secular academy is the graduation exercise. Academically garbed bodies—principally adult, white, and male—are rendered inarticulate, demonstrating the same body-mind hierarchy. In these—perhaps our grandest cultural rituals—the robed, heavily garbed body reflects and enacts our deepest cultural and religious beliefs. The body below the neck is suspicioned and its articulation, its sexuality, its fleshiness, is to be covered, suppressed, denied. Though as academics we study ritual and as religious people we construct and practice liturgy, though we consider powerful both the study and the practice of ritual, we are rarely sufficiently self-aware or self-reflective to recognize that, in the most common of our cultural acts, we are effecting our theologies through our embodiment of them. From this perspective, we must recognize that the supposed objectivity and disinterest of the academy is based on inherited beliefs (a theology and an anthropology) that the head (the mind) is superior to the rest of the body, that education is, for the most part, the training of the mind. The University of Colorado's (my university) current advertising sound byte is "Minds to Match Our Mountains."

As I will show through specific examples, the results of intellectual and academic research are not simply shaped by, but rather almost fully determined by, various unarticulated and unacknowledged theories of body held by scholars. Further, I believe such theories, because they are tacit in their natural embodiment, must be understood as theologically based, a reflection of who we are, rather than consciously and reasonably chosen as part of the intellectual process. Our academic studies are shaped to a far greater extent than we acknowledge by who we are, by our most fundamental beliefs, than by the propositionally held academic theories we espouse. Though criticism is well developed to evaluate the application of theory, it scarcely exists for how theory is chosen, yet once theory is chosen, all else is largely determined.

Given this perspective, the discussion of the rightful place of theology in the academic study of religion seems naive at best. Of course, I suspect what is really being addressed by this question is the relationship of church and state, the distinction of church-supported seminary studies and state- or privately supported intellectual academies, the distancing of explicitly espoused branded theologies felt necessary by those who champion some objectivity of the academy. The naiveté stems from the failure to acknowledge that both Western religious theologies and Western secular intellectual academies deny the gross body, the body below the mouth. This denial is not only shared, something held in common, by both; it also distinguishes both and arises from a common history. As fundamental embodied beliefs reflect and affect the lived experiences of truth and reality, it is impossible to entirely separate religious theology from secular grounds for belief. While from the perspectives of either the church or the secular academy the other seems vastly different, from the global perspective of the diversity of world cultures these two seem barely distinguishable, particularly as they are embodied. Walter Capps' recent book, *Religious Studies: The Making of A Discipline*, is insightful in this respect.[1] From within the so-called discipline of religious studies, there appears almost overwhelming diversity among the hundreds of figures presented in Capps's book. Yet, from but a short distance outside this frame, the discipline comprises almost exclusively European Christian white males. The proximity of religious and secular is reflected in the term "religious studies" as the name of the discipline, which uses the adjective "religious" to distinguish itself rather than some more nominal form. While the case I am making is most acute with regard to the academic study of religion, I think it holds for the entire Western academy. For the white European male ethnic gender profile remains the same across the academy.

The battle over the rightful place of theology in the academic study of religion is rather like the squabbles between Methodists and Presbyterians—it is a big thing only if you are one or the other. And it is on this very point that as a career academic I feel disenchanted. I chose the academy as a career where I might participate in what I believed was the grand humanistic enterprise of understanding others simply for the goodness, the rightness, of doing so without any intention to affect or influence or shape them; to understand them "in their own terms," as we so often say. Yet, time and postmodern insights have shown not only the impossibility but also the negative potential of these goals. While most academics now have at least nominally given up the possibility of objectivity and altruism, few to none have pondered an adequate alternative. To the postmodern challenge, the response has either been ostrich-style retrenchment, or entry into a postmodern discourse that is too often a hermetically sealed community that purposefully generates ambiguity endlessly. While I chose the university over the seminary because I did not want my work to be based in an explicit religious theology and I did not want my work to be directed toward proselytizing or even judging my subjects, I have come to see that my work will always be shaped in a determining way by my embodied theology and the results of my work cannot help but affect, often in colonizing ways, my subjects. In choosing the secular intellectual academy, I have effectively chosen only that my theology remain unarticulated.

I have come to see that much of our work must be characterized as amounting to "preceding simulacra," to use a term offered by Jean Baudrillard.[2] That is, the results of our research, seen in this light, are primarily projections onto our subjects of ideas, concepts, and expectations that we hold prior to our encounter with them. Such preceding simulacra are not so much reflections of the reality of our subjects as they are hyperrealities, concoctions that, in being almost entirely self-referential, provide their own confirmation. Consequently, if our actual subjects are to have any existence in our world, they are forced to conform to the preceding simulacra we project on them, thus changing themselves to confirm our projections.

To more fully consider where we can stand in this complex situation is not my concern here. I have attempted this in other works.[3] Basically I am interested in promoting multi-perspectivality, in rigorous and self-conscious comparison, and in relentless self-awareness. And in the following presentation I want to show that our embodied theologies, though they remain largely tacit to us, determine the character, the goals, the domains, and the results of the academic works even of those who do not consider themselves religious and who would deny that theology has anything to do with their academic work.

It might be argued that this set of embodied beliefs is best referred to as worldview rather than theology. I would not contest this reference, yet I rather like and welcome the emotional charge carried by the word "theology" because it reminds us that all argumentation and value are based in belief that is outside our usual frame of propositionality and that such belief is not universal or simply human, but depends on our cultural, historical, religious, personal, and situational

conditioning. Our theologies, because they are embodied, tacitly direct our interests, give us the feelings of conviction regarding our choices, shape the hunches
and guesses we formalize as hypotheses, and fuel the passion of our arguments,
which are almost never simply or even primarily logical.

I want to trace specific body histories to show how bodies are variously and
differently constructed and, in turn, how such body histories correspond with and
even determine how the world is encountered and seen as meaningful. I will do
this in fairly general terms, depending on and extending the detailed study of the
history of Central Australia that I provided in *Storytracking*. Here I choose embodied theologies as the category of comparison. I will trace the determining influences of the embodied theologies of a number of figures and groups that encountered one another in Central Australia. This will give us insights about the shape
and significance of the often conflicting encounters among these parties, thus
advancing our comprehension and appreciation of this fascinating Central Australian story, but more so for my purposes here, illuminating the roles embodied
theologies play in shaping human encounters, including those that are explicitly
religious and explicitly of the secular academy. The example is intended to provide
a base on which to comment further on the relationship of theology and the academic study of religion.

Let me begin with aborigines in Central Australia as they existed in the mid
to late nineteenth century.[4] Aborigines lived in intimate relationship with the land.
They manufactured little in the way of clothing, their housing was but temporary
brush shelters, and their tools were limited to spears, clubs, digging sticks, and
boomerangs. As hunters and gatherers, they did not plant or harvest. The intimacy
of their relationship with the land is evident in both the practical necessities of survival (non-aborigines generally cannot survive the scarcity of resources or the
harshness of the climate) and also the identity of the stories that tie their personal
identities to tracks across the landscape. The cultures of Central Australia powerfully and decisively shape the bodies of aborigines. Circumcision, subincision
(often repeatedly done), nail pulling, tooth extraction, bloodletting, the insertion
of bones in the nasal septum, and scarification are done extensively and purposefully connected with rites of passage, social status, and prestige. Diet, absence of
protective clothing, exposure to sun and flies and other insects that we consider
pests, the work habits of hunting and gathering, and the obvious experience of this
powerful landscape all leave distinctive impressions on the bodies of aborigines.

Tony Swain has argued effectively that aboriginal ontology is spatially, rather
than temporally, based.[5] The bodied experience of time, in the sense of experiencing sequences of change, is supported by the experience of marked interval or
change. The cycle of day and night, the cyclic lunar phases, and change of aging
(birth and death) exist in Central Australia, but there is little else that marks inter-
vals or sequences of change. Even seasonal changes and weather patterns are irreg-
ular. Droughts may last years. Aboriginal languages have few ordinals; they count
to three or five. Aboriginal languages are not written. Aborigines have intimate

knowledge of land and particularly tracks across the land identified with ancestors who are seemingly both present and absent. Conception identifies one's body with specific ancestral bodies and with specific tracks of land. Body is land; land is body. Body is ancestor; ancestor is body. Body is story; story is body. Body is community; community is body. Land, ancestors, story, community are all immediate; immediate as body. The individual and cultural bodies of an aborigine are physically molded as these identities are realized. The visible markings on the body and the actions of the body can be easily understood by any member of the community. For example, circumcision marks when a boy leaves the women's camp to begin being molded as an adult of his male skin group. Subincision marks accomplishment of adulthood performed in a ritual counterpart to our graduation exercises. Though less well known, women have their own body-shaping actions, including scarification and body decorations to mark similar cultural values. Though I skip ahead, the reason the lives of aboriginal women are not well known is because the embodied theologies of the European male ethnographers blinded them to the existence of aboriginal women.

Education in aboriginal life is invariably accompanied by pain, the felt pain of the body. There is the pain experienced in the ardors of hunting and gathering in a hot and scarce physical environment but more importantly there is the culturally prescribed pain, which is required to be stoically borne, of surgical and intrusive procedures performed on genitals, skin, nails, and teeth. Aboriginal education is invariably body active and body changing. Learning to hunt and gather is done by performing these tasks. Stories and songs are learned most commonly in the performance of ritual dramas. The land, a counterpart to the community shared body, is surveyed by walking about on it. The world known to aborigines during this period was the world known through their physical experience. Since there appears to have been little interest in origination or in worlds beyond their present physical world, it seems unlikely that much of the knowledge of aborigines could be characterized as propositional or theoretical. The mind is the body; the body is the mind.

In aboriginal life, the body is the principal thing made. It maps the territory and vice versa; it holds and enacts the stories; it maintains tradition and continuity by incarnating ancestors; it marks gender; it marks education, politics, and power. Aboriginal life unfolds as a cultural encounter with the body. The body is central and integral to all meaning in aboriginal life.

Late in the nineteenth century, a group of Lutheran missionaries from Hermannsburg, Germany, entered this Central Australian landscape.[6] As Christians, they held a powerful mind–body duality, considering the body of lesser value than the mind or soul. The body is to be disciplined to support the cultivation of the soul. They were willing to risk body and endure hardship and pain to accomplish the task of winning their own salvation by bringing their god to the godless. Their god was attached to no land, for he was the creator of the world, the whole world. He existed in heaven, a place sufficiently vague in location as to be equally accessible to all believers, wherever geographically located. The physical world, like the physical body, was understood as but a place of transit, a temporary and dangerous place to be overcome, transcended. The physical world and the physical body were suspect in offering temptation and distraction. Both required careful discipline, measures of control, and vigilance.

These men in black entered the landscape of Central Australia bearded, shod, and hatted. They were accompanied by cattle and sheep. They brought books with them, particularly the Bible. It took them eighteen months to make their first trek from South Australia to their new home. Their bodies suffered the harshness of their mission, which collapsed within a few years primarily because their bodies could not adjust to the demands of the territory.

As Europeans and Christians, their body stories are told in terms of the architecture and furniture they considered necessities. Immediately upon arriving in Central Australia, they set about building. First, corrals were built to hold their domestic animals and gardens were cultivated in the attempt to produce food. Then they built houses to shelter themselves. Their basic bodily needs dictated by their cultural heritage even took priority over their spiritual mission. Once their basic bodily needs were met, they built a chapel and a school, both seen as essential to the accomplishment of their mission.

To bring god to the aborigines meant to bring aboriginal bodies into line with Christian body theology. They clothed the naked. Clothing obscures the aboriginal cultural markings on the body that indicate identity, gender, status, and power. Clothing also served to bodily mark those aborigines who were influenced by Christianity. The missionaries brought aborigines into the chapel to sit in pews to listen to the word of god. In schools, the aboriginal children were taught to sit at their desks to learn to read and write. To achieve the nourishment of spirit, soul, and mind, Christian missionization requires that proselytized bodies be disabled and discouraged through the discipline of architecture and furniture and clothing.

The aborigines, it seems, were willing to subject their bodies to clothing and Western architecture and furniture to meet their bodily need for food during times of scarcity. Missions attracted aborigines mostly during times of protracted drought. They also attracted orphaned children, their only full-time residents, who likely would otherwise not have survived. Aborigines understood missions primarily in terms of their bodily needs.

Coincident with the arrival of the missionaries was a stream of European-Australian miners, cattle ranchers, administrators, telegraph builders and operators, and scholars.[7] They were all Europeans and thus shared a common history of body, although this general history was certainly shaped in various ways by their individual physical, psychic, and occupational experiences.

I want to consider here only those we identify as scholars, for their stories are most germane to our chosen concern. I want to consider them in two groups: the first is the group of scholars who physically experienced Central Australia—Baldwin Spencer, Ted Strehlow, Géza Róheim—and the second is the group who did not—Mircea Eliade and Jonathan Smith.

Baldwin Spencer was an Oxford-trained biologist who was hired by the University of Melbourne to create the study of biology in Australia; Ted Strehlow was born of missionary parents at Hermannsburg in Central Australia and learned Arrernte language along with German and English as a child; and Géza Róheim was a Hungarian Freudian psychologist who traveled to Central Australia to confirm Freud's positions, as advanced especially in *Totem and Taboo*, and to establish a field of psychoanalytic anthropology. It is not difficult to construct the general theologies these men embodied and to articulate their various understandings of the body.

A biologist and an evolutionist, Baldwin Spencer studied aborigines in Central Australia as he did species of plants and animals.[8] It was during his travels with the Horn Expedition to study Central Australia that in Alice Springs he met the telegraph operator Francis Gillen, with whom he wrote the famous work *Native Tribes of Central Australia*.[9] Spencer, known to aborigines as "All-day-pick-em-up-pick-em-up," collected, classified, photographed, and sketched plants, animals, and people. His understanding of body was a biologist's understanding. Consequently, he saw aborigines as objects to arrange in given classificatory schemes. Actual bodies were secondary, if relevant at all, to the demands of the general patterns, classifications, and theories forged by such major theorists as James George Frazer and E. B. Tylor. Still, as a biologist, Spencer clearly valued the body, the physical world. He repeatedly traveled to Central Australia to collect not only biological specimens, but also, increasingly important to him, cultural specimens. His collection was accomplished by written description, photographs, and drawings. As a cultural evolutionist, Spencer saw aboriginal bodies as primitive bodies, as specimens representing an early period in human evolutionary history. Spencer was interested in aborigines solely because their physical bodies marked them categorically as primitives. Spencer's world was a world oriented to time. His traveling to Cental Australia was the experience of a wrinkle in time, a visitation to human origins.

Spencer's body was an academic's body. He spent most of his life teaching and researching at the University of Melbourne. One of his first tasks in creating an Australian study of biology was to design a building to house such a study at the university. Central Australia was his field for work, a place to visit to collect specimens he took home to study.

Ted Strehlow is distinguished among European-Australian scholars in having been born at Hermannsburg and, having learned Arrernte language as a child, he claimed it as a mother tongue.[10] Consequently, though there are detractors, he retains the reputation as the most trusted student of aborigines, a valuation shared it seems by both aborigines and his scholarly colleagues. Throughout his life Strehlow claimed the position of aboriginal spokesman, sometimes even to the exclusion of aborigines, an exclusion that he justified by comparative body histories—that is, he claimed more bodily experience in Central Australia than some aborigines. It seems clear that Strehlow's reputation is the result of his specific bodily history as much as the evaluation of the scholarship he produced.

Géza Róheim,[11] an interesting contrast with Strehlow, is routinely dismissed because of the disposition he held, as a Freudian, toward the body. Róheim, in contrast with most other students of aborigines, centered his attention on the sexual body and on the bleeding, suffering, scarred body. Although these body matters are unquestionably important to aborigines, no other scholar gave more than passing interest to aboriginal sex, blood, and pain. No other scholar gave so much attention as did Róheim to children, whom he engaged in a play-based form of psychoanalysis, and to women, whom he interviewed extensively, usually about their sex lives. Because of his disposition toward the body, Róheim's many publications remain obscure and the target of dismissive criticism. Interestingly, Róheim's psychoanalytic anthropology anticipates Baudrillard's preceding simulacra in that he understood all field studies and encounters with others in the psychoanalytic terms of projection and counter-projection.

I am arguing that among this group of Europeans who went to Central Australia to study aborigines, their personal and cultural embodied theologies powerfully shaped the academic work each did, and also have been significant factors in the way each has been valued by the academic and aboriginal communities. The theologies embodied by each of these scholars were consistent with that of the European or Western intellectual heritage they held, which I will soon trace a bit more, yet each was shaped, even determined, by specific physical, psychic, historical, cultural, and intellectual factors, factors that can be more fully accounted for only through biography and more specific storytracking.

While these scholars differ significantly from one another, they shared the tacit commitment that body experience is essential to their contribution to the academic enterprise. While each tended to reconstruct his subjects unconstrained by his physical experience, as I show in *Storytracking*, each believed that one must go, physically, bodily, to Central Australia, even if briefly, to study aborigines.

Let me turn now to Mircea Eliade's and Jonathan Smith's studies of the aborigines of Central Australia. Neither went to Australia. Because of their stature in the field, I consider Eliade and Smith exemplary of modern education in the West. Their body history is in broad terms identical to that of the Western academy; their history of body is ours. Modern educational instutions have inscribed this attitude toward the body on us all. These institutions have molded our bodies, as well as our understandings of the body.

From the earliest days of school, our children are taught to read and write in a manner that invariably, even necessarily, is accompanied by a discipline of the body. Children are told to "sit still and pay attention," to "sit down and be quiet," to "read silently so as not to disturb others." Writing requires a supported surface and tools—a desk and pencils—both of which limit body mobility. Educational architecture and furniture are designed to disembody. Classrooms at all levels have chairs. Students sit at desks that confine the body, often by having the desktop fold across students' laps. Desks are often bolted to the floor to prevent disorder and student socialization. Students all are forced to face the same direction, towards the teacher, thus establishing in the body a hierarchy of learning. Teachers enjoy a bit more body freedom, though many cannot tolerate a room without a lectern. Teachers' desks and chairs are larger, likely as much a sign of the status of the learned as a product of the necessity of their more abundant stuff.

Books, videos, filmstrips, pictures, and now the Internet bring the world to the bodiless minds of the students. Microsoft advertises "Where do you want to go today?" Or "Who do you want to be today?" The increasing privilege of the mind at the expense of the body changes the body's relationship to space. Bodies need not move to learn; indeed, it appears all we need are eyes and an index finger. Virtual and actual lose their distinction; distance and immediacy are indistinguishable. Universities are rapidly embracing the concept of "distance learning," learning via the Internet, and in doing so, proclaim the utter uselessness of the body to learning.

In the university, faculty members "hold positions" and "occupy chairs." As Elaine Scarry has shown, all things we make are somehow projections of our bodies.[12] Skinny legs, a big seat, and a straight back seem a pretty apt description of the typical academic, all, of course to support the all-important enlarged bespectacled talking thinking head. Stereotypes of professorial clothing styles and personal grooming habits reflect our admiration for bodily neglect by the learned.

Western education has incorporated as distinctive to it the contestability and arguability of ideas, of thought. Thus, we improve our minds, we change other's minds, we criticize ideas, we argue positions. Yet, the body is disciplined, denied, and disabled seemingly without even our awareness, much less our consent. Unquestioned and unprotested acceptance of educational architecture and furniture hugely shapes who we are. It is through these methods of disciplining and shaping our bodies, more so than through intellectual methods of argumentation, that our theologies are transmitted.

Academic bodies are not natural bodies; they are bodies disciplined from their earliest days of school to privilege the head part and to develop agnosia with respect to everything from the mouth down. As I noted earlier, the academic body correlates well with the Christian body. Academic garb differs little from Christian liturgical garments. Both render the body inarticulate. Such garments transform the human body into a cloth-covered pedestal on which is prominently displayed the all-important head, the domain of mind and spirit. In the study of religion, with Christianity serving as the tacit prototype for our definition of religion, it is not surprising that the correlation is especially strong.

Eliade's *Australian Religions* is one of the few general treatments of the religions of aboriginal Australians.[13] His frequent use of aboriginal examples was important to ground and illustrate his influential understanding of religion. While Smith did not write about Australian religions in such breadth, his use of aboriginal examples and particularly his criticism and reinterpretation of Eliade's use of aboriginal examples have been important in establishing his understanding of religion and the academic study of religion.[14] Yet even though Eliade had extensive embodied experience in religious study in India, neither he nor Smith considered it necessary to go to Australia or to have any bodily experience whatsoever to complete their respective studies of aborigines. Though both scholars are accomplished in the study of languages, neither considered it necessary to learn any aboriginal languages. While we must still consider these seemingly peculiar aberrancies, given the tracking of the various histories of bodies—various embodied theologies—that intersect in Central Australia, can we expect anything other than that the body histories of Eliade and Smith have played a major role in what they understood and how they came by their positions and understandings?

Both Eliade and Smith focused their attention on myth texts and ethnographies. Eliade even confused mythic events with ethnographically observed ones. Neither scholar was interested in the extensive bloody and painful genital and body operations or in other bodily aspects of aboriginal life. As I show in *Storytracking*, Eliade concocted the aborigines as exemplary of "religious man" in that, according to him, their lives were unliveable should their world center, which gave them access to their god, be destroyed. His presentation of aborigines is not an interpretation of extant sources, but rather is a constructed simulacrum that ignores and is unconstrained by the actual aborigines or even by the ethnographic records he cited.

Smith's interest in the aborigines is primarily in service to his refutation of Eliade as representing a model for the study of religion. Smith focuses on aboriginal myth texts collected by ethnographers. By rejecting Eliade's interpretation of the aboriginal myth as establishing the synonymy of religion and the sacred center, Smith gives a more historically and contextually oriented alternative interpretation. Smith's understanding is certainly more embracing of actual aboriginal life, yet analysis shows that even his alternative interpretation is not adequately constrained by his textual sources.

For both Eliade and Smith, aborigines were reconstructed in text from other textual sources to support the advancement of existing general theory. The physical bodied existence of aborigines is of no concern to either scholar. Aborigines exist as texts, writings, examples, not as bodied people. There is no concern for the flesh-and-blood aspects of aborigines that, one would think, establish the most primary base for authority and authenticity. It seems Smith and Eliade hold the tacit assumption that none of their readers has any interest in actual embodied aborigines. And the broad acceptance of their work seems adequate confirmation.

The distinction I am making here between the two groups of scholars is that one group met the aborigines in the flesh, while the other group did not. I suggest that there are two poles within which the continuum of scholarship is conducted: studies that focus on specific cultures and studies that are broadly theoretical. Though we all know that theory and application are inseparable, that all specific culture studies are theory driven, we still make the distinction and often identify one or the other pole as descriptive of our own work and concerns. I think this division is but another face of the body-mind duality. Works such as Spencer and Gillen's are seen as nontheoretical. Indeed, in their correspondence, James George Frazer warned Spencer to leave the theory to him. Spencer thought he was complying, yet much of his work was actually done at Frazer's specific requests for corroborative ethno-graphic evidence to support his culture theory and, of course, everywhere is the imprint of his perspective as an evolutionist. Still, in the academy, most ethnography is considered descriptive and nontheoretical, as transparent to the embodied theolo-gies of the ethnographers. Smith and Eliade appear to see their work on Australian aborigines at the other pole, as working primarily with texts rather than people. But it seems to me that rather than holding a view that the texts are perfectly transpar-ent, that is, that they perfectly present the actual people, both scholars were uninter-ested in the actual people. Rather, both considered the texts, even in their opacity, even in their disembodying their subjects, completely sufficient.

In the past, I have argued for a clear distinction between a religious study of reli-gion and an academic study of religion.[15] In broad terms, I continue to believe that such a distinction is important. Without such a demand, the academy is indistin-guishable from the church, on the one side, and fiction, on the other. In the terms I have presented above, the religious study of religion presumes a position identified with a particular religion among other religions. This approach both overdetermines and inappropriately limits the categories of comparison and the terms of evaluation. On the other hand, the academic study of religion, a child of our broadly humanis-tic efforts, of our efforts to embrace anew a plural and richly diverse world, must stand lightly and temporarily (a style of standing that does not well suit explicit West-ern religious traditions) in order to conduct comparative analysis in terms of some self-consciously constructed and expectantly modifiable categories. We do so not to find truth, but to enact who we—determined to a degree by our historical, cultural, and religious particularity—are, who we want to become. What I have suggested in this paper is that while we must distinguish between religious and academic approaches, these positions are finally not separable because the most basic premises of the Western academy are interwoven with fundamental beliefs and understand-ings of reality—theologies—that are continuous with the more explicit theologies of Western religious traditions. Such theologies inform the very architecture, furni-ture, pedagogy, and research methodology of the Western academy, which, in turn, determine to a degree far greater than we commonly acknowledge the way we con-duct academic business. The necessity, yet impossibility, of making a clear distinction here is what characterizes us at this moment.

There is no place in the academic study of religion for explicit religiously the-ological positions of any kind, but the entire Western academy—not simply the academic study of religion—is shaped by general theological positions that, though tacit, are nonetheless so determining, particularly as they are embodied, that the academy could not survive their eradication.

The question then is not whether theology has a rightful place within the aca-demic study of religion, because the academy is in important ways a Western the-ological project. The question is rather how theology can be reconstructed and reimagined beyond explicit religious theologies, as perhaps an academic theology, so as to contribute to the challenges of the modern academy, indeed, in the service of embracing the modern plural and diverse world. An academic historical and descriptive theology should contribute to the growing self-awareness of the specific religious/theological conditioning of the academy in all its subtlety and to the descriptive, comparative, and interpretive study of the theological elements in cultural practices of others. An academic constructive theology should endeavor to develop the operative theological positions of the academy, to make them more explicit than tacit, so as to achieve systems of belief and specific strategies of inquiry that invite greater interaction with the world's religions and culture—that create openness to change, modification, and even abandonment; that celebrate the play of interaction—bodied as well as minded—with others in the world; that recognize that our academic efforts to understand others, to focus on such constructed categories as "religion," and to engage in processes of the mind we call "academic" are but the ways we embody our own theologies.

Notes

1. Walter Capps, *Religious Studies: The Making of a Discipline* (Minneapolis: Fortress Press, 1995).

2. Jean Baudrillard, *Simulacra and Simulation*, trans. Sheila Faria Glaser (Ann Arbor: University of Michigan Press, 1994), 1–2.

3. *Storytracking: Texts, Stories, and Histories in Central Australia* (New York: Oxford University Press, 1998); "No Place to Stand: Jonathan Z. Smith as *Homo Ludens*, The Academic Study of Religion *Sub Specie Ludi*," *Journal of the American Academy of Religion* 66, no. 2 (1998): 283–312; and "Play," in *Critical Guide to the Study of Religion*, ed. Russell T. McCutcheon and Willi Braun (London: Cassell, 2000), 451–462.

4. See *Storytracking*, chapters 3 and 6.

5. Tony Swain, *A Place for Strangers: Towards a History of Australian Aboriginal Being* (Cambridge: Cambridge University Press, 1993).

6. See *Storytracking*, chapters 2 and 5.

7. See *Storytracking*, chapter 2.

8. See *Storytracking*, chapter 6.

9. W. Spencer Baldwin and Francis J. Gillen, *The Native Tribes of Central Australia* (London: Macmillan, 1899).

10. See *Storytracking*, chapter 6.

11. See *Storytracking*, chapter 6.

12. Elaine Scarry, *The Body in Pain: The Making and Unmaking of the World* (New York: Oxford University Press, 1985), 244.

13. Mircea Eliade, *Australian Religions: An Introduction* (Ithaca: Cornell University Press, 1967).

14. See *Storytracking*, chapters 1 and 7.

15. Sam D. Gill, "The Academic Study of Religion," *Journal of the American Academy of Religion* 62, no. 4 (1994): 201–211.

7

From Theology to theology: The Place of "God-Talk" in Religious Studies

WILLIAM D. HART

The house of religious studies is full of strange beds and even stranger bedfellows. One often finds oneself in a strange bed, embraced by a stranger, not knowing how one got there or how to get out. No wonder so much effort goes into policing the boundaries between the scholarly self and the dogmatic other, between the academic study of religion and the promotion of an ecclesiastical agenda in the guise of scholarship. For when this boundary is blurred, there can be a dreadful and palpable sense of violation. I use this sexually inflected term because being forced into a bed that one finds undesirable is still the privileged way of talking about such matters in this culture. This sense of violation may provide a useful account of why some in religious studies want to separate themselves from theologians. According to some proponents of religious studies, the presence of theologians raises real questions of intellectual respectability. The proponents of this view do not want to be regarded by fellow academics (guilt by association) as intellectually promiscuous. These intellectual Victorians (bourgeoisie who are so easily shocked, shocked!) want to guard their chastity. They fear being caught with their pants down, of charges that they consort with the wrong crowd. For these Victorians, to be caught in the company of a historian of religions is a venial sin and to be caught with a theologian is a mortal sin. Besides, don't they risk madness by engaging in these unnatural relations? What are respectable academics to think? Imagine the gossip, raised eyebrows, and the sardonic laughter. Imagine scientists and humanists, already suspicious of the academic study of religion, saying, "And these people think they belong in the arts and sciences?"

All jesting aside, I admit being tempted by the view that the intellectual health of religious studies demands that theology be strictly quarantined. But I am skeptical of this view as well. In this essay, I attempt to negotiate the tension between my temptation and my skepticism by exploring two interlocking questions: What is the relation between theology and religious studies? and Does theology have a place within religious studies? In response to these questions, I offer five theses. First, theology and religious studies, if not Siamese twins, are as closely related as mother and daughter; indeed, the former gave birth to the latter. Second, Theology has left powerful traces within the academic study of religion, which is evident in the way that religious studies departments are organized. Third, these Theological traces are a source of discontent. Fourth, standard ways of distinguishing theology from nontheological forms of religious studies fail. Fifth, while denying any role for Theology within the academic study of religion, I argue that the place of *theology* is secure.

I distinguish between Theology and *theology*. Theology with an uppercase "T" refers to a devotional, confessional, and dogmatic enterprise, a professional, church-based enterprise; *theology* italicized with a lowercase "t" refers to a liberal, academic, and humanistic enterprise, a philosophical enterprise. Theology is fideistic; *theology* is fallibilistic. The former is absolutism born of skepticism. The latter is an open, revisable, hypothetical form of inquiry that rejects the either/or of absolutism and skepticism. I use theology, nonitalicized with a lowercase "t," to convey a meaning that is neutral between Theology and *theology* or where a distinction is not being made. My use of Theology is analogous to Derrida's pejorative use of "philosophy." But a better analogy is Rorty's distinction between Philosophy, which he doesn't like, and philosophy, which he commends to a post-Philosophical culture. In this paper, I commend *theology* to a post-Theological culture.

A SHORT HISTORY OF *THEOLOGIA*

The best account of which I am aware of the development of theology as an academic discipline is Edward Farley's *Theologia: The Fragmentation and Unity of Theological Education*.[1] Farley identifies two premodern notions of Theology: Theology as "a sapiential and personal knowledge of God" and Theology as a self-conscious scholarly discipline, an Aristotelian science. On the one hand, Theology was *opinio,* and on the other hand, *scientia*. This ambiguity, according to Farley, was constitutive of Theology in medieval Christianity. As *scientia, theologia* was a demonstrable set of conclusions about God and things related to God. The major proponents of this disciplinary notion of Theology were Aquinas and the scholastics. In their view, Theology not only had a legitimate place but the chief place in the university, which was just emerging during that period. If Theology was a qualified science because of "the supernatural origin of its principles," this only ensured its status as queen of the sciences. These developments, however, only intensified tensions with the much older and more common notion of Theology as practical knowledge (wisdom) rather than theoretical knowledge. This wisdom was understood as a salvific knowledge of God and godly things.

This ambiguous notion of *theologia* was exported to colonial America, where no clear distinction was made between ministerial education and an ordinary college education. Theological education had not yet been professionalized. Future clergymen did not pursue a specialized course of study but took the same courses as everyone else. *Theologia* was not a curriculum but an ethos that pervaded the curriculum. This was the time in American education, before the rise of seminaries, that Farley calls "the period of pious learning," or divinity. While ministers did not receive specialized training, it was common practice for them to apprentice themselves to a pastor who would educate them in the knowledge of divinity. By increment and degree, these informal arrangements were formalized and institutionalized. Harvard in 1721 and Yale in 1755 appointed chairs of divinity whose sole responsibility was to teach divinity, that is, about God and things related. Students would soon return to college for "a special two-year course in divinity"— an incipient graduate program. These trends were greatly influenced by developments in Germany where the secularization of the German university undermined the intellectual legitimacy of Theology as an academic discipline. This challenge led to a re-conceptualization of Theology as a field of study whose purpose was to train ministers. The formal establishment of seminaries at Andover and Princeton, with their German-trained faculty, consummated the transformation of *theologia* into the specialized, ministerial training of theological education. Along with their training, these faculty members brought with them the "fourfold division of theological sciences (Bible, dogmatics, church history, practical theology)" that was standard in Germany.[2] These specialized disciplines were governed by a professional ethos designed

> . . . to prepare the student for designated tasks or activities which occur (or should occur) in the parish or in some specialized ministry. To the degree that this is the case, the theological student neither studies divinity nor obtains scholarly expertise in theological sciences, but trains for professional activities.[3]

The consequence of these developments, according to Farley, was the fragmentation and thus the loss of *theologia*.

Farley's account is helpful not only for understanding the complex history of Theology, but also for understanding the emergence of religious studies, the way religious studies was configured, and why there are growing tensions within religious studies between Theological and nontheological approaches to the discipline. The ambiguity between Theology as "individual cognition of God" (or devotion) and Theology as a self-conscious scholarly discipline, combined with the tension generated by scholarly specialization that characterized Theology during the colonial period, is still evident today. If the contemporary university remains suspicious of theology, and this includes many well-meaning critics within religious studies, this has much to do with the failure to distinguish *theology* from Theology.

THE BIRTH OF A RELIGIOUS STUDIES DEPARTMENT

We get some sense of the suspicions that the modern university harbors toward theology by examining the establishment of the Religion Department at Princeton University. The same tension between a devotional and a scholarly self-understanding that characterizes *theologia* is evident during the gestational period that eventually led to the birth of religious studies at Princeton. The precursor institution was a two-course curriculum and standing committee, which are described in the following abstract from "Report of the Special Committee of the Faculty on Religious Education," 11 April 1935:

> This report was presented first to the Faculty and later to the Board of Trustees of Princeton University. On recommendation of the Faculty, the Trustees have approved the following actions:
>
> 1. Authorization of a first-term junior course on "The Development of the Religious Thought of the Hebrews," and a second-term junior course on "Religious Thought in the Gospels."
> 2. Institution of a standing committee of the Faculty which shall stand to these courses in lieu of a department, and which shall select and nominate a scholar to conduct them.[4]

The authors try to allay any suspicions that this proposal might engender among their colleagues. Religious studies, they are careful to note, is a liberal art, not a professional or devotional enterprise. The fourfold theological sciences exported to American seminaries and divinity schools during the colonial period will not be their model. On the contrary, the study of religion will have nothing to do with religious practice. For intellectual inquiry, when mixed with religious practice, generates the very suspicions that led to the expulsion of religious studies from Princeton University in the first place. So the report insists that the distinction between the study and the practice of religion be "thoroughly and permanently adhered to" as the practice of religion is "rightfully the concern and function of the chapel and its ministers."[5]

A historical methodology, they suggest, should guide the study of religion. The object of that study is the "essence, development, and effects" of religious forces. Here the authors anticipate a problem. How can a department of religious studies be justified when religion can easily be studied in other departments within the arts and sciences? What justifies this apparent duplication of intellectual energy and financial resources? What makes a department of religious studies necessary? Or, to put this differently, what makes religious studies a discrete academic discipline? The authors' answer is this: "The religious forces in history are distinct with their own essence, development, and effects. Consequently the study of them is a study in itself and not a by-product of the study of other phenomena."[6] This account of religion and its method of study reflects a *sui generis* understanding of religion, which means that religion must be understood on its own terms and according to its own method. Other academic disciplines within the arts and sciences (anthropology, sociology, psychology, etc.) offer some insights, but they are partial and, more important, external. They tell us something about religion's function but nothing about what religion is in itself.

The argument for a separate program or department of religious studies, and for a religious methodology that is appropriate to religious studies, echoes the argument of the *Religionswissenschaft* School in Europe. This school would be exported to the United States, where it was called the history of religions. Its chief advocates were émigrés such as Joachim Wach and Mircea Eliade. The notion that there is an "in itself" of religion, an essence that requires a special, religious method of investigation, is one I do not find persuasive. But the notion that the study of religion ought to begin with the tradition that the inquirers know best, namely Christianity, seems right. One of the virtues of beginning this way, although the writers seem unaware of it, is that one avoids much of the chauvinism that accompanies what the authors call the "anthropological approach," in which the observer draws inferences about "advanced" religions such as Christianity from "primitive" religions. Unfortunately, the authors exemplify this chauvinism by situating their account within a pseudo-evolutionary narrative characteristic of the colonial *mentalité* or discourse of the time. Christianity, as they say explicitly, is "the best presentation of what Religion *is*." The study of Christianity naturally pulls the Hebrew tradition in its train, according to the authors of the Princeton Report, since an adequate understanding of the former requires an understanding of the latter.

Toward the end of the Report, the authors take time to disabuse the reader of the idea that they are recommending the exclusive study of Christianity. While Christianity and its Judaic precursor are privileged, the authors suggest that other traditions ought not be neglected. Ultimately, the study of religion is inadequate without the study of "Mohammedanism [*sic*] and the religions of India and the Far East." The study of primitive religions, by which the authors presumably mean among others African and Amerindian religions, is relegated to the "approaches" section of the report under the heading "Anthropological Approach." To repeat what the authors said earlier, the anthropological level is the wrong place to begin the study of religion. But once "genuine insight into the essence of religion in its more developed form has been attained, a knowledge of its primitive beginnings is illuminating, indeed essential." "Primitive" religions, presumably, can properly be understood on the anthropological level; they are properly regarded as data for how "we" understand the religions of the *civilized*. Here the authors reflect the standard scholarly practice of the time and perhaps of our time where "primitive" religion is the *ersatz* subject of religious studies, the *real* subject being Christianity and the "world religions." Even the world religions are rank ordered. That order looks something like this: first Christianity, then Judaism, and then, in an order that varies with the commentator, "Mohammedanism" [*sic*], Buddhism, Confucianism, and Hinduism. So while the study of religion will be Christianity-centered, the reasons for this go beyond the purely practical one that the authors cite—that Christianity is the religion that Americans know best. The authors choose Christianity for normative reasons as well.[7] Christianity is not merely familiar—it is superior.

In the end, the authors recommend against establishing a formal department of religion and call instead for a permanent committee of the faculty called the Committee on the Study of Religion, which would oversee the hiring and supervision of a scholar to teach the courses described in the Report. The authors suggest that the establishment of a department of religious studies would be premature. Whatever motivates their caution, the authors conclude the Report with what amounts to a credo:

> There is no theological school connected with the University to dictate the professional approach. We are free to pursue the study of religion as an element of liberal culture and as one of the humanities. Except as such, this Committee must refuse to recommend any religious instruction whatsoever as part of the curriculum of the University.[8]

Although one should not generalize too broadly from this particular case, there are some appropriate generalizations to be made. Religious studies emerged from a theological matrix whose cultural geography is European and American. Its ideological presuppositions are derived from the ambiguous legacy of the Enlightenment, from its "Rights of Man" topside and its imperial underside.[9] These assumptions include the separation of government (*imperium*), church (*sacerdotium*), and university (*studium*). This triangulation defines the space in which religious studies is done.[10] What this means, among other things, is that religious studies has always been Christianity- and Western-centered, closely associated with the emergence of the modern state and the "Europeanization" of the world that resulted from the voyages of "discovery" and conquest. These voyages unleashed a crusading-imperial-colonizing disposition (what the authors of the Report call the "anthropological approach") that has been the dominant approach to the religious other for half a millennium: from Muslim "heretics," to African "fetish-worshipers," to Amerindian "idolaters."

Religious studies is best understood, perhaps, in reference to the Enlightenment, the underside of which includes the history of religious "othering" that I just described, and in light of the fourfold theological sciences that emerged from the dismembered corpse of *theologia*. This is apparent even in an atypical case such as Princeton University, where religious studies is not housed in and did not grow out of a divinity school. The curricula priorities that guide the Special Committee are largely incomprehensible without the history that Farley narrates. With the formal establishment of the Department of Religion, the fourfold would undergo a metamorphosis: Bible, dogmatics, church history, and practical theology became biblical studies, theology and philosophy of religion, church history, and Christian ethics. There was the oddball offering, perhaps in the history of religions. But the new religious studies fourfold provided the core curricula of what over time, through a process of accretion, came to include "world religions" and "primitive religions." This colonial model with its Christian center, "oriental" periphery, and "primitive" outer periphery is still the dominant way of organizing religious studies departments. Note well! This does not contradict my previous claim that the authors of the Report were right to start with Christianity, since that was the tradition they and their students knew best. The object of my critique is not *that* they privilege Christianity but *how* they privilege it. This how, which has much to do with the afterlife of powerful Theological residues within departments of religious studies, which in turn are tied, in complex ways, to notions of Western superiority, is a current source of discontent.

RELIGIOUS STUDIES AND ITS
THEOLOGICALLY INDUCED DISCONTENT

The discontent with Theology in the development of freestanding departments of religion is complex and long-standing. This is evident in the Princeton Report itself when the authors assure their intended readers that the proposed courses in the Hebrew Bible and the Christian gospels will not be driven by a theological agenda, by what they call "'Bible Study' or apologetics." These courses should not be an occasion for religious confession or a site where professors dole out pastoral care. In recent years, the most organized and sustained criticism of theology's place in religious studies has occurred in the journal *Method and Theory in the Study of Religion* (MTSR) by scholars such as Donald Wiebe and Robert Segal.[11] MTSR is the organ of the North American Association for the Study of Religion (NAASR), which is portrayed by Charlotte Allen's "Is Nothing Sacred? Casting Out the Gods from Religious Studies"[12] as a renegade, antitheological group of scholars. An editorial from the inaugural 1989 issue gives the following rationale for the establishment of the journal: "there is no journal exclusively devoted to the discussion and debate of issues concerning method and theory in the study of religion." Well, MTSR has certainly made its mark.

There are at least two ways of being disaffected with the place of theology in religious studies. Some critics are opposed to theology in all of its manifestations. Others are opposed to confessional forms of theology and to the confessional ethos that pervades departments of religious studies. For the former group of critics, theology by definition is a noncritical, apologetic, or confessional activity. It is irremediably tied to the Christian religion, if not the Christian church, and is therefore an ethnocentric way of approaching religious studies in the modern, liberal academy. This approach to religious studies, critics argue, may be appropriate in the freestanding seminary or divinity school, but not in a Ph.D.-granting institution. According to these critics, theology is not a scientific discipline. What they mean by scientific, however, is often fuzzy. Do they mean scientific in the Aristotelian sense of demonstrable knowledge (*scientia*), in the modern experimental sense of the biological sciences, in the highly speculative and mathematical sense of theoretical physics, or in the social scientific, value-neutral sense? Proponents of this latter view have traditionally been called empiricists, positivists, or modernists. This tradition includes the British empiricists (Locke, Berkeley, and Hume); the French positivism of Auguste Comte, Emile Durkheim, and the *Annee Sociologique* group; and the logical positivism of the Vienna School of analytic philosophy. This is precisely the tradition that philosophers and critical theorists on both sides of the North Atlantic have called into question. This paradigm has been on the defensive for some time, indeed since Charles S. Peirce's anti-Cartesian philosophical papers of the 1860s and 70s. Consequently, positivism (or crude empiricism) has become an epithet. The epistemological privilege of science in all its forms has been undermined. Science is no longer viewed as monopolizing legitimate knowledge claims, of being the paradigm of knowledge, of being coextensive with knowledge. Science and knowledge are not synonyms.

Although aware of these contemporary sensibilities, the second group of critics takes a different tack. Their criticism is pragmatic, rather than epistemological. Jeffrey Stout is exemplary in this regard. Stout does not begin with the assumption that theological language is unscientific nor is that his conclusion. The language of scientific and unscientific is not his idiom. It is not a privileged idiom as it is, though in very different ways, for the Chicago and the Lancaster schools of the history of religions.[13] Stout assumes that rational arguments for theology can be made, since rationality, from a pragmatist perspective, is a weak and minimalist form of praise. The claim that something is rational is simply an invitation to listen sympathetically. It tells us little about the seriousness of the argument, the value we should accord it, or what our deliberative judgments should be. Thus the pragmatic question: "Can theology even be heard among the cacophonous voices of a culture that doesn't view itself as needing what theology has to offer?" Even if theologians can make rational arguments, what can they possibly have to say to a secular culture[14] that "atheists don't already know?" But isn't this precisely the theologian's choice: to mimic the rest of the culture and thus tell atheists what they already know, or to speak a confessional or apologetic language that few people outside the church are interested in hearing and that most people believe has no place in the liberal academy? Stout supports this point through a reading of James Gustafson's theocentric ethics, where he questions the persuasiveness, much less the necessity, of God in Gustafson's account of ethics and piety. In the end, Gustafson isn't saying anything about the natural finitude of human beings that a sensitive nontheist wouldn't say. Thus Stout asks, "Why add, as Gustafson does, that there is an Ultimate Other who deserves our ultimate concern? What difference does it make for ethics to place Mystery at the center once Humanity has been displaced?"[15] At no point does Stout question the rationality or scientificity of Gustafson's theology. What he does question is its persuasiveness for those who do not share Gustafson's theological presuppositions—indeed, the uncertain and even unnecessary relationship between Gustafson's ethical piety and his theology. Stout's disavowal of the positivism of people such as Wiebe and Segal—that is, the scientific pretension of their rationalist and empiricist (as opposed to rational and empirical) epistemology—is what distinguishes his pragmatic critique. Stout knows what he is for and against, but abjures the fetishizing of purity.

PURITY AND DANGER

Some critics want to throw theology out of the academy. They have a purity fetish; thus they fail to distinguish between Theology and *theology*. For them, theology is a source of epistemic danger. It endangers open inquiry, the reason for being of the liberal academy. Were their objections merely political, ethical, or aesthetic, they could be disposed of quickly, since politically, ethically, and aesthetically despicable beliefs are illegitimate reasons, with the rarest of exceptions, for excluding a discipline and its advocates from the academy. In contrast, the question of epistemology, of making publicly accessible hypothetical knowledge claims goes to the very core of what academe is all about. Does theology contribute to the fund of knowledge? Or is it merely dogma and religious propaganda?

Undoubtedly, there are some critics for whom theology is not a purity issue but merely a bore. But I suspect that they are a minority. For many, theology is hardly a bore. They find it endlessly exciting in an adversarial kind of way. The desire to get rid of theology, to make a clean sweep of things, is a sign of their ardor. In their view, theology is an anomaly that confounds the distinction between church and university. Theology fudges the distinction between knowledge and opinion, fact and value, objectivity and subjectivity. As the anthropologist Mary Douglas tells us, purity is always about dirt, about keeping the dirty and the clean apart and policing the boundaries between the same and the different, the self and the other. Dirt is "matter out of place." Pollution is a result of those things that are anomalous with respect to cherished classifications. "Gender-benders" such as Boy George and Ru Paul are "confused" about whether they are men or women and thus make chaos of standard gender classifications, sexual difference being a prototypical site for the production of things dirty. According to Douglas, we adopt one or more of the following strategies when confronted with the anomalous: we reinterpret, control physically, subject to disapprobation, label dangerous, or appropriate for ritual use.[16]

How does Douglas's notion of purity and pollution help us understand the conflict between theology and religious studies? It does so by analogy, of course. Take Jeffrey Stout's critique of theology, to which I referred earlier. I interpret Stout's stance toward theology and its place in religious studies as an act of reinterpretation. As I read Douglas, this is clearly the most generous response (within the economy of purity and pollution) to anomaly. It is an attempt, short of regarding them as mad or morally vicious, to understand why others might engage in practices we deem strange. It is tantamount to trying to make sense of the anomalous other in ways that do not move us to think and do the worst. Thus Stout can give an account of theologians so that, under specific circumstances, they need not be regarded as irrational, non-scholarly, or dangerous. Theologians need not be seen as "epistemological monsters" that confound the distinction between church and university, between the certainties of dogma and the fallibility of knowledge.[17] In this view, the theologian's hermeneutical circle is no more vicious than any other.

Good fences make good neighbors. Fences are a way of delimiting and policing boundaries. Boundary policing isn't bad in itself and need not have the nasty purity fetishism that often comes with the practice. Erecting a fence is a way of saying, "We like this, we don't like that!" Douglas uses the dietary restrictions of Leviticus to make this point. By specifying what the ancient Israelites could not eat, the dietary code of Leviticus cast a different light on what they could eat. The code had a certain pedagogic and identity-maintenance function. In similar fashion, religious studies has legitimate reasons for policing the church-university boundary and resisting the encroachment of an ecclesiastical agenda and ethos. Perhaps religious studies needs its own Levitical code since much of what they "eat" in seminary and divinity schools we should not eat.

The notion that theology is dangerous, like the plague, is the result of taking the necessity of boundary making and boundary policing too seriously, with too much dogmatism and rigidity. This approach to theology, I suggest, characterizes the views of Wiebe and Segal. In arguing for religious studies as a science, they are caught in an epistemological time warp. Like Nietzsche's madman who hasn't heard that God is dead, they do not realize that science is no longer Science.[18] In many respects, they are men of the nineteenth and early twentieth century, the age that gave us "scientific socialism" and "Christian Science." For them, science is the intellectual phallus, *the* signifier of truth and validity. Now far be it from me to be an uncritical critic of science. I believe that no area of study has established a closer connection among its aims (prediction and control), methods, and results. But this is merely to say it is easier to predict and control the behavior of microorganisms in a petri dish, the rate at which a five-pound ball dropped from the leaning Tower of Pisa will fall, or the effects of high doses of radiation on Y chromosomes than to predict and control human behavior. It does not tell us that prediction and control are the only way, much less the best way, of producing knowledge. For the questions can always be asked: Knowledge for what purpose? Best according to what scale of value? Science (can we understand a poem scientifically?) is inadequate for some purposes. But, and this is crucial, the purposes for which it is inadequate are not less true or valuable.

My skepticism should not be read as disagreement with everything that Wiebe and Segal hold. Like them, I believe that much that goes by the name of religious studies is apologetic, confessional, and dogmatic. A great deal of "postliberal" and "radical orthodox" theology, for example, which is more noisy than radical, is merely dogmatism with a bow tie. The apologetic, confessional, and dogmatic habits of mind that characterize these forms of theology are the bane of the open, revisable, and hypothetical mode of inquiry that some of "us" value. But these bad habits are hardly limited to Theology; they cut across the Theology-religious studies distinction and across the theology-nontheology distinction within religious studies as well. Nor are apologetic, confessional, and dogmatic advocacy exclusively religious studies problems. There isn't a sector of the academy that is immune to arguments that go beyond the evidence, resist contrary evidence, or tailor the evidence to fit their theories about what ought to be the case. Besides, epoch-making ideas often run ahead of the evidence, ahead of what the conventions that govern what counts as evidence will allow. Even so, I share much of Wiebe and Segal's Enlightenment ethos. But I am also persuaded by the contemporary critique of the Enlightenment, which questions the notions of light, vision, clarity, and transparency. I, too, am critical of the Enlightenment prejudice against prejudice and of enlightened notions of truth. If, however, the Enlightenment ideal is a myth, including its notion of transparent, scientific vision, then it is my preferred myth, the myth by which I live. Thus I agree with Alfred North Whitehead who, speaking of science, said: "Seek simplicity and distrust it."[19] I commend those who strive for a simple explanatory account of the complex facts of religion. This is what religion scholars, among other things, *should* do. I have high praise, in particular, for Stewart Elliot Guthrie's *Faces in the Clouds*, which construes religion as a highly developed form of anthropomorphism, as a tendency to look for humans in the environment, which characterizes all forms of human perception. But I distrust his account also. My distrust has nothing to do with cheap piety, the piety of agnostic descriptivists (piety in the face of mystery), which Weibe, Segal, and others rightfully criticize. If I distrust Guthrie's account, and perhaps distrust is too strong a word, it is only because I have questions that he doesn't answer and because he offers answers to questions I see no good reason to ask. Thus my own piety, let's call it "the piety of infinite inquiry" or natural piety (which to be sure has its own consummations along the way) gets in the way of me fully accepting Guthrie's account.

I guess I distrust Wiebe and Segal, too. But here my reasons are more substantial and the word distrust *is* apropos. Unlike them, I do not believe that there are persuasive, non-controversial, explanatory accounts of religion that *ought* to elicit the assent of reasonable people. This does not mean that we should necessarily accept the beliefs (habits of action) of religious people or refrain from offering explanatory accounts of religion that challenge the truth of religious claims. What religious people believe may be false and the consequences for them and for us may be bad. This is sufficient reason for speaking the truth and exposing lies. But to think that there is a method derived from science that will at last allow us to make indisputable sense of religious people's nonsense is nonsense. As a religious studies scholar *qua* scientist, I may think that God is merely the deification of social life or the "titanic" image of "daddy" written large on the cosmos as "big-daddy" or the symbolization of my unresolved Oedipal desires, a family romance between "mommy, daddy, and me." But this is simply one (complex) candidate for truth among others. It has no irresistibly coercive or "knockdown" effect that only irrational or unscientific people such as theologians and Chicago School types can resist. If these truth candidates succeed, or if Guthrie's cognitive explanation of religion prevails, they will do so because they better account for the evidence, however contested the evidence might be. My problem with the likes of Wiebe and Segal is that they are too religious; their position is the inverted image (*camera obscura*) of Theology. They play the same game that theologians play. The logic is the same. They may be antitheologians, but they are theologians just the same. Thus having gotten rid of God, they would replace him with Science.

Wiebe and Segal use theology as a ritualized term of abuse, a use that has a long pedigree. Marx and Nietzsche, for example, use theology as an insult, as a way of describing cognitive error, ideology, or *ressentiment*. Heidegger uses theology, ontotheology, to describe a wrongheaded view of reality. On Edward Said's use, which resonates with the views of Marx, Nietzsche, and Heidegger, theology is a synonym for moral, epistemological, and political manichaeism, where the world is divided into the "sons of light" and the "sons of darkness." The use of theology as a term of ritual abuse can also be found in religious studies circles, where it serves as a metaphor for those things that "we" do not like or that "we" think are dangerous. I have often used the term this way myself. It functions as shorthand, a dismissive epithet, which is a cipher for notions such as apologetics, confession, or dogma. Thus in departmental discussions about filling faculty vacancies or about the future direction of the department, I have used theology to tar those with assumptions, foci, and methods I think are contrary to those that ought to characterize a department of religious studies. In doing so, I failed to make the distinction that I offer here between Theology as a closed, dogmatic, and fideistic form of reason and *theology* as an open, revisable, and hypothetical form of inquiry.

If philosophy is the successor subject of Philosophy, then *theology* succeeds Theology. But the problem in using theology as a term of ritual abuse and as a descriptive term for a legitimate style of religious studies scholarship is a predictable misunderstanding by literal-minded and humorless colleagues, by dogmatic Theologians on the one hand and by dogmatic anti-Theologians on the other. Either one is mistakenly regarded as antitheological when one is anti-Theological, or as pro-Theological when one is merely indifferent to *theology* in a vaguely "live and let live" sort of way. While I cannot imagine calling myself a Theologian, I can imagine calling myself a *theologian*. But why bother? I have a hard time understanding what makes theologians (besides love of a particular language game called "God-talk") different from philosophers and theorists. I cannot mark the (imaginary) place where *theology* ends and the philosophy of religion and the theory of religion begin.

The idea that there is something—call it "the way things really are," Science, Rationality, or Rigor—that, apart from a particular description, distinguishes what nontheologians do from what *theologians* do dies hard. It is a view that has hardly

died. But in the view that I defend, this "methodological atheism" and "methodological rationalism" are as phony as Descartes' methodical doubt. This is true not
because everybody believes in God or doesn't believe in reason but because everyone believes in some things without evidence or agreement on what counts as evidence that are the basis of them knowing anything at all. Thus the significant differences between *theologians* and nontheologians do not lie on the level of evidence
and facts but on the hypothetical or metanarrative level—of Wittgenstein's "primitive behavior" that funds our language games, Quine's web of beliefs, and Indra's
Net. Our web of beliefs can be rewoven, but we cannot climb out of the web to
gain leverage against it; we cannot, that is, produce evidence of what the world is
like as a whole.[20] That we are "caught" in such a web is simply another way of saying that we are finite, which is not to say that our web cannot be rewoven. Thus
the besetting sin of philosophers, according to Whitehead, "is that being merely
men, they endeavor to survey the universe from the standpoint of gods."[21] The
philosophers' sin has become the scientists' sin has become the sin of would-be scientists such as Weibe and Segal. But suppose there is no God's-eye point of view,
no God-substitutes such as Rationality, Science, Method, or Rigor (Mortis?) that
can settle disputes on the rarefied level of primitive behavior, web of beliefs, Indra's
Net, or what Rorty calls our final vocabulary.[22] In this case, which I think is the
case, what "we" take to be better or worse arguments are relative to (and persuasive
within) particular epistemic contexts between which there are no noncontroversial
reasons to choose. I suspect that Weibe and Segal think they can have more than this.

I think that this desire is vain, even as I admit its residual effects on me. I confess to an ambivalent, if not embarrassed, desire. Thus I sometimes long for the day
when we (and I mean everybody) stop speaking theologically, when God-talk in its
hallowed and explanatory senses is as quaint as ether-talk. But I cannot provide a
persuasive argument, and I certainly do not have a method, whose logic, facts, or
evidence is such that those who speak theologically will be convinced that they
shouldn't talk that way. I think that it is better to speak of nature rather than God,
of our necessary finitude as one species among others, of the natural contingencies
that cast us into the world as foundlings,[23] of landing in places that we could not
anticipate, of coping with our environment as best we can. We cope as agents and
patients, by acting and suffering, by transforming our environment and being transformed by it, by adapting to circumstances we did not choose. And so we cope by
dreaming dreams and telling stories, by making simple tools and constructing complex machines, by organizing ourselves into "simple" clans and into complex social
groups. But there is nothing apart from the sheer *seductiveness* of my account, assum-
ing that it is seductive, that would lead others to accept it. Here we run into a matter of taste; thus where *theologians* (of the open, hypothetical, and inquiring type)
speak of God, I speak of nature. In either case, we offer a hypothesis, a higher-level
hypothesis that helps order our lower-level hypotheses about this and that. But the
important point is that they are hypotheses, "guesses at the riddle" of things (of why
there is something rather than nothing) that invite further inquiry.

CONCLUSIONS

I had imagined writing a different kind of paper. But if writing is the most rigorous form of thinking, then writing this paper has forced me to rethink the conclusion that I had first anticipated. Academic theology, I initially thought, should not elaborate upon the tradition but simply tell us what the tradition is. Theology within the religious studies context should be a strictly historical and methodological enterprise, a constructive elaboration of the tradition being strongly discouraged, since theology is a Christian and church-based endeavor. The rule against constructive elaboration would also apply to other traditions of religious thought. My concluding argument would read something like this: that theology should not be constructive since constructive theology is the task of the church and church community, including its educational institutions such as Bible colleges, seminaries, and divinity schools. This is an argument that I cannot make without qualification, without relating the argument, that is, to the difference between Theology and *theology*. To say that theology should not be constructive is to say that it is intellectually illegitimate: that theology is to religious studies as alchemy is to chemistry and astrology to astronomy—that is, a historical curiosity. On this view, theology is an intellectual appendix, a useless developmental vestige that does no work but when inflamed can cause a lot of harm. Thus, constructive theology is improper as an academic subject, as are constructive alchemy and astrology. Only as a historical phenomenon is theological study legitimate. But how does one go about making this argument without being foolish? I do not believe, as much as I might have wished, that the argument can be made that there is a nondogmatic argument of this sort. So I am forced to make a different argument, an argument against Theology, which is an all-purpose term for dogmatism and "professional creep" in the academic study of religion. According to this argument, the academic study of religion and the professional study of theology (in the broad sense of the fourfold theological sciences) are very different enterprises. The professional study of theology (or Theology) is the province of Bible colleges, seminaries, and divinity schools, which to varying degrees are committed to training clergy and to advancing the goals of "the" church. This professional, "illiberal," and sectarian enterprise—which doesn't mean that it is a bad enterprise—ought to be kept separate from the academic study of religion. The differences between the two should be institutionally maintained.

There is no place at all for constructive Theology in religious studies departments. But what about *theology*? Here we speak of a different animal altogether. That I have been forced to reject false arguments against the inclusion of *theology* in religious studies departments only heightens the importance of the issue that the editors of this volume asked the contributors to address: What is the proper relation between theology and nontheology in religious studies? If *theology*, as I have argued, is open, revisable, and hypothetical inquiry into the nature of the divine, then it has a proper place within departments of religious studies, within the arts and sciences. To speak of *theology* as one methodology among others is to misspeak, for there is no methodological difference between *theology* and the methodologies employed in the arts and sciences. *Theology* (lower case "t") is, among other things, a philosophical enterprise,[24] a species of speculative metaphysics, an effort to give a hypothetical account of the nature of things. Critics often question the value of such accounts because of their abstract character. But all theory abstracts. General theory requires a higher level of abstraction (a systematic vagueness) because it has more to explain. And metaphysics as the most general of all general theories requires the highest degree of abstraction. Critics deny that metaphysical accounts can do useful explanatory work. But that depends, of course, on what one is trying to explain and on what counts as a useful explanation.[25] On these points there is deep disagreement. I do not think that the critics of hypothetical (nonfoundational) metaphysics can make good on their complaint. Thus I conclude that *theology* is a legitimate mode of inquiry within the methodological plurality of religious studies. It is a "guess at the riddle," one among many hypotheses on an open road of inquiry.

NOTES

1. I rely upon this work in the following section; see, especially, Edward Farley, *Theologia: The Fragmentation and Unity of Theological Education* (Philadelphia: Fortress Press, 1983), xi, 6–11.

2. Edward Farley, *Theologia*, 10.

3. Ibid., 11.

4. P. A. Chapman, T. M. Greene, C. G. Osgood, R. M. Scoon, T. J. Wertenbaker, A. M. Friend, Jr., "Report of the Special Committee of the Faculty on Religious Education," (Princeton University, 11 April 1935).

5. Ibid., 2.

6. Ibid.

7. Ibid., 11.

8. Ibid., 12, 14–15.

9. The Enlightenment, of course, was multiple: French, German, English, Scottish, and American. There are important similarities between these sites of Enlightenment and important differences.

10. This is true for both private and public universities. In private universities, especially those that have historical affiliations with a Protestant church, the greatest tensions are between university and church. In public universities, the tension is between university and government, which has everything to do with how the state interprets the establishment and free exercise clauses of the First Amendment. Theology is likely to cause more angst in a public (government-funded) than in a private (non-government-funded) university. This distinction is of course only relative inasmuch as "private" universities receive huge amounts of government funding.

11. See Donald Wiebe, *Religion and Truth* (The Hague: Mouton, 1981), and *Beyond Legitimation* (New York: St. Martin's Press, 1994). Also see Robert Segal, *Religion and the Social Sciences* (Atlanta: Scholars Press, 1989), and *Explaining and Interpreting Religion* (New York: Peter Lang, 1992).

12. See *Lingua Franca* 6 (1996): 30–40.

13. The Lancaster School (as opposed to the Chicago School of Mircea Eliade, Joachim Wach, and those in their orbit) refers to Ninian Smart and those trained or influenced by Smart. This would include much of the religious studies scholarship that comes out of the University of Toronto. Many of the contributors to the journal *Method and Theory in the Study of Religion* are associated with the Lancaster School.

14. The concept of secularism is as controversial as the concept of religion, on which it is parasitic. A casual use of the word may be more trouble than it is worth.

15. Jeffrey Stout, *Ethics After Babel: The Languages of Morals and Their Discontents* (Boston: Beacon Press, 1988), 183.

16. Mary Douglas, *Purity and Danger: An Analysis of the Concepts of Pollution and Taboo* (London: Routledge, 1991), 35–36, 39–40.

17. Douglas's account is darker than the one I present. Citing E. E. Evans-Pritchard, she writes: "If a monstrous birth can be labeled an event of a particular kind the categories can be restored. So the Nuer treat monstrous births as baby hippopotamuses, accidentally born to humans and, with this labeling, the appropriate action is clear. They gently lay them in the river where they belong. (39)"

18. For a wonderful discussion of this issue, see Richard Rorty, "Is Science a Natural Kind?" and "Texts and Lumps," in *Objectivity, Relativism, and Truth: Philosophical Papers I* (Cambridge: Cambridge University Press, 1991).

19. Alfred North Whitehead, *The Concept of Nature* (Cambridge: Cambridge University Press, 1926), 163.

20. Rorty makes this same point as follows: "The anti-scientific, holistic pragmatist who adopts the latter attitude ('the laissez-faire attitude that sees religion and science as alternative ways of solving life's problems, to be distinguished by success or failure, rather than rationality or irrationality') wants us to adopt naturalism without thinking of ourselves as more rational than our theistic friends. He begins by granting the Quinean point that anything can, by suitably reweaving the web of belief, be fitted either into an anti-naturalistic world-view in which Divine Providence is a central element *or* into a naturalistic world-view in which people are on their own. This is to admit that James was right against Clifford: 'evidence' is not a very useful notion when trying to decide what one thinks of the world as a whole." Richard Rorty, "Pragmatism Without Method," *Objectivity, Relativism, and Truth*, 66.

21. Alfred North Whitehead, "Remarks," *The Philosophical Review* XLVI (1937): 179.

22. For a description of final vocabularies, see Richard Rorty, *Contingency, Irony, and Solidarity* (Cambridge: Cambridge University Press, 1989).

23. See Robert Corrington, *Nature's Religion* (Lanham, Maryland: Rowman and Littlefield, 1997), xiii, 97, 102.

24. Of course, theology is more than philosophy and speculative metaphysics, since no methodology in the arts and sciences is beyond its purview.

25. See Robert Cummings Neville, *The Highroad Around Modernism* (Albany: State University of New York Press, 1992). I depend heavily on Neville's notion of metaphysics as a systematically vague and hypothetical (nonfoundational) mode of inquiry.

8

Territorial Disputes: Religious Studies and Theology in Transition

LINELL E. CADY

The resurfacing of the debate over the relationship between religious studies and theology—a debate that remains implicit when not explicit, given their genealogies—is, to put it simply, a good thing. Although the most recent turns in this debate have again, and not surprisingly, failed to generate any consensus, the exchange overall has proved illuminating. The most recent chapter of this conversation has continued to serve the useful purpose of highlighting the contours of these distinct, though related, scholarly traditions. But it harbors the potential to offer more. The recent exchange has been marked by increased recognition that the conventional mapping with its sharp boundary between these traditions of inquiry is problematic. The overlap has been too great, the boundary too jagged, to take that map at face value. But exposing the limitations of the map has not led to a shared response. Quite the contrary, it has sharpened and polarized the voices.

Recognition of this particular instantiation of "map is not territory" has provided the analytic space to move past the oppositional construction of the conventional mapping, exposing the more complex dialectic that characterizes these scholarly traditions. It has helped to pose new questions regarding their respective character and relationships and in the process, it has helped to make limitations more visible. In so doing, it has created opportunities to facilitate an internal transformation in each that is driven by a mutually corrective engagement. Seeking to nurture such lines of development is, I shall argue, more appropriate, intellectually and politically, than either advocating the inclusion of theology in religious studies or stepping up the campaign to eliminate all theological traces from it, the two most visible positions on the current scene that for convenience I will label "theological inclusivism" and "naturalist exclusivism."

All too often, calls for including theology in religious studies resemble a form of postmodern soup, overaccentuating their similarities and glossing over their dif-

ferences. They overlook the extent to which the discipline of theology remains
deeply shaped, due to its history and current institutional embodiment, by assumptions, methods, and interests that are more aligned with church than academy. It is
hardly surprising that scholars of religion remain deeply skeptical of opening the
door to a tradition of intellectual inquiry whose historical ballast keeps it moored to
the periphery of the modern university. On the other hand, scholars overly sensitive
to the continuing presence of theology within religious studies—either explicit or
implicit—have gone on the offensive, waging a highly visible campaign to eradicate
all traces. Although there is merit to this critique, it goes too far in its quest to wipe
out the theological presence that continues to inform religious studies. If ever fully
successful, the result would be an impoverished religious studies that was largely
unresponsive to the clearly existential motivations and concerns that drive most of
its students. Although neither the "theological inclusivist" nor the "naturalist exclusivist" position is finally compelling, each captures something important. In this essay,
then, I shall consider the emergence of these alternative positions, and, without
embracing either one alone, suggest ways in which taken together they contribute
to the further evolution of the contested domain of religious studies.

The Reigning Map

Although the conventional disciplinary mapping of religious studies and theology
appears increasingly misleading in fundamental respects, it has nonetheless exerted
considerable power in configuring the landscape in its image. That the map has lost
some of its transparency is a reflection of the larger intellectual, social, and cultural
shifts associated with what is widely identified as the postmodern turn. The most
salient feature of the reigning map is the clearly delineated border that divides theology from religious studies. Put differently, religious studies has largely secured its
academic credentials for admittance into the modern university by accentuating
its differences from religion and theology. Although the academic study of religion
has roots that extend back centuries, its modern incarnation institutionalized as
religious studies is largely a post-World War II phenomenon.[1] It occurred at a
period in American history marked by the further disestablishment of religion, the
displacement of Protestant Christianity from its overarching role in American life.
     This historical trajectory is evident in the increasing secularization within
higher education aptly captured by George Marsden in his title: *The Soul of the
American University: From Protestant Establishment to Established Nonbelief*. In this historical context, the development and institutionalization of religious studies as a
disciplinary field within the arts and sciences was contingent upon establishing its
secular credentials. The 1963 Supreme Court case *Abington School District v.
Schempp* proved exceedingly helpful in this regard, providing both the language
and judicial stamp of approval to differentiate the study of religion from the profession or practice of religion. In the language of this ruling, there was a distinct

difference between the teaching *about* religion and the teaching *of* religion. Implicit in this distinction is the presumption that one can approach religion from a neutral, objective point of view. The ready acceptance of this distinction, and its success in facilitating the development of religious studies in secular and public institutions, must be seen against the backdrop of a centuries-long trajectory wherein the secular and the religious were essentially coconstructed in a mutually defining dialectic. The secular was identified as a neutral, public domain, explicitly contrasted to the religious, which was relegated to the private sphere, the province of individual passions and parochial identities. Within this framework, reason was construed as universal and trafficking in the realm of objective facts. Religion, on the other hand, was assimilated to feelings and beliefs that could be confessed but not publicly defended.

There were a multiplicity of purposes and forces converging in this trajectory, not least the need to demarcate a social space free from sectarian religious strife. As Talal Asad argues, however, this process served primarily to contain and disempower religion as it "was gradually compelled to concede the domain of public power to the constitutional state, and of public truth to natural science."[2] The differentiation of spheres, and their progressive secularization, which marks the modernist trajectory helps forge a distinctively modern view of religion as "anchored in personal experience, expressible as belief-statements, depending on private intuitions, and practiced in one's spare time."[3] The secular assumes the mantle of the reasonable, securely located within the bounds of the natural; religion, in contrast, is tethered to the supernatural, and primarily a matter of faith. This discursive formation, although showing significant signs of weakening, has been widely taken for granted in both popular and scholarly contexts. Consider, for example, Bruce Lincoln's highly condensed methodological reflections on religion and academic inquiry: Religion, he posits, "is that discourse whose defining characteristic is its desire to speak of things eternal and transcendent with an authority equally transcendent and eternal. History, in the sharpest possible contrast, is that discourse which speaks of things temporal and terrestrial in a human and fallible voice, while staking its claim to authority on rigorous critical practice."[4] Or consider Stanley Fish's comments about the effort to de-divinize religion: "I confess myself as never having been able to understand these assertions, except as a determination to retain the name of something even after you've cut its heart out. It's like Hamlet without the prince, or like veggie-burgers. Where's the beef?"[5]

Within the modernist framework, the scholar has assumed the position of the detached observer, one who surveys as if from above. It is a position of epistemic privilege in which a barrier separates the knower from the known. The scholar inhabits the "view from nowhere" capable of reaching objective knowledge about the object under study. The ultimate quest is for explanation and general principles that result from abstracting from the historical embeddedness of both the knower and the known. By stepping into this paradigm, the scholar of religion is able to preserve the necessary distance from the object of study, thereby ensuring that the study of religion is categorically distinct from the practice or profession of religion. This is particularly important for the scholar of religion since her object of study is the most polluting to the secular mind. Given this culturally pervasive discursive framework, it has been essential for religious studies in its quest for scholarly legitimacy to situate itself over against the discipline of theology, buttressing its own academic credentials through accentuating the latter's religious roots. Disciplinary histories, such as J. Samuel Preus's *Explaining Religion,* have helped to sustain this conceptual landscape through the construction of a narrative in which the scholarly maturation of the academic study of religion is tied directly to the jettisoning of religious and theological assumptions and sensibilities. The secular, naturalistic study of religion marks the coming of age of this intellectual lineage, achieved through the rejection of the supernatural and authoritarian elements indelibly inscribed on religion and theology. The dominance of this narrative in western liberal society and the modern university context has made it all but inevitable, then, that religious studies has defended its academic credentials through the disavowal of any significant overlap with the religious or the theological.

THE SHIFTING TERRAIN

Recent scholarship has called into question the adequacy of this map, exposing the assumptions that have driven it, the interests that have benefited from it, and the terrain that it has failed to illuminate. The modernist liberal project that it has reflected has been increasingly challenged from multiple angles, as fundamentalists, postmodernists, feminists, and inhabitants of colonized cultures, among others, have taken exception to some facet of its purportedly neutral, universal agenda. The collective result has been the historicization and contextualization of this project, its exposure as a partisan agenda in the service of particular interests, primarily associated with the modern, western, capitalistic nation-state and the "autonomous man" that has inhabited it. The presumptive epistemic privilege of the scholar has been shaken as the epistemological foundations upon which it was based have crumbled. The scholar inhabits a particular place and time, limited and enabled by the discursive fields within which she is situated. Rather than occupying a position above the data, so to speak, the scholar is enmeshed in a dialectical relationship with the data. Disciplines from physics to anthropology have reconceptualized the model of the knower and the known, emphasizing the interactive relationship that obtains between the two.

For our purposes, we can glimpse the significance of this shift for conceptualizing the boundary between religious studies and theology by considering Donald Lopez's recent AAR award-winning book *Prisoners of Shangri-La: Tibetan Buddhism and the West.* In this work, Lopez explores the western take on Tibet and Tibetan Buddhism that has alternated between denigration and romanticization, extremes that Lopez correlates with Tibet's relationship to colonial powers and interests. Lopez traces the growing idealization of Tibet in this century as a place set apart, spatially and temporally, an idyllic haven protected from the corruptions of the world and entrusted with the preservation of an ancient spiritual tradition. It is, as the 1932 classic film *Lost Horizon* symbolized it, utopia. Far from capturing the "real Tibet" this representation is primarily a western myth in which, Lopez suggests, "the West perceives some lack within itself and fantasizes that the answer, through a process of projection is to be found somewhere in the East."[6] Although the construction of this myth has many sites, one of the more salient in the twentieth century has been the academic. Lopez provides a fascinating portrait of the rise of Tibetan Buddhist Studies in the past few decades, focusing in particular on the influential career of his teacher Jeffrey Hopkins at the University of Virginia. Hopkins's pedagogical approach was essentially a highly abbreviated version of the training accorded a Tibbetan monk. The student was trained in the translation and exposition of the ancient texts. Critique of these texts, according to Lopez, "was considered presumptuous and somehow unseemly. It would be impossible for us to ever surpass their understanding; our task was to represent it accurately in English."[7] Through this endeavor, Lopez notes, the student essentially partook in "a form of salvation by scholarship."[8] Not surprisingly, most of the graduate students in this field were also practitioners of Tibetan Buddhism.

Lopez's case study of western representations of Tibetan Buddhism constitutes a powerful refutation of the modernist epistemological conceit that imagines that the knower occupies a transcendent vantage point, outside of time and context, from where objective knowledge can be secured. His study underscores the extent to which the personal, the political, and the popular shape the formation of knowledge, including its scholarly production. The implications for the conventional portrait of religious studies are extensive. The presumption that the scholar can escape from the influences of time and place, and transcend personal interests and motivations—whether religious or not—is belied by the evidence he amasses. Tibetan Buddhism in the twentieth century is as much, if not more, the construction of a tradition, serving the confluence of interests of exiled Tibetans, and, most especially, alienated Westerners, including "scholar-adepts." The conventional portrait of religious studies as the neutral, objective study about religion serves to veil this constructed dimension. Perhaps most importantly, it effectively hides the religious motivations and interests that circulate freely in the production and reception of knowledge of Tibbetan Buddhism. In short, Lopez convincingly demonstrates that the border between religious studies and theology is far more porous than the conventional mapping indicates.

To some scholars, i.e., the naturalist exclusivists, this is hardly news. From their perspective, religious studies is, and has always been, implicitly theological regardless of the ideology it has appropriated to mask this character. The problem, from their perspective, has been the general refusal to acknowledge the continuing and deep influence of theological assumptions and interests in the academic study of religion. Hence, to this camp, these recent theoretical studies provide further ammunition in the service of their cause to eradicate theology from the academic study of religion. The proper response to this recent theoretical work, in their eyes, is not to fine-tune the cartography but to intensify the battle to purge the field of its theological traces.

According to the naturalist exclusivists, there are a number of indicators that point to the continued religious/theological underpinnings of the field of religious studies, its objectivist ideology notwithstanding. Donald Wiebe, for example, analyzes the AAR presidential addresses from 1964, the year the professional organization changed its name from the National Association of Biblical Instructors, to 1993. Although much significance was attached to the name change as indicative of a paradigm shift within the field, Wiebe concludes that virtually all of the presidential addresses in the ensuing years have continued to reflect its theological, even Christian, roots. Most of the addresses "insist that the academic student of religion concern him- or herself not only with accounting for religions and religion, but also with religious matters."[9] For Wiebe, then, the AAR has not advanced the objective study of religion, but has "worked strenuously to . . . support a normative approach to the study of religion which involves not simply teaching about religion but a teaching of religion."[10] Advancing a similar critique, Ivan Strenski argues that the inclusion of a category labeled the "The Constructive-Reflective Study of Religion" among the AAR Awards for Excellence is indicative of the influence that theology continues to exert within the field. The award—"listed proudly in first position"[11]—is either trivial or problematic: to the extent that all scholarship is constructive and reflective, it is trivial, and to the extent that it endorses constructive thought, it crosses the line between scholarship and religion. As Strenski puts it, "'constructive study' of religion is not about religion; it is religion itself. It is not empathetic contemplation and understanding of religion; it is religion-in-the-making."[12]

While Wiebe and Strenski focus on the more explicit manner in which a theological agenda remains operative within religious studies, other scholars within this camp have begun to pay increasing attention to its clandestine presence within the field. Even in the absence of any overt theologizing in religious studies scholarship, so this general argument goes, implicit theological assumptions and interests are conveyed through its central analytic category, "religion." This work is a further elaboration and extension of J. Z. Smith's observation that religion, far from having an empirical referent, is "solely the creation of the scholar's study. It is created for the scholar's analytic purposes by his imaginative acts of comparison and generalization."[13] With this as a jumping off point, scholars have turned their attention to tracing the evolution of this modern category, exposing the multiple vectors that have intersected in its discursive formation.

Russell McCutcheon's *Manufacturing Religion* is, as the title suggests, one such effort. For the most part, North American scholars, McCutcheon argues, have unreflectively operated with a particular model of religion as if it were essentially a natural category. According to this dominant model, religion "is best conceptualized as sui generis, autonomous, of its own kind, strictly personal, essential, unique, prior to, and ultimately distinct from, all other facets of human life and interaction."[14] As

McCutcheon rightly notes, this model of religion is a constitutive element in the modern liberal project that has sought to carve out a common secular public sphere by relegating religion to the private realm. Rather than focus primarily on the way in which this construction allows the differentiated spheres of the market and politics to escape from the influence of religion, McCutcheon, facing the other way, attends to the ways in which it protects religion. Identifying some experience or feeling as essentially religious suggests that it demands interpretation on its own terms. In other words, the emergence of the distinctively religious generates methods of study that can explicate it, which in turn legitimates and perpetuates this cultural construction. This dialectical relationship between object of study and methods of study in the case of religion has contributed to the dominance of interpretive and phenomenological approaches that privilege the emic view. Perspectives that seek to interpret and explain religion through other frameworks with naturalistic assumptions are marginalized, routinely criticized for failing to explore religion "on its own terms." Failure to subject the central analytic category of "religion" to scrutiny, therefore, allows it to continue its cultural work, aided and abetted by scholars of religion. The dominant model of religion, McCutcheon concludes, "effectively brackets not only the datum but the researcher as well from critical scrutiny."[15]

Mounting a similar critique in his recent book *The Ideology of Religious Studies*, Timothy Fitzgerald contends that there is "no coherent non-theological basis for the study of religion as a separate academic discipline."[16] Determinations of what counts as religion and what doesn't, particularly as they become more removed from Christianity, are notoriously difficult and reflective of the western theological roots of the category. Fitzgerald argues that religion is the "basis of a modern form of theology" which he terms "liberal ecumenical theology," but this has been obscured by claims that all human beings have the capacity for religious feeling or experience.[17] Religion is a form of liberal ecumenical theology insofar as it is construed as a cross-cultural phenomenon and its varied expressions interpreted as alternate modes of relating to the ultimate or the transcendent. In this fashion, myths and rituals across the globe are abstracted from their local cultural complex and reinscribed in terms of the self's relationship to God—though more generically framed to preserve the illusion of cross-cultural universality. The ways in which these myths and rituals are embedded in the concrete life of a particular time and place, including its sociopolitical and material dimensions, are largely eclipsed.[18] Lifting them out of their own contexts and relocating them in terms of the world religions discourse facilitates their interpretation as alternate forms of religiosity that are indicative of the multiple paths that humans purportedly travel toward the same goal. Differences are acknowledged, but rendered irrelevant, subsumed under a homogenizing framework that perpetuates a Christian view, properly muted.

Fitzgerald, however, is even more concerned about exposing the ideological function that this complex—religion, religious studies, liberal ecumenical theology—plays within a wider political, social, and cultural arena. This requires locating it in relationship to the construction of the secular in the modern West:

The construction of 'religion' and 'religions' as global, crosscultural objects of study has been part of a wider historical process of western imperialism, colonialism, and neocolonialism. Part of this process has been to establish an ideologically loaded distinction between the realm of religion and the realm of non-religion or the secular. By constructing religion and religions, the imagined secular world of objective facts, of societies and markets as the result of the free association of natural individuals, has also been constructed. This latter construction, which is the ideology of liberal capitalism, . . . is actually far more important since it is the location of the dominating values of our societies, but it has to be legitimated as part of the real world of nature and rational self-realization that all societies are conceived as evolving toward.[19]

The modern category of religion and the academic study of religion that has developed in its wake are critical elements in making room for the nonreligious. One might say focusing on religion distracts attention from the real action that is taking place offstage. Scholars of religion, Fitzgerald and McCutcheon conclude, are participants in the western, liberal, capitalist project insofar as they allow the analytic category of religion to perform this ideological work.

As noted earlier, the recent scholarship that has explicitly or implicitly challenged the prevailing disciplinary map for religious studies and theology has spawned two opposing, highly visible camps: the naturalists seeking more successfully to exclude the theological from religious studies, and academic theologians seeking to use these recent theoretical shifts to secure membership in full standing in religious studies and the university. A growing number of theologians have begun to argue that recent critiques of modernism radically undermine the standard rationale for their exclusion from religious studies.[20] According to one variant of this argument, once the secular is contextualized, it loses its status as the neutral, public domain and shares the mantle of particularity with religious traditions. With this shift, there is no intellectual warrant for excluding theology simply because it is rooted in a particular religious tradition. In *Theology and Social Theory*, John Millbank mounts an extensive case for this position. Through a genealogical analysis of the coconstruction of the secular and the religious in the modern period, he seeks to expose the particular interests and assumptions underlying the emergence of secular forms of reason. His project is, in the final analysis, to show that "'scientific' social theories are themselves theologies or anti-theologies in disguise."[21] Other variants of the argument to include theology in religious studies build upon the impossibility of sustaining a pure distinction between description and construction. Rather than explore these arguments in more detail, in the interests of space I want to turn our attention at this point to negotiating between these respective camps.

BROKERING THE DISPUTE

The current debate on the relationship of religious studies and theology in relation to the modern university is primarily framed in terms of the question of the inclusion or exclusion of theology, and that is unfortunate. First, it is unnecessarily inflammatory, tending to foster caricatures on both sides, no doubt due to the intellectual legitimacy that is at stake for both. Even more importantly, however, this framing of the problematic does not clear sufficient space to consider reasons why each side might have something important to contribute to the evolving shape of these respective disciplines—and yet, not be persuasive in its final goal of achieving exclusion or inclusion. In the remainder of the paper, I want to consider what each camp in this highly charged debate has to offer, and yet also indicate why each is wrong in its final goal of excluding or including theology in religious studies.

The critique of religious studies developed by scholars of the naturalist exclusivist persuasion has convincingly exposed the extent to which the central analytic category "religion" and the primarily interpretive methods developed to study it have been profoundly shaped by the modern liberal agenda. The presumed universality of this category, and the resulting emergence of the world religions discourse, has allowed a western, liberal mold to frame the data, wrenching it from its own material and sociopolitical context. Not only has this distorted our understanding of other cultures, but liberal ecumenical theological interests have been served in the process. This scholarship has helped to account for the privileging of religious interpretive frames in the academic study of religion and the marginalization of alternate discourses, particularly those with naturalistic assumptions. This literature has been critical to making this development visible and troubling.

On the other hand, acknowledging the importance of this corrective literature in no way entails that only naturalistic redescriptions are appropriate.[22] The presumption in much of this writing is that the only responsible stance of the scholar toward religious discourse is its deconstruction. It is possible to distinguish at least two rationales, often intertwined, that drive this position. First, and most importantly, religion is taken as a category whose essential role is that of sacralizing views, values, and practices. In Lincoln's formulation, this is its "defining chacteristic," and most visible in contrast to the historicist, fallible frame of the scholar. Insofar as religion is essentially an "authorizing strategy" the only proper role of the scholar of religion is that of critic.[23] A second rationale advanced in support of this position is the more specific concern that religious discourse necessarily advances the liberal agenda, and scholars remain complicitous in this project if they perpetuate one of its central conceptual planks. Given the ideological freight of the analytic category of "religion," then, translating it into other non-religious discourses is essential.

Although certainly much is gained through such translation, it is also important to recognize what is lost. Let me frame the issue in terms of a distinction that Russell McCutcheon uses to compare the approaches of Ivan Strenski and David Chidester. Strenski, McCutcheon notes, focuses primarily on the individual agent making choices in a particular context; Chidester, on the other hand, shifts the focus to consider the "material and theoretical preconditions that make the production and use of knowledge possible."[24] The danger of focusing on individual action,

McCutcheon warns, is that it may lull us into thinking that human behavior, including scholarship, can "somehow float free of its sociopolitical preconditions." True enough. But scholarly attention to the sociopolitical discursive constraints within which individuals move should supplement and inform, but not replace, attention to the issues as they are framed at the level of the individual. Ignoring the more immediate horizon of the individual fosters its own acontextual bias. Given how deeply embedded the religious/secular discursive formation has become in modern western life, it is inevitable that individuals inhabit this formation. If individuals can legitimately appropriate religious discourse to articulate insights about the human condition, by extension it is legitimate for the scholar to do so as well. Arguments to the contrary reduce religion entirely to a sociopolitical function, ignoring the ways in which it serves as a vehicle for other interests and concerns. In a similar vein, reading religion exclusively in terms of its "sacralizing function"— understood in opposition to discourses that are self-consciously historicist—privileges a single interpretive lens that does not do justice to the data. Attention to the variety of religious discourses and practices in the West makes clear that increasing numbers of individuals inhabit this rhetoric "lightly," fully cognizant of their role in its appropriation and interpretation. Religion in America, as Wade Clark Roof describes it, has increasingly become a "spiritual marketplace." In this context "responsibility falls more upon the individual—like that of the bricoleur—to cobble together a religious world from available images, symbols, moral codes, and doctrines, thereby exercising considerable agency in defining and shaping what is considered to be religiously meaningful."[25] This is a very significant shift; it reflects trends that efface the authoritarian and supernatural marks that have defined religion in the modern West in sharp opposition to the secular. Given these developments, the presumption that religious discourse necessarily sacralizes and secular scholarly discourse historicizes is much too simplistic.

The naturalists' model for religious studies suffers from a bias against the personal that has become deeply engrained in the ethos of the modern university. Looking more closely at this bias, and its problematic consequences, helps to demonstrate the limitations of the naturalist alternative and simultaneously indicate the sort of contribution that a more theological approach can bring to the study of religion. As we have seen, within the modernist paradigm, knowledge is essentially impersonal, consisting of purportedly objective facts and broader principles and laws. The objectivity of knowledge is secured by bracketing particularity and values and locating them within the domain of the personal. Despite the extensive critique that has been leveled at this epistemological framework, its powerful legacy continues to shape the modern university. Knowledge as information and technical mastery that is passed from teacher to student is the dominant pedagogical form. In this model, the student is accountable for receiving the public knowledge, but any integration of that knowledge with his own experience is done "after hours." Indeed, the personal experience of either the teacher or the student is considered irrelevant to the educational context, and hence is policed within the classroom.

Impersonal knowledge transmitted to disembodied minds is the norm. The individual is left entirely on his own to relate this knowledge to a personal life narrative, with its constellation of experiences, values, emotions, and hopes.

The naturalist exclusivist camp wants to place the spotlight on the wider social-political-material context that individuals inhabit, making the persuasive case that this level of analysis is critical to analyzing what is going on. In the process of focusing there, however, the individual is more or less abandoned. No effort is made to occupy the standpoint of the individual, who is presumably the recipient of the insights gained by attending to the wider configuration within which she lives. After all the analysis is said and done, the question still remains: What is the most responsible integration of such analysis into the framework of an individual life? That question has been deemed illegitimate, out of bounds, within the liberal paradigm given the abstract model of reason that dominates. The integration of public knowledge and the private realm of emotions, values, and experiences takes place offstage, under the rhetorical control of "subjectivity," or "emotion," or "faith," or "personal opinion." This reflects the trajectory of twentieth century scholarship that, as Richard Rorty argues, has come to favor "logic, debunking, and knowingness" and increasingly lost its capacity for the imagination and self-transformation. A humanistic discipline, he rightly insists, needs both, but the forces of professionalization and academicization have privileged "dry, sardonic knowingness."[26] In a similar vein, literary scholar Jane Tompkins diagnoses the problem with American education as a lack of "respect for the whole human organism, emotions, body, and spirit, as well as mind."[27] The naturalist exclusivist approach simply perpetuates the biases and limitations of the modern academy insofar as it brackets attention to the personal or the embodied individual.

One of the features that has distinguished theology as an intellectual discipline—and rendered it suspect within the modern university—has been its concern with the personal domain. Insofar as theology attends to the religious worldviews that individuals inhabit, it necessarily takes into account the horizon as it is framed in terms of the individual. Insofar as it attends critically to these worldviews, it is not simply repeating the emic perspective, but seeking to analyze and assess it in terms of other perspectives, including naturalistic frameworks. Insofar as theology attends constructively to these religious worldviews, it is seeking to integrate the emic and etic perspectives in a synthesis that is intellectually and morally responsible. Understood in this fashion (although clearly *not* all theology can be understood in this fashion), the discipline of theology offers a model wherein the public and the personal can be brought together into the same frame for critical exploration. Failure to consider the topic of religion from the perspective of the individual is disappointing to students. Much student interest in the field is driven by existential interests, by the desire to explore various religious orientations and practices in relation to the student's own life. As Kimberly Patton notes in her reflections on teaching religious studies, the "process of evaluation happens even when the student is unconscious of it." The teacher can choose to "ignore this ontological and existential melee" or "attempt instead to mediate or even to deploy it in the learning process."[28] The pedagogical challenge is to bring together the public realm of facts and the personal world of experiences, values, and emotions.

This challenge has grown larger in recent decades as the dialectical trends toward globalization and pluralization have intensified. In a fascinating study of the crisis facing the modern university, Bill Readings argues that it is rooted in a loss of purpose that was formerly tied to the imperative to acculturate students in a common national culture.[29] The forces undermining the nation-state, and the increased pluralism within its borders, have undermined this cultural purpose of the university, and allowed economic rationales to dominate. The contentious disputes over a western canon constitute one of the more visible signals of these trends. Insofar as students are not collectively socialized into a common culture, they are left on their own to integrate a personal narrative that is both intellectually and morally responsible. Religious studies ought to be one of the academic sites that facilitate this integration. But it will not realize this potential unless it escapes from the model that has long controlled it, a model that advances both secular liberal and liberal ecumenical theological interests. The liberal variant of this model underscores the imperative to locate religions on a level playing field, approaching them neutrally and objectively. The ecumenical variant celebrates them all as essentially different but equal paths to the same transcendent goal or ultimate. Although these variants can be analytically distinguished, in practice they coalesce to control the shape of religious studies. It is essential to recognize that this dominant approach reflects a normative model, but it is not itself a model that provides for normative reflection on religion. It can be construed as theological in the very limited sense that it reflects a particular theological position, but it does not facilitate theological reflection about religions. Quite the contrary. Insofar as all religions are championed as equally legitimate paths, critical normative assessments about beliefs and practices are ruled out of court. Hence the naturalist exclusivists and the theological inclusivists have a shared opponent: the reigning liberal/ecumenical theological model that protects religions from critical judgment. This certainly does not mean that these two camps can replace the liberal model that currently dominates, for much of the work carried out under this banner is indispensable to gaining an understanding of the multiple religious worlds, past and present, that humans inhabit. But its dominance has served to marginalize, if not preclude, other approaches to religion that warrant inclusion.

Although religious studies can benefit from incorporating some of the features associated traditionally with theological reflection—such as its attention to the individual's horizon, and its commitment to making critical judgments about religion rather than simply celebrating all that falls under its mantle—it is misleading to argue from these points to the conclusion that theology belongs as a subfield within the wider field of religious studies. It is misleading because the discipline of theology remains deeply rooted in confessional contexts that determine

its shape, audience, and self-understanding. To select only those features that res-
onate with and enrich religious studies leaves out too much of the picture. Such
selective theological disciplinary portraits, although exceedingly important, are
primarily efforts to reconfigure the discipline, but scholars of religion, not surprisingly, fixate on its present rather than its future shape when considering its
appropriate institutional location. Here I can only allude to a few of the factors
that would seem to preclude any simple incorporation of theology within religious studies.

Theology is still largely construed—by its practitioners, audiences, and critics—as reflection in the service of a particular faith tradition or community. There
is a confessional identity and purpose that stamps theology. A deep commitment to
sustaining the identity of a particular traditioned community contributes to a tendency to pursue theological "salvage operations" in which the desire to sustain the
tradition trumps compelling counters to it.[30] The concern for fidelity too often out-
paces the concern for plausibility.[31] Although this risk is not exclusive to theologians, the disciplinary self-understanding that presumes location within an identifiable religious tradition clearly exacerbates the problem. This receives powerful
institutional reinforcement—through such mechanisms as hiring and tenuring—
insofar as theology is institutionally located in religiously affiliated divinity schools
and seminaries. It is of course highly significant that some theologians have increasingly come to challenge this state of affairs, arguing for thoroughly historicist
understandings of religious life and thought.[32] Too much theology, however, remains
rooted in authoritarian forms of argumentation that privilege a tradition's particular texts or doctrines that have been central to the formation of the tradition.

Finally, it is important to keep in mind the political risks associated with this issue.
To some extent, we are dealing with a definitional matter. Theologians arguing for
the inclusion of theology within religious studies typically defend a subset of the
discipline called "academic theology," thereby signaling agreement that not all theology belongs within the liberal arts and sciences. However, such definitional finesse
overlooks the rhetorical meaning of theology in our age. It is located in a discursive field that places it on the side of faith, subjectivity, and authority rather than
reason, objectivity, and open inquiry, and definitional discriminations stand little
chance against this cultural complex. Just consider how the latter is powerfully rein-
forced through the recent publicity regarding the Vatican's policy on "orthodoxy
tests" for Catholic theologians.[33] One might well counter that this simply concedes
the term to retrograde forces, and that it is important to rehabilitate the term. There
is certainly some merit to this argument, particularly if retaining the designation
"theology" allows academic versions to stand as alternatives, and possibly correctives, to popular or religious variants. However, from a more global perspective, the
picture looks quite different. Far from serving as an appropriate designation for normative reflection about religion in a comparative, global context, the term "theology" is indelibly marked with theistic, and to a great extent Christian, overtones
that preclude its serviceability for identifying this intellectual enterprise.

My point is not to undermine efforts within theology that seek to foster its development as an academic discipline, and align it more closely with religious studies and wider studies in culture. In fact, I share that agenda, and have written in its support.[34] However, retaining the label of "theology" to capture the transformation of religious studies that is warranted is inflammatory and misleading. It fails to convey the extensive modifications needed in theology, leaving the impression that the aim is to incorporate theology-in-its-current-form into a more inclusive religious studies. Given the changes demanded, and the institutional weights that keep theology anchored to its current configuration, it is more likely and politically less risky for religious studies to pursue its self-transformation from within.

Although neither the theological inclusivists nor the naturalist exclusivists should win the day, each camp offers important insights into the limitations of religious studies as currently configured. Most scholars of religion belong to neither camp, embracing the liberal model that has effectively blocked criticism—whether internal or external—from center stage. Countering that model, as each camp does from a different location, holds out the promise of a religious studies that welcomes naturalistic explanations of religion as well as humanistic explorations and assessments of religion.

NOTES

1. See, for example: Eric Sharpe, *Comparative Religion: A History*, 2nd ed. (La Salle: Open Court, 1986); *Religion in the Making: The Emergence of the Sciences of Religion*, ed. Arie L. Molendijk and Peter Pels (Leiden: Brill, 1998); Walter H. Capps, *Religious Studies: The Making of a Discipline* (Minneapolis: Fortress Press, 1995); *Religious Studies, Theological Studies and the University-Divinity School*, ed. Joseph Mitsuo Kitagawa (Atlanta: Scholars Press, 1992).

2. Talal Asad, *Genealogies of Religion* (Baltimore: John Hopkins University Press, 1993), 207.

3. Ibid.

4. Bruce Lincoln, "Theses on Method," *Method and Theory in the Study of Religion* 8, no. 3 (1996): 225–27.

5. Stanley Fish, *The Trouble With Principle* (Cambridge: Harvard University Press, 1999), 297.

6. Donald S. Lopez, Jr., *Prisoners of Shangri-La: Tibetan Buddhism and the West* (Chicago: University of Chicago Press, 1998), 6.

7. Ibid., 171.

8. Ibid.

9. Donald Wiebe, "A Religious Agenda Continued: A Review of the Presidential Addresses of the American Academy of Religion," *Method and Theory in the Study of Religion* 9, no. 4 (1997): 371.

10. Ibid.

11. Ivan Strenski, "Our Very Own 'Contras': A Response to the 'St. Louis Project' Report," *Journal of the American Academy of Religion* 54, no. 2 (1986): 331.

12. Ibid., 321.

13. Jonathan Z. Smith, *Imagining Religion: From Babylon to Jonestown* (Chicago: University of Chicago Press, 1982), xi.

14. Russell T. McCutcheon, *Manufacturing Religion: The Discourse on Sui Generis Religion and the Politics of Nostalgia* (New York: Oxford University Press, 1997), xi.

15. Ibid., 26.

16. Timothy Fitzgerald, *The Ideology of Religious Studies* (New York: Oxford University Press, 2000), 3.

17. Ibid., 5.

18. Steven M. Wasserstrom sheds considerable light on the roots and implications of this religion discourse in his recent study *Religion After Religion: Gershom Scholem, Mircea Eliade and Henry Corbin at Eranos* (Princeton: Princeton University Press, 1999).

19. Timothy Fitzgerald, *The Ideology of Religious Studies,* 8.

20. See, for example, George Marsden, *The Outrageous Idea of Christian Scholarship* (New York: Oxford University Press, 1997); David Ray Griffin, "Professing Theology in the State University," in *Theology in the University: Essays in Honor of John B. Cobb., Jr.,* ed. David Ray Griffin and Joseph C. Hough, Jr. (Albany: State University of New York Press, 1991); Gordon Kaufman, "Critical Theology as a University Discipline," *God, Mystery, Diversity* (Minneapolis: Fortress Press, 1996); Delwin Brown, "Believing Traditions and the Task of the Academic Theologian," *Journal of the American Academy of Religion* 62, no. 4 (1994): 1167–1179.

21. John Milbank, *Theology and Social Theory: Beyond Secular Reason* (Cambridge: Blackwell, 1990), 3.

22. June O'Connor makes a persuasive case for the importance of multiple scholarly approaches in "The Scholar of Religion as Public Intellectual: Expanding Critical Intelligence" *Journal of the American Academy of Religion* 66, no. 4 (1998): 897–909.

23. See, for example, Russell McCutcheon, "A Default of Critical Intelligence? The Scholar of Religion as Public Intellectual," *Journal of the American Academy of Religion* 65, no. 2 (1997): 443–68.

24. Russell McCutcheon, Review of *Savage Systems: Colonialism and Comparative Religion in South Africa* by David Chidester, *History of Religions* 39, no. 1 (1999): 73–76.

25. Wade Clark Roof, *Spiritual Marketplace: Baby Boomers and the Remaking of American Religion* (Princeton: Princeton University Press, 1999), 75.

26. Richard Rorty, *Achieving Our Country: Leftist Thought in Twentieth-Century America* (Cambridge: Harvard University Press, 1998), 129–135.

27. Jane Tompkins, *A Life in School: What the Teacher Learned* (Reading, MA: Addison-Wesley Publishing, 1996), xii.

28. Kimberly Patton, "'Stumbling Along Between the Immensities': Reflections on Teaching in the Study of Religion," *Journal of the American Academy of Religion* 65, no. 4 (1997): 839–40.

29. Bill Readings, *The University in Ruins* (Cambridge: Harvard University Press, 1996).

30. In his classic study of the conflict between historical knowledge and Christian faith, Van Harvey describes twentieth century efforts to bridge the conflict as "salvage operations" that ultimately fail. See *The Historian and the Believer* (New York: Macmillan, 1966), 246.

31. Wesley Wildman analyzes theology in relationship to these two poles in his book *Fidelity with Plausibility: Modest Christologies in the Twentieth Century* (Albany: State University of New York Press, 1998).

32. See, for example, Gordon Kaufman, *An Essay on Theological Method* (Missoula, MT: Scholars Press, 1975); Gordon Kaufman, *Theology for a Nuclear Age* (Philadelphia: Westminster Press, 1985); Sheila Davaney, *Pragmatic Historicism: A Theology for the Twenty-First Century* (Albany: State University of New York Press, 2000); William Dean, *History Making History: The New Historicism in American Religious Thought* (Albany: State University of New York Press, 1988).

33. Reporting on this development, a recent article in *The Chronicle of Higher Education*, for example, notes: "Unlike professors in religious-studies (*sic*) programs, who examine religion from a cultural and historical perspective, theologians focus on interpreting practices and beliefs of a particular religion—usually their own. 'Faith seeking understanding' is the quick definition of the field. Such a blending of subjective belief and objective analysis has led academics in other disciplines to view theologians somewhat skeptically, as if they were not true scholars." Although the article profiles several Catholic theologians with different responses to the new policy, the article leaves the reader with the impression that theology is aligned with faith, church, and authority in a manner that is not the case with religious studies, or the university more generally. In the words of one Catholic theologian quoted in the article, "To me, theology is a form of ministry, and it's something I do within the context of the church." See, Beth McMurtrie, "Three Theologians Face a Dilemma for Themselves, Their Colleges, and the Church," *The Chronicle of Higher Education*, 20 July 2001, A8.

34. Linell E. Cady, "The Social Location of the Theologian: Intellectual, Legal and Political Considerations," *Bulletin of the Council of Societies for the Study of Religion* 22, no. 1 (1993): 3–7; Linell E. Cady, "Loosening the Category that Binds: Modern 'Religion' and the Promise of Cultural Studies" in *Converging on Culture: Theologians Dialogue with Cultural Analysis and Criticism,* ed. Delwin Brown, Sheila Davaney, and Kathryn Tanner (Oxford: Oxford University Press, 2001).

9

Academic Theology in the University
or
Why an Ex-Queen's Heir Should Be Made a Subject

Delwin Brown

S hould theology be a subject in the university? Answers to this question presuppose answers to other questions, such as: What is a university? What kind
of inquiry is appropriate to it? What is theology? Does the term refer to
more than one kind of study? If so, what kind of theology is at issue in the question? What is the nature of this inquiry? Is this kind of theological inquiry consistent with the form or forms of study appropriate to the university? This series of
questions reflects a formal approach to the debate about theology and the university: What is the class of university inquiries, and is there any form of theological
inquiry that falls within this class? This is an important set of questions, with both
historical and conceptual components.

We would be mistaken, however, to suppose that the relationship of theology to the university is not also a material or political issue, or, indeed, many such
issues. What is at stake in the culture when these kinds of questions are posed?
Whose agenda is being promoted or challenged? What is at stake in the academic subculture when this question is asked, and whose agenda is being threatened
or advanced there? In short, what is to be lost or gained depending on whether
some form of theology is admitted as a university inquiry? These, as I say, are
political questions.

Theology in the most general sense is the critical analysis of religious beliefs.
Even from the standpoint of quite confessional, even authoritarian, perspectives,
theology is not simply religious beliefs themselves; theology is their examination.
I contend that there is a type of inquiry properly called theology that is appropriate to the university. I hold, moreover, that the inclusion of this kind of theology

126

is culturally and politically important. I shall attempt to make both the formal and the political case in this essay. First, however, I will provide a background for the emergence of these considerations.

THE QUESTION OF AN ACADEMIC THEOLOGY

Is there an "academic theology," a type of theology appropriate to the university? The background of this question is the gradual freeing of the university from ecclesiastical control and more broadly from the domination of any particular religious perspective or even that of "religion itself," whatever that might mean. Although the meaning and value of this development is debated in many respects, for our purposes it can be summarized quite simply.

Once upon a time in the Western world the generation of knowledge was dominated by religious values and their concomitant religious norms. If it did not claim to be the sole source of legitimate knowledge, Christianity in particular sought to govern the production of all knowledge, both conceptually and politically. It delimited what could be claimed true in every other sphere according to the perceived compatibility of these claims to its own truth. And whatever was thus permitted to be "true" conceptually was admitted politically. The control of the church and religious tradition over the production of knowledge was gradually broken in a political and intellectual process that includes at least medieval nominalism, Renaissance humanism, the rise of science, the growth of nationalism, Enlightenment rationalism, nineteenth-century historicism, and the secularism of the twentieth century. The most significant form of inquiry thus liberated emerged within the universities. In one respect, this was a conservative liberation, since in many cases these were the same universities that had been the bastions of religiously dominated knowledge. But perhaps for this very reason the transformation was all the more radical—the old domain had itself been taken over from church control and freed for open inquiry.

Although freed from religious domination, university inquiry, or alternatively "academic" inquiry, is decidedly not free in all respects. Indeed, what is characteristic of academic inquiry is not simply the negative feature of being outside the control of religion in any of its traditional forms, but also the positive feature of having a particular criteriology that governs its investigations. At the most general level, this is the requirement that all claims to knowledge be based on forms of evidence that are open to reproducible processes of examination by any and all qualified investigators. Of course, what kinds of evidence are appropriate in this or that field of knowledge, what the appropriate qualifications of an investigator are, even how these are to be determined, etc., are debatable and debated. This is only to say, however, that the criteria of academic inquiry are as open to investigation, critique, and revision as are the products of inquiry. What follows is important for the questions at hand: The academy and its specific formation as the university is not an egalitarian assembly of all points of view in a culture. The academy, and therefore the university, which is its chief institutionalization, is itself a particular subculture. It is a subculture defined formally at any given time by certain rules of investigation and rules for revising these rules of investigation, which of course intermingle and interact with all kinds of quasi- and noncognitive passions and practices, as in any other culture or subculture. Therefore, while claims to knowledge arising from any and every cultural perspective and practice are proper *objects* of academic investigation, only those types of investigation that can be defended in relation to the current criteriology of the university are proper *participants* in academic investigation. Since, however, not only the knowledge claims from other cultural sites, but also their implicit or explicit critiques of the university's criteriology, are proper objects of academic investigation, the transfer between the university and other subcultures is a two-way process, made even more complex by the fact that academics are also members of other subcultures. The point, however, remains: Although its boundaries are quite porous, the academy is a subculture, most visibly institutionalized in the university, defined by its own dynamic and revisable criteria and practices of inquiry with their concomitant material formations.

Because the academy is constantly vulnerable to critique and revision, its character and structure are always subject to question. This is altogether evident today with respect to the university, where questions of self-understanding abound. For example: What is the relationship of the liberal arts to the cultural products of particular communities? What is the relationship of the liberal arts to professional education? What is the relationship of the norms of the academy to the norms of the professions being studied within it? What is the relationship of the humanities to the sciences, with their distinctive methods, subject matters, and norms? What is the relationship of theory to practice, and inquiry to advocacy? And more generally, what does the public funding of education imply about public control?

The relationship of the university to religion and, especially, religious belief is a particularly complex issue, in part because of the American version of the tradition of the separation of church and state.[1] The value of this separation has been abundantly clear. Hence, when the topic of religion and the academy has arisen, the separation doctrine has been invoked rather automatically to say an initial "no" to whatever is being proposed. One consequence of the social upheaval of the 1960s, however, was the gradual "refinement" of the separation doctrine so that religion could be "studied" but not "practiced" in the university. In the great public universities, this kind of inquiry was admitted more readily with respect to "foreign" and thus exotic religions, but once the distinction between the "study about" and the "practice of" a religion became comfortable, the dominant American religious traditions, too, were deemed legitimate academic subject matter.

A special problem remained, however, with respect to the *beliefs* of religions, whether familiar or foreign. One can study a religious ritual, such as the eucharist or the vision quest, without performing the ritual, and one can study the roles of religious figures, such as tent preachers and medicine men, without performing their characteristic activities. But when the study moves from rituals or organizational roles or social structures or even grand myths to the particular constructions of religious *beliefs* embedded in these contexts, the distinction between "studying" and "practicing" becomes much more complicated. What is the difference between thinking about the logic of a particular complex of beliefs as it relates to other beliefs and to its material context, and doing what the adherent does when he or she thinks analytically about these same beliefs? One can think about ritual without doing ritual, but can one think about a set of beliefs, as analytically as one might think about the components and functions of a ritual process, without doing something very close to what reflective practitioners might do when they think about the same set of beliefs?

Instructors in university religious studies departments sometimes have the experience of lecturing on what is to them an alien religious worldview and its attendant beliefs, only to hear later that some students thought they were articulating their own beliefs. The experience is at first flattering ("I obviously set aside my biases") but then frustrating ("Don't they understand that I am functioning as an objective scholar, not a believer?"). The students' mistake, however, is instructive. In certain respects, "thinking through" a set of beliefs is the same for the scholar as for the practitioner, just as, were it actually to happen in a classroom, the performance of a ritual could be very much the same for the scholar as for the practitioner. The peculiar problem with religious belief remains, however, because the basic form of academic inquiry is thinking, not physical performance. This fact makes the distinction between study and practice in the area of religious belief uniquely complicated—thinking about a particular line of religious thinking is in many respects quite like the religious thinking itself.

Not, however, in every respect! There is a way to distinguish the thinking of the scholar and the thinking of the adherent. This, I argue, is the distinction that justifies, at least formally, the introduction of a certain type of thinking about religious beliefs, quite properly called theology, into the university. This argument on behalf of an academic theology has both an historical and a conceptual component.

THE CASE FOR AN ACADEMIC THEOLOGY

The earliest clear Western antecedents of what I am calling "academic theology" are to be found in a segment of thirteenth-century scholasticism. These beginnings could be pushed back to Anselm and, especially, Abelard in the eleventh century, but until the end of the twelfth century theology was overwhelmingly an exegetical enterprise nourished by the works of the Fathers and a Christianized version of neoplatonism. Exposure to Aristotle through the work of the Arab philosophers, and to a degree the views of the philosophers themselves, then began to create a distinction between theology as an exegetical exercise and another theological undertaking oriented toward different criteria and purposes. While the starting point of the latter inquiry remained the dogmas of faith, they were investigated now via an autonomous reasoning process. To be sure, this autonomy was enabled early on by the assumption—in some quarters at least, by no means in all—that independent reasoning, Aristotelian in style, was not inimical to Christian faith and for many, such as Aquinas, this confidence was sustained.[2] But whatever the degree of perceived compatibility or of tension, this rational mode of investigation was pressed forward.

In Paris, by the middle of the thirteenth century, the *theological* curriculum permitted, alongside exegesis and commentary, a second form of theology characterized by independent thinking. In fact, Aristotelian thought was not only a methodological model but also an autonomous source of truth for this kind of theology, while theological exegesis on the other hand continued to be governed by inherited Christian norms. Thomas Aquinas valorized these dual theological tracks, confident, as we have noted, that they were complementary. But others, in particular the Christian Averroists as they came to be called, found that critical theological inquiry often conflicted with the exegetical one and yet held that this theology freed from authority should nevertheless be pursued without restraint. These theologians were condemned in 1270 and 1277, and by the fourteenth century, as epitomized in Ockham, the critical methodologies were sharply separated from the exegetical ones as philosophy and theology, respectively, and all hope of maintaining their mutuality was abandoned. Indeed, *all* independent inquiries on topics about which revelation had already spoken were now deemed "philosophical." In much subsequent Catholic thought and in most of Protestantism until the nineteenth century "theology" referred only to those studies of religious belief that conformed to the needs and norms of the religious tradition itself.

For our consideration, the important issue in the thirteenth century was not the adequacy of Aristotle's philosophy, as such, but what it was taken to represent, namely a perspective based on "general plausibility" rather than "authority," to use the distinction Duns Scotus later put forth. Theology as one aspect of this critical mode of general inquiry was answerable to whatever canons of truth were widely defensible; theology in this sense was a "secular" enterprise. But while Aristotelian thought as such was not the fundamental issue, its substance was important for our purposes because it redirected all forms of independent inquiry toward the empirical world. Theologians like Aquinas taught that observable reality exists in and for itself and hence should be studied for what it is, not simply for what it is thought to reflect about the divine. After the condemnations of 1270 and 1277, however, that purpose was not again espoused for theology per se for several centuries, but it was nevertheless now set out as a new (for the time) form of possible inquiry— empirical analysis, based on generally defensible criteria of scholarship.

Implicit in this medieval undertaking is the idea of a specifically theological inquiry whose objects are the "dogmas" of traditions, i.e., religious beliefs, whose interest is the actual historical functioning of these beliefs, and whose methods of analyzing and evaluating religious beliefs are those defensible in the community of scholarly inquiry. This is what I mean by academic theology. Academic theology differs from what might be termed "religious theology." Religious theologies are analyses of religious beliefs for the purpose of clarifying, extending, and defending the conceptual practices of particular religions or religious communities. They are governed by the purposes and therefore the norms of their "host" or sponsoring religious community. Academic theologies are also analyses of the beliefs of religious communities, but they are governed by the purposes and therefore the norms of a different community, namely the academy. Of course, religious and academic norms will overlap to some degree, sometimes perhaps to a significant degree. The distinction, however, remains: the desire to understand religious beliefs, employing analyses and argumentation defensible in the academy, not religious traditions, motivates academic theology in the same way that the desire to understand ritual practices or economic behavior motivates ritology (the academic study of rituals) or economics. Academic theology is rooted in purposes and values defensible in the academic community, and its historical roots extend back into the Middle Ages.

The medieval worldview of rational scholastic thought gradually disappeared. Theology was eventually removed from her place as queen of the sciences. But an offspring of medieval theology, theology as an analysis of the meaning and function of religious beliefs responsible to scholarly standards, lived on as a distinct conceptual possibility. That mode of analysis emerged again into prominence in the nineteenth century. Here it took two somewhat different, though not necessarily inconsistent, forms. One was a more speculative reconstruction of religious ideas; the other was more empirical and analytical. The first enterprise was primarily philosophical, not simply in the medieval sense of reasoning freed from the constraints of religious authority, but also because it was grounded in various of the philosophical traditions being developed in university settings. In Germany, for example, theological speculation for the most part followed Kantian or Hegelian lines. In Great Britain, the most interesting independent theological constructions reflected idealistic or evolutionary philosophical presuppositions. British and German thinkers both had their impact in the United States, with creative adaptations, beginning in the last half of the nineteenth and continuing into the twentieth century. One thinks, for example, of the early religious naturalists and evolutionary theologians, the Boston personalists, Henry Nelson Wieman's empirical theology, the Death of God theology, and the speculative strand of process theism. This kind of theology is speculative, as I have said, but also entrepreneurial. It is more concerned with developing new and better religious ideas than with conducting a theory-conscious analysis of beliefs within actual religious traditions and subtraditions.

The other type of academic theology also reemerged in the nineteenth century. It is more descriptive and analytical, beginning with the conceptual data of particular religious traditions, asking what these ideas mean, and how they are to be evaluated in terms of various criteria of adequacy, internal and external. What do these religious beliefs mean in this specific context? What job are they doing? Whose interests do they serve? Are they functioning as they are intended? What unintended or unacknowledged consequences do they have? How are they being evaluated, according to internal criteria? Are those evaluations sustainable? How are they being evaluated by external criteria, including those of the academy? How should they be? Alternative reconstructions of beliefs within particular traditions may also be undertaken, but they are preceded by an elaborate analysis of actual forms of language and behavior. How might adherents of this tradition adapt their conceptual scheme so as to meet better the various tests being applied to these beliefs, either their own tests or those proposed from other quarters?[3] Finally, this kind of academic theology is theory-conscious, asking these questions within the framework of hypotheses about the nature of religion, the character of religious traditioning, the function of conceptualizing processes within traditions, and the relationship of believing to other forms of religious practice.

Ernst Troeltsch was the first widely influential practitioner of this kind of academic theology, but it was perhaps most clearly developed in the sociohistorical studies of the evolution of Christian beliefs conducted by members of the "early Chicago School" of theology. It was practiced by the more empirical strand of process thinkers and is advocated today under the formal guise of a distinctively American version of "theological historicism."[4] Acknowledged or not, this kind of theological analysis is often evident in college and university courses on "religious thought." Its purpose is not advocacy but, at its best, a "thick" analysis of religious beliefs, much as other scholars might study religious rituals and religious institutions. This is the kind of academic theology I believe to be appropriate subject matter in a university setting.

I do not reject in principle the more speculative forms of academic theology. After all, academic studies of political and economic data sometimes give rise to constructive proposals by the academician—political or economic philosophies, for example—that are quite speculative in character. So long as they depend on public evidence and are open to public scrutiny, they are deemed appropriate to the academy. My view, however, is that speculative proposals from academic theologians tend to be of rather limited usefulness. At their best, they usually adapt or revise currently persuasive philosophical perspectives to make more credible particular religious visions and their attendant practices. Hence, they are sometimes referred to as philosophical theologies and are located, often, in philosophy departments. Whatever their locations, they too easily slip into universalizing proposals for understanding religion itself or particular forms of religious expression in general. As such, they obscure the richness of particular conceptual formations in concrete religious contexts and thus the contexts themselves. At their worst, speculative theologies are individualistic flights of fancy that even the most open and pluralistic university department should discredit—eccentric prescriptions for salvation proffered by tenured gurus seeking disciples.

Compared to the most credible proposals of the speculative theologian, the kind of academic theology best suited to the university is what I have elsewhere described as the "ethnography of belief," if, that is, "ethnography" (following James Clifford) is rescued from the illusions of descriptivism.[5] Its data are the beliefs-rooted-in-practice of particular religious traditions, its purposes are to analyze beliefs just as other scholars of religion attempt to make sense of, for example, a tradition's rituals, and its criteria are those deemed defensible in the debates of the academy. Its primary conversation partners are cultural theory and the various social sciences, including ethnographies of the particular traditions in which it is interested.

My primary reason for preferring this kind of academic theology has to do with the nature of religious traditions. Religions are fluid processes, internally diverse, and porous at their rough and inexact boundaries. They are not internally consistent monoliths, unfolding organically through time from some primitive core or essence that marks their "true" natures. Therefore, they take quite different forms in different settings. Their various dimensions, moreover, are intertwined in distinctive ways. In other words, the particularity of a religious tradition at any point is as important as its dynamism over time, and the two are related. Thus, the study of religious beliefs ought to be quite specifically located and tied into explorations of that tradition's rituals, power relations, stories, institutions, etc. Concepts of deity, salvation, liberation, destiny, enlightenment, authority, land, and law may have general meanings, but even if they do, these thin remainders tell us very little about the different ways of being in the world in which these concepts do their work. In short, a religious tradition's beliefs must be examined concretely. I believe this concreteness is best provided by the methods and conclusions of non-reductionistic social sciences and in particular theoretically self-conscious cultural studies. An academic theology should work primarily in relation to these inquiries, rather than being governed by its historical allies, philosophy and biblical studies.

None of this is to say that there should not continue to be a form of disciplined reflection, such as Christian theology, whose task is the propagation of inherited doctrine for the edification of the believing community, governed by its own special criteria of adequacy, and located in its own educational institutions. Indeed, without these tradition-governed theologies, as well as the everyday reflection of ordinary believers on which they depend, academic theology would be deprived of its subject matter (and, more important, religions would be deprived of internal analysis and critique). My point, instead, is that theology need not be only that. There is also the possibility of, and a precedent for, another form of theological inquiry. Initiated in the thirteenth century and further developed in the nineteenth, this inquiry treats the cognitive phenomena of religions as data whose social meanings and functions are to be studied in themselves; its studies are conducted and its conclusions defended in relation to criteria elaborated, scrutinized, and revised within the academy.

My position, then, distinguishes theologies whose norms are those of the religious community, which I refer to as "religious theologies," from academic theologies whose analyses are guided by canons of humanistic inquiry defended within the university.[6] That the term "theology" should be used to refer to both may on occasion be confusing but is not without precedent or utility. "Biblical studies" can denote both the pious study of Scripture inspired and constrained by the heritage of a religious community, and the varied humanistic and social scientific studies of sacred texts, including the Bible, that are entirely at home in the university. And, in fact, terms such as "philosophy," "economics," and "politics" also have dual meanings, referring both to the "interested" opinions of "believing" segments in the society at large, and to the disciplined inquiry of specialists within the university. Moreover, despite the confusion it sometimes causes, the dual use of these terms has a practical justification. Whatever the subject matter, the two forms of practice—popular and scholarly—are not entirely disconnected. For one thing, the scholarly inquiries in almost every case arose from the popular inquiries. In addition, the two are not necessarily inimical and, even when they are, they may contribute to each other, at least as data, if not also as useful critique. Finally, the university is itself best understood as a "believing" community, one among others, with no need or right to control the meaning of terms even if it has every right to contend for its definitions, methods, and criteria in the culture at large.

A particular conception of the academic community, represented by "the university," is important to my understanding of the kind of theology appropriate to it, and the proper and improper reasons for locating theology there. The university both is and is not a public community. It is but one subculture within the broader corporate life, the public. The university has its own varied traditions of research, with their proximate and tentative agreements on practices such as proposing judgments of fact and the criteria whereby they are to be evaluated and alternatives adjudicated. In these general respects, it is like traditions of business or sport. The discourse of the university is not automatically open to all comers simply by virtue of their membership in the larger corporate life. In that respect, the university is not a "public square." All claims, methods, and criteria are not accorded equal hearing. Only those are given a place that can defend their credibility in relation to established criteria or plausible alternatives to established criteria.

The university *is* public, however, in the sense that none of its claims is immune to critique from any quarter, and in principle at least no one is prevented from participating in its critical and constructive processes. There are no conditions of membership except the knowledge of applicable procedures and criteria and the capacity to use them to extend, revise, or replace them. Its claims and criteria are open to change, but to introduce change one must either show claims to be warranted in relation to current criteria, or, taking these criteria into account, show how they can be revised or replaced. Since critiques, to be successful, must be mounted in relation to its own canonical process of evidence and argumentation, the university is a particular tradition, one dynamic and internally plural tradition among others, not the gathering place for all.

Academic theology is appropriate in the university because it operates within the complex criteriological tradition of the academy. Its presence in the university is not, and should not be, grounded in a genial openness to all interesting and serious perspectives on life,[7] or in a willingness to have "native informants" (i.e., theologians) readily available to the scholar of religion.[8] Neither is it justified, in the final analysis, by the postmodern denial of the objectivity and universality of knowledge.[9] The fact that all inquiries are contextual and interested does not entail that all contextual and interested inquiries belong in the university. The humility proper to postmodernism undercuts all absolutist illusions, those of the academy as well as the religions. The taming of universalistic pretensions, however, heightens our awareness of the importance of particular traditions, their values and their goals. Traditions are internally diverse and externally porous and therefore inevitably dynamic and changing. They overlap, too. But their rough and complex particularity enriches the cultures they inhabit and compose. The academic tradition is one of these fallible, partial, and dynamic perspectives, not the pretentious inclusion of them all. Academic theology is an appropriate subject in the academy only because it is academic.

THE POLITICS OF AN ACADEMIC THEOLOGY

Academic theology, I have argued, is governed by the canons of discourse debated, defended, and transformed within the university. It is therefore a permissible discipline within this community of inquiry. Academic theology's purpose, like that of other scholarly disciplines, is to gain understanding. Its methods, like theirs, are those of evidence and reasonableness. Its conclusions, like theirs, are subject to critique from all quarters. This, however, is only to show that academic theology is a possible university discipline, an inquiry that cannot on theoretical grounds be excluded from the modern university. There are, in my judgment, additional reasons for concluding that theology *ought* to be located in the university. They are political in the sense of pertaining to the health and vitality of the polis, the human community.

The academy has become an increasingly influential arbiter of knowledge during the modern period in Western culture. Until mid-century in the United States, the influence of the university persisted through the education of a small privileged class in a group of select universities. Until that point, the process of producing knowledge was relatively protected precisely because it was largely restricted to elite places for elite people. Since mid-century, the academic subculture has become less protected, more vulnerable to various forms of attempted social control, but that is because its role has broadened and thus become more publicly visible and influential. The social aftermath of World War II, represented first by the entry of women into the workforce and later by the GI Bill, rapidly increased the number of young men and women educated in American universities. If university education was itself significantly adapted, even altered, in this process, the gain is its much wider role in society. Disciplined education in most of the professions, arts, and political and social perspectives is and for the foreseeable future will be centralized in the vast system of public and private secondary studies that falls under the umbrella of "university" education.

Today the university is our culture's central and most comprehensive producer of knowledge. Individuals, especially young people, who once were educated in homes, religious communities, guilds, community organizations, social movements, and the like, now complete their education in the university, with its own relatively distinctive criteriological heritage. The massive influence of the university is the best argument for including within the academic curriculum the study of any phenomenon of social and cultural importance. That is the argument for studying the physical world and the social, political, and cultural dimensions of the human world. Each of these is of such significance that a sensible society cannot afford to exclude them from careful academic scrutiny. The same considerations hold for religions, their histories, rituals, organizational structures, and patterns of influence and change—and, of course, religious beliefs. For the university to omit a disciplined examination of the beliefs-rooted-in-practice of particular religious traditions would be as foolish as excluding an examination of the philosophical presuppositions, economic practices, and gender roles operational in society. The driving question is not whether this or that religious outlook is true or truer than others, but how it is to be understood and appraised in relation to the various criteria, conceptual and practical, that are defensible within the academy. To dismiss the need for an academic theology in the university would not only be unwarranted theoretically, it would be unfortunate practically, and tragically so. Religions possess a remarkable potential for good, largely because of the comprehensiveness of their applicability and their appeal to the whole person—intellectual, volitional, and affective. For precisely the same reasons, however, they are capable of enormous evil. It is simply irresponsible to exempt either potential from the careful forms of analysis that the academy offers, or, indeed, to deprive believers of the benefits that can come from disciplined studies of their religions and their religious beliefs.

To this argument, one can imagine a sympathetic but not entirely persuaded response, as follows:

> To be sure, the study of religion is important even within the academy and that holds, too, for religious beliefs. And it is unfortunately true that the study of religion, including especially the study of religious beliefs, has been neglected, perhaps even repressed, in the university. That neglect should be remedied. More than that, we can agree that the type of inquiry characterized as "academic theology" in this essay is a valid academic enterprise that can and should be included in the university curriculum. But it need not and should not be called "theology." Even if there is an explicit historical precedent for labeling as "theology" this way of assessing religious beliefs, precedent is not destiny. The term "theology" is today too closely tied to the self-serving reflection of believers—whether ordinary practitioners, tele-apologists, or self-styled gurus—to also be used to designate a

university discipline, even when modified by "academic." It will be misunderstood within the university, and it will mislead the public about what we are doing in the university.

There is no "knockout" reply to this argument. The common usage of terms, such as "theology," does create preconceptions that are hard to challenge and correct. Thus the risk of misunderstanding in the case of "academic theology" is real. It may indeed be the case that the term "theology" should be avoided with reference to the academic analysis of religious beliefs. I do not think so, for two reasons.

First, it is a demonstrable mistake, I think, for intellectuals to cede to other advocacy traditions—and the academy is also an advocacy tradition that promotes certain types of evidence, adjudication and the like—terms that possess cultural and social power by virtue of their historical lineage. In the area of politics, for example, intellectuals of a liberal stripe abandoned for a long time emotional carriers of historic aspirations, like "values," "responsibility," "patriotism," and "America," because they had become trivialized, if not downright corrupted, in popular discourse. The result was to give these terms over to reactionary forces that exploited their power to gain a hearing in social and political controversy. The term "theology" (like "professor") is also loaded with cultural power; its use in popular culture is honorific, even when treated satirically. Its broad cultural potency will increase, moreover, as the American separation doctrine continues to be qualified,[10] and as the social influence of communities of color, for whom "religion" and its attendant categories are generally quite positive, continues to grow. In short, "theology" does and will continue to connote thinking about matters of fundamental significance for human life, issues of special importance for human well-being. If religious beliefs have, or even purport to have, this fundamental significance, the analysis and critique of these beliefs are of vital importance. To forego a term like "theology" is to forego an opportunity to make a claim about the great significance of the academic analysis of religious beliefs. To use the term may risk associations with other connotations of "theology," such as religious dogmatism and narrowness. Realistically, however, that is a minimal risk; at this point in history, the chance that inquiries within the university will be mistaken for religious special pleading is remote indeed. The real question is not whether the university will be misunderstood; it is whether the university wishes its discourse about religion and religious beliefs to be heard in the public debate. To call its analysis of religious belief a form of theology, i.e., "academic theology," is to increase greatly the chance that its analyses will be taken seriously, even if in opposition from those who wish to reserve the honorific term "theology" for themselves.

Second, to insist on calling an academic inquiry by the term "theology" is more than implicitly to call to accountability other inquiries in our culture that go by that designation or endeavor to do the many things that theologies historically have done. Put another way, the attempt to gain a wider hearing for university discourse about religious beliefs is justified, not only as an end in itself, but because extra-academic forms of religious reflection badly need explicit, public, and sustained academic (positive and negative) analysis. On the one hand, the religious credulity of the popular mind today may well rival that of the masses in antiquity. On the other, there is a widespread misunderstanding of religion, the function of religion, and in particular the contextual roles of religious beliefs. To say that today people believe anything religious and understand nothing about religion is an overstatement, but an instructive one. An important factor in this situation is the failure of the humanistic disciplines within the university to be intentional and strategic advocates for their methods and conclusions in the broader society. There is a reason for this failure. The solution to the religious wars of the early modern period was in part the removal of religion from the social sphere, making it a private affair. The secular university accepted this arrangement, largely exempting religious belief from disciplined scrutiny (though not necessarily from unanalytical disdain). The exemption is without justification. For one thing, religions have social and public implications that cannot to be "privatized." For another, if the university is faithful to its social purpose, no body of knowledge claims can legitimately be exempted from its systematic analysis. This is especially important in the case of religious beliefs, which are so pervasively employed as the reasons or at least the rationalizations for so much that affects social well-being. The meanings and implications, conceptual and practical, of religious ideas are as much in need of examination as are ideas about the economy, race and gender, popular culture, democratization, and the host of other beliefs that drive human conduct. An academic assessment of these ideas should enter the public fray with the expectation, indeed the demand, that its claims deserve to be taken as seriously as those of any *other* set of "theological" claims in the public arena.

Theology is customarily understood to be the analysis of religious beliefs, not simply the beliefs themselves. That being the case, so long as its distinctive norms are clear, the academic analysis of religious beliefs is entitled to enter the public field of debate about religious ideas claiming itself to be a form of "theology." It is *academic* theology because it adheres to criteria defensible in the university. It is academic *theology* because it stands in a lineage of the disciplined assessment of religious beliefs that is independent of religious restrictions. Academic theology is *important* because the power of religions for good and ill is too great to be ignored by the academy, and because the scrutiny of academic analysis is too valuable to be denied to religious beliefs.

NOTES

1. On this, see the work of Linell E. Cady, especially *Religion, Theology and American Public Life* (Albany: State University of New York Press, 1993).

2. For a lovely, if wholly unpersuasive, contemporary expression of this Thomistic confidence, see Nicholas Sagovsky, "Thomas Aquinas, *Ratio Dei*, and the University," *Theology* (September/October 1998): 353–358.

3. The evaluation process appropriate to an academic theology is exploratory and hypothetical about options, rather than advocative. It takes the form of: "This pattern of action seems to have these consequences and these consequences in turn seem to be or not to be compatible with these values, if these are one's values." Or "This conceptual formation does not appear to measure up to this criterion, so if consistency is a value either the formation or the criterion or both should be reconsidered." Or "If the value you affirm is X, then you should consider whether X might be more fully affirmed by employing this resource in your tradition rather than that." Or "Have you considered the possibility that your tradition is incapable of providing resources for X, and if so, what consequences follow from that?" Or "If the value you wish to defend and support is Y, then here are some reasons for and against your adopting this conceptual position, institutional affiliation, or lifestyle in support of Y." Of course, these are artificial formulations; the give and take of a vigorous academic environment is not likely to tolerate such cut-and-dried conceptual moves. But they do convey the logic underlying the evaluative approach of an academic theologian.

4. For a discussion and assessment of this form of historicism, see Sheila Greeve Davaney, *Pragmatic Historicism: A Theology for the Twenty-first Century* (Albany: State University of New York Press, 2000).

5. Delwin Brown, "Refashioning Self and Other: Theology, Academy and the New Ethnography," in *Converging on Culture: Theologians in Dialogue with Cultural Analysis and Criticism*, ed. Delwin Brown, Sheila Greeve Davaney, and Kathryn Tanner (New York: Oxford University Press, 2001).

6. Delwin Brown, "Believing Traditions and the Task of the Academic Theologian," *Journal of the American Academy of Religion* LXII, no. 4 (Winter 1994): 1167–1179. See also "Constructive Theology and the Academy," *Council for the Study of Religion Bulletin* 22, no. 1 (February 1993): 7–9, and "Academic Theology and Religious Studies," *Council for the Study of Religion Bulletin* 26, no. 3 (September 1997): 64–66.

7. Eric J. Sharpe, "The Compatibility of Theological and Religious Studies: Historical, Theoretical, and Contemporary Perspectives," *Council for the Study of Religion Bulletin* 26, no. 3 (September 1997): 52–60.

8. Jonathan Z. Smith, "Are Theological and Religious Studies Compatible?" *Council for the Study of Religion Bulletin* 26, no. 3 (September 1997): 60f.

9. Garrett Green, "Challenging the Religious Studies Canon: Karl Barth's Theory of Religion," *The Journal of Religion* 75, no. 4 (September 1995): 473–86.

10. On this, see the entire issue of the *Notre Dame Law Review* 75, no. 2 (December 1999), entitled "Fostering Harmony Among the Justices: How Contemporary Debates in Theology Can Help the Divisions on the Court Regarding Religious Expression by the State," by Kathleen A. Brady.

10

Rethinking Theology and Religious Studies

SHEILA GREEVE DAVANEY

What is the nature of religious studies and what is its role within the contemporary university? How should theology be defined and what place is there for academic theologians in the academy? Are religious studies scholars and theologians enemies, siblings, versions of similar academic impulses and commitments? Do current developments in theory, especially cultural theory, challenge how these questions have been answered historically, suggesting ways to reinterpret both theology and religious studies and reconceive their relationship? Do they challenge ways in which religious studies has construed itself so as to exclude theological reflection and do they call for the relinquishment of claims historically made by theology to epistemic and experiential privilege?

Before delving into some of these questions it is important to consider the immediate atmosphere in which the current discussions are situated and to trace, if briefly, their historical background. To but it bluntly, religious studies has increasingly become inhospitable toward theology. Almost everywhere one looks in the academic study of religion there is the denunciation of theology, the denial of its academic status, and its segregation to nonacademic (religious) communities or pseudoacademic locales (seminaries and religiously related schools). To use Ray Hart's politically incorrect phrase, theology has become the *bête noire* of religious studies.[1] Not only are theological studies and religious studies to be distinguished in subject matter, purpose, and methods but also they are to be relegated to different institutional locations and those locations are to be given differing intellectual status. Moreover, an insidious linguistic convention has developed whereby scholars of religion attack their intellectual enemies by virtue of announcing they are really theologians in disguise or their theories or methods are really theological and, hence, ruled illegitimate.

A few recent examples may suffice to suggest the flavor of the conversation. Russell McCutcheon, in his 1997 book *Manufacturing Religion: The Discourse of Sui Generis Religion and the Politics of Nostalgia*, attacks the enterprise of religious studies, especially the trajectory associated with the history of religions, arguing that it has invented the category of religion and indeed reality of religion in order to create and defend itself as an academic discipline.[2] In particular, he asserts that religious studies as a separate academic discipline, deserving a place in the modern university, is predicated upon the notion of religion as a separate, autonomous realm that can only be identified and studied by specialized scholars. Such an idea of religion as *sui generis* is, according to McCutcheon, really theological, i.e. the problem with religious studies is that it remains theology. Or, again, Ray Hart, in reporting on the views of scholars of religion who separate themselves from theologians, states that the former "are more agreed on what is 'wrong' with the study of religion than what should be 'right' about it. What is wrong is that it still 'includes theology.'"[3] Another example can be found in Mark C. Taylor's "Introduction" to the much discussed book *Critical Terms for Religious Studies.* Taylor traces the relation of theology and religious studies, indicating the various permutations in their relationship, including the current divorce between the two. He then goes on to state that the opposition between theological and religious studies should not be oversimplified. However, the theologian's sense of reprieve at this caution is only momentary. Taylor does not, as I had hoped, suggest that theology has been construed in a too essentialist and nonnuanced manner but goes on, like McCutcheon, to suggest that many critics of theology are really closet theologians. The problem of oversimplification is not that theology has been distorted but that scholars of religion have unself-consciously continued to embody the pretensions and desires of theology. According to Taylor, "critics of theology embrace the methods of the social sciences ranging from history and psychology to sociology and anthropology with an enthusiasm bordering on the religious. . . . The Cartesian promise of a proper method is in fact a secularized version of theology's dream of an unconditional principle of principles. For those with eyes to see, theology casts a long . . . shadow."[4]

Is such a dream—the longing for absoluteness, for an unconditional principle of principles—the dream of theologians today? While certainly one can point to historical and contemporary examples of such longings on the part of theologians, as Taylor notes, so too can one find endless examples of philosophers, other scholars of religion, and a wide variety of representatives of other intellectual disciplines who shared such dreams or continue to pursue them today. But as is evidenced across all of the academic disciplines today, many scholars and intellectuals have forsaken such pursuits and have come to construe their endeavors, to conceive their scholarly identities and disciplinary definitions, in radically new ways. Are theologians alone of all intellectuals and scholars unable to reconsider our tasks? In an age that repudiates essentialism on so many levels, is theology to be rejected out of hand by virtue of an essentialist rendering of it that by definition disallows the changes that have transformed other disciplines? Do, in particular, theologians who have also repudiated ahistorical, universalistic, essentialist claims, and have come to view theology as a form of cultural analysis and criticism, recognize ourselves in these characterizations or are they someone else's fantasies imagined for purposes that do not further open conversation among scholars? Before we can answer these questions we need to ask how we reached this juncture.

Intellectuals steeped in the forms of cultural and historical insight and theory that have such widespread influence today, and have transformed the self-understanding of so many disciplines, are well aware that the versions of history we tell ourselves are not straightforward depictions of uncontested facts. Instead, histories are constructed selectively; from among the welter of conflicting elements of the past, some things are emphasized, others ignored, and others creatively distorted to create narratives that support one perspective rather than another. Such imaginative reworking of the past is not only the province of politics and family life. It is also the process by which intellectuals map out disciplines, delineate scholarly boundaries, and legitimize practices and methodological approaches. Today we are confronted with just such a narrative in religious studies that tells the story of how the study of religion was born, how it rejected all theological impulses, and how it thus became a legitimate and acceptable member of the academy.

The most often cited version of this narrative is really quite simple. It is that, for the first fifteen centuries or so of the Christian era, theology reigned supreme, was controlled by the church, and served the religious needs of the believing community. Theology, concerned with knowledge of or discourse about God, was carried out primarily through interpretation and commentary on Scriptures and eventually upon the creedal and dogmatic productions of the church. Its purpose was the enhancement of piety, its practitioners were faithful believers, and its authorities were ecclesial.

With the development of the medieval university, theology became more associated with the university and its intellectual pursuits and less fully encompassed by the requirements of piety. While theology as personal and communal knowledge of God remained a focus, with commentary on Scriptures and dogma central to theological reflection, there also developed new intellectual trajectories that sought knowledge through rational analysis and argument. Contrasts between the monastery and the university, between faith and reason, between theology as a habit of the soul and theology as a rational discipline all began to emerge.

But, importantly for this story, there emerged with the humanism of the fifteenth century not only a contrast *within* theology but also one that was to separate religious reflection from other kinds of human knowledge, that is, there developed a clearer separation of the humane sciences and the divine sciences. As Jonathan Z. Smith, a sometimes practitioner of this narrative, has stated, for the emergent humanism, "if the study of religion was anything, it was the study of that which was utterly different from the human sciences. The two were perceived to be mutually exclusive."[5]

This separation of the humane and divine sciences was to be greatly accentuated in the modern period, the era to which we are most directly heir. This part of the story is well known: the demise of Catholic Europe; the Reformation and its aftermath of religious warfare; the Enlightenment and the development of the modern sciences with their promise of objective and final truth; in some quarters, the criticism of religion and religious authority and tradition; and in others, the growing identification of religion with the depths of human subjectivity and the progressive relegation of religion to the emergent private sphere in newly secularized nation-states. If, for fifteenth century humanism, the divine and humane sciences were increasingly separated and all things to do with religion were placed within the divine sciences, a new twist takes place by the eighteenth and especially the nineteenth centuries. New scientific studies emerged that claimed as their object "religion" and located themselves within the objective human sciences and set themselves over against theology. Religion became a proper object of academic study, its practitioners, scholars who served the pursuit of objective truth, unbeholden to ecclesial authorities or the constraints of piety. To use Van Harvey's terms, "the morality" of critical judgment replaced the "ideal of belief."[6] For many tellers of this tale, the best symbol for these developments is the Dutch Universities Act of 1876, whereby the sciences of religion became a field of study within Dutch state universities and dogmatic and practical theology were remanded to denominational seminaries. According to Jonathan Z. Smith again, the sciences of religion now took theology's place and were "assumed to be more 'neutral and scientific.'"[7] Increasingly, theology appeared to have less and less of a place in the modern university; if it was permitted to stay in the university, the argument for its retention often followed Kant's and Schleiermacher's appeal that it was in the interest of the state to have an adequately trained clergy.

When we move to the United States, the narrative intensifies the distinction not now between humane and divine sciences but between theology and all other academic disciplines. Originally, the study of religion, including theology, was located in divinity schools and denominational colleges and universities and hence was tied to the training of clergy and the preservation and transmission of religious traditions. But in a country in which the separation of church and state has played so central a role, the study of religion was not surprisingly absent in public educational institutions. In the last thirty years, the situation has greatly changed. The pivotal point in the United States, is, according to many commentators, the 1963 Supreme Court decision, known as *School District of Abington v. Schempp*, that distinguished the teaching *about* religion and the teaching *of* religion. That case dealt with a Pennsylvania law requiring the reading of Bible verses in public schools. In a concurring opinion supporting the main ruling of the Court, Justice Goldberg made the now famous distinction between the teaching *about* and the teaching *of* religion, the distinction between studying something and proclaiming something. The former was now deemed acceptable in public institutions as long as it was clearly distinguished from the teaching of religion, i.e., from the induction of students into particular religious traditions, beliefs, and practices. Religious studies, as the exploration of religion, could finally claim its rightful place in the academy as a neutral, objective, and nonreligiously driven intellectual discipline. For those who articulate the logic of the court ruling in defense of religious studies, public universities are to progressively take over the academic study of religion and divinity schools and theological schools, identified with religious commitments, fade in academic importance. Theology, for its part, becomes interpreted as one religious practice among others—something to be studied as one studies the ritual practices of a religious community, but not to be viewed as an equal intellectual endeavor or a legitimate means of studying religion itself. The long journey from theology as an expression of religious life and a vehicle of ecclesial power to religious studies as disciplined inquiry into human phenomena serving the dictates of the university is now, the story goes, almost complete.

There are a number of assumptions embedded in this version of our history that lead to certain normative conclusions about scholarship, the university, and who rightfully might claim a place within academic disciplines. One set clusters around the notions of academic study as objective, neutral, impartial. To be a scholar is to retain a judicious distance from one's subject matter. As Donald Wiebe has stated, "the break with the theological or religious perspective was a deliberate attempt to move towards an intellectual impartiality towards religious traditions other than one's own and to be objective in a detached and scientific manner."[8] For some scholars, this judicious distancing entails the bracketing of one's own religious beliefs in the academic context, the steadfast maintenance of the difference between as Martin Jaffee puts it "professing religion" and "religious confession."[9] For Jaffee, a scholar certainly may have "personal beliefs" that in and of themselves do not discredit his/her scholarly identity. Moreover, such a religious identity and its acknowledgement might well serve educational purposes. However, these religious commitments must, in the practice of scholarship, take a back seat to at least a methodological "impartiality." One way of doing this is to understand religious studies as primarily a descriptive endeavor that relinquishes any interest in evaluating beliefs or practices or making normative proposals of its own. Questions of "truth," however defined, or even utility are left out of the discussion. A scholar might report on the fact that some Christians believe in God, but avoid the issue of whether or not such a reality in fact exists or even whether beliefs of this sort are "healthy," "useful," or "serve particular political purposes," etc.

Another version of what I am labeling judicious distance has somewhat different repercussions. That approach suggests a real tension between the personal holding of beliefs, convictions and values identified as religious and the scholarly enterprise. Here, a more active "disbelief" is the requirement for the "objective" or scientific study of religion. This perspective has taken varied forms, ranging from the somewhat mild suggestion that one should never study one's own group to the stronger assertion that "disbelief" is the partner of the naturalized study of religion. In the latter view, religious perspectives are often taken to assume the transcendent, supernatural nature of religions and their objects, while the academic, i.e. objective and scientific study of religions, assumes their "natural" status, seeing religious beliefs and practices as open to explanation and indeed criticism. It is precisely, according to Bruce Lincoln, "the refusal to ratify its (religion's) claim of transcendent nature and sacrosanct status" that is the starting point of religious studies.[10] While for Lincoln himself this starting point does not necessarily entail "cynicism" toward the objects of religious study, it does rule out, for scholars *qua* scholars, being advocates for religious communities and perspectives, or, as he puts it, becoming "cheerleaders, voyeurs or retailers of import goods."[11] For others, the repercussions are even stronger—the secular assumptions of the university require both the naturalizing of religion, that is its treatment as a human phenomenon, and a certain skepticism about and even antagonism or hostility toward the objects of its study. The perspective of the academy, epitomized in the secular university, is not a "view from nowhere" but one that assumes and embraces a secularized and naturalized view of all phenomena and hence, at its core, is not only non-religious but in fact antireligious.[12]

Where does theology fit into this scenario? For many, many thinkers, theology is located on the religious side of the equation. This can be seen on several closely interrelated levels. The first has to do with what might be termed the identity or motivation of the theologian. Theologians are assumed to carry out their tasks in the service of the preservation and extension of a particular religious community. Theologians are taken to variously assist their traditions, indoctrinate, or, put less pejoratively, induct their students into particular ways of life, act as advocates on behalf of particular religions, be caretakers or proselytizers. That is, theologians are classic insiders, motivated by commitments to a religious worldview or community. By both religious studies scholars and conservative religious proponents, theologians are assumed to be believers and practitioners—for many the unbelieving or religiously unattached theologian is an oxymoron. While other scholars are designated according to their subject matter, theologians are identified by their presumed motivations as servants of religious values and then ruled out on this basis as legitimate academics.

It is not only the religious identity of the theologian that carries with it certain assumptions but also often presuppositions about the subject matter of theology. As noted above, many religious studies scholars assume that "religion's viewpoint" entails assumptions of the supernatural or nonhuman status of religious claims, experiences, and practices. Theologians, too, are taken to share this assumption, and thus naturalized interpretations of religion are assumed to be nontheological or antitheological in nature and vice versa. If a scholar interprets religious beliefs and practices as historical human constructions, then he or she is no longer thought to be a theologian but now to be something else. To be a theologian, thus, entails not only being a practitioner and a believer, but also someone who shares assumptions about the supra or at least nonnatural status of religions and their objects of devotion.

Finally, given their motivation and religious identity, their loyalty to religious communities and traditions, and their sense of the supernatural character of the objects they study, theologians are taken to argue on behalf of their claims, not according to the canons of public reason, but by recourse to special or privileged sources. To argue theologically, it is presumed, *is* to present reasons that make sense according to the dictates of a tradition, *not* to offer arguments that would carry weight within an academic context. In sum, theologians are believers or practitioners whose audience is fellow believers or practitioners and whose purpose is finally religious as opposed to academic. If outsiders are addressed, it is for apologetic or proselytizing purposes. Theologians may be intellectuals but who they are, the audience they address, the reasons they carry out their work, and the place they should be carrying it out all locate theologians outside the parameters of the academy.

This historical narrative, with its assumptions and implications, is, I believe, a prominent, perhaps the reigning, narrative of the academy. And in many ways it helps us understand where we have come from and how the current debates and positions have taken shape. But it is not one that is going unchallenged or at least unrevised. There are those who have attempted to complexify the story by pointing out, as McCutcheon has, that the very notion of religion as a *sui generis,* autonomous sphere is not only the product of theologians and believers but also the product of the emergence of religious studies itself, as scholars sought an appropriate object of analysis. In particular, McCutcheon and others have identified those thinkers associated with the history of religions' trajectory and especially Mircea Eliade as major proponents of this interpretation of religion. Other scholars have raised different kinds of issues about the idea of religion and the discipline that studies religious phenomena. José Casanova, in *Public Religions in the Modern World,*[13] and Linell E. Cady, in an essay entitled "Loosening the Category that Binds: Modern 'Religion' and the Promise of Cultural Studies,"[14] each note that this idea of religion developed along with that of the secular and that it cannot be understood except in relation to modern nation-states and their secularized public sphere—precisely as religion emerged as an autonomous sphere, it was simultaneously privatized and set over against a supposedly secular public sphere. In these views, both the religious and the secular spheres become problematized. David Chidester, in his work *Savage Systems: Colonialism and Comparative Religion in Southern Africa,* has argued that modern notions of religion were not just the province of either scholars or believers in Europe but developed in the context of colonialism in frontier situations in which explorers, colonial representatives, clergy, and merchants all used religion to further the colonialist project.[15] And, in an article in a recent book, *Religion in the Making: The Emergence of the Sciences of Religion,* Arie L. Molendijk offers a far more nuanced interpretation of the famed Dutch Act on Higher Education. Far from being a clear-cut case of theology vs. the sciences of religion, the Act represented, according to Molendijk, the attempt to reshape theology, not do away with it. The debates about the science of religion were not about how to accomplish "emancipation from the patronizing power of theology" or about how to establish a new academic discipline. They were, rather, about the proper way to do theology. Moreover, the Act's major proponents were liberal Protestants who sought to put theology on a more scientific footing, doing so not out of antagonism toward religion, but to prove their own religion was the best. In Molendijk's words "they (liberal Protestants) believed in an unbiased, non-confessional study of religion, which would in the end prove the superiority of their own liberal Protestantism."[16]

In many ways, the greatest challenges to the interpretations of theology, religion, and the academy have been side effects of developments in cultural theory broadly conceived. I cannot rehearse all the arguments that have been taking shape in current cultural theory. But I do want to raise up several central claims and then explore how they might change the dynamics described above and in particular inquire whether they are suggestive about ways to rethink religious studies and theology. For this discussion, the most important claims relate to the assertions concerning culture and religion as a dimension of culture. Increasingly, cultures are being conceived as dynamic processes of historical invention and negotiation, which are neither unified nor stable, but in which continual struggles for power, meaning, and identity take place. Culture, in this sense, does not refer to some separate sphere. Certainly culture or cultures are not only the domain of elites; in the postmodern theories of culture prevalent today, "high" and "popular" culture exist on a continuum, with no absolute delineation possible. Nor does the term refer only to the realm of ideas or symbolic production, as though symbolic and ideational forms exist in separation from the material aspects of human history. This all pushes toward the conclusion that there is no "culture in general" but only the particular configurations of specific human groupings that can be studied only in their concrete specificity. Culture thus becomes an encompassing heuristic term that allows us to trace the multiple, complex, and conflictual interactions of various dimensions of human life, especially as those relate to the distribution and circulation of power.

When such assumptions are the starting point, the modern notion of religion as an autonomous sphere also falls apart. First, as culture in general disappears, so too does the idea of generic religion, of an essential religious experience, set of beliefs, or common practices that are the same everywhere. Religion is replaced by religions, by concrete traditions of belief and practice that can never be known abstractly but only concretely. Second, the idea that has accompanied that of generic religion—the idea that the religious constitutes a separate, *sui generis* sphere—also is questioned. There are no spheres of human life that are cut off or nonentangled with other aspects of culture. The claims that there exists a singular religious realm demanding specialized scholars practicing unique methods thus begin to collapse: the "religious" becomes one aspect of cultural reality and hence open to the same efforts at interpretation and explanation as are other aspects of human culture. The challenge here has been not only to the proponents of *sui generis* religion or generic religion but also to other contemporary thinkers who emphasize the particularity of religious traditions while seeing them as self-contained or self-referential, able to be explained without reference to things such as economics, politics, or other cultural or religious traditions. Both self-enclosed particularity and amorphous generality are ruled out here. Thus, to study religions is not only to analyze particular traditions and configurations but also to see them as part of wider cultural interactions and mechanisms. If culture cannot be understood without reference to religion, neither can religions be adequately interpreted except as part of culture. Third, the methods and approaches for the study of religions should not be assumed to be unique to the subject matter but to be the same theoretical tools that are appropriate to the rest of human realities. Religious studies has neither an utterly unique subject matter nor distinctive methodologies; it is one humanistic endeavor among others.

On many levels, these claims appear to be the culmination of those tendencies in the modern period that did not take the turn toward religion as a uniquely autonomous realm but sought to naturalize religion and bring its study into the modern academic enterprise, especially in its social scientific mode. According to some, what current cultural theory has done is challenge and render problematic lingering essentialist and "theological" tendencies that have continued to corrupt religious studies and render it suspect in the academy. Dreams of absolute principles, of supernatural origins, of ahistorical authorities, of pure traditions shaping but not shaped by worldly realities may all continue to be objects of study but should no longer infect how religious studies conceives of itself as a discipline or how it delineates the object of its study.

But the naturalizing or, perhaps better, the culturalizing of religion is only part of the story. For contemporary cultural theory, analysis, and criticism have also raised serious questions about the claims to objectivity, impartiality, and neutrality that have been the hallmark of the modern academy. The academy, too, is a cultural reality; it like everything else is thoroughly implicated in cultural interactions. Far from being the site of neutral and value-free analysis, the university is one more juncture in the circulation of power, the manufacture of symbolic and material goods, and the construction and deployment of cultural values and visions. What it is not is some still point in the cultural universe that stands above or outside the cultural fray. Just as the distance is narrowed between high and low culture and popular religion and venerable religious traditions and institutions, so too the distance is narrowed between academic practices and the cultural practices such as religion that scholars seek to study.

What does this "culturalizing" of both religion and the academy suggest for theologians and theology? Several proposals or models have emerged that take these developments seriously and hence seek to rearticulate the relation between theology, as an academic enterprise, and the academy.[17] Often these draw upon, though not always consistently, the arguments just noted. One approach sees religious studies and theological studies as separate enterprises, with differing purposes and locales. The change here is that they need not be related in a hierarchical or antagonistic manner but can be interpreted to have the status of separate but equal intellectual endeavors; the pejorative connotations associated with theology are muted. Theologians are still understood as believers and practitioners and are still understood to serve religious communities. Religious studies scholars just serve other communities. This is, I think, a widespread current compromise that we find in the AAR today, institutionalized in the language that refers to religious and theological studies as distinct enterprises that share, we might say, the same building or at least the same annual meeting program.[18]

A second possibility is that the academy's pretensions of objectivity, neutrality, and impartiality have now been unmasked and such unmasking should lead to a new understanding of what is permitted in the university. As we turn our critical gaze to the academy, what is revealed is not impartiality at all but the antireligious assumptions and commitments of the secular university. The academy embodies, as Page Smith put it in his book, *Killing the Spirit: Higher Education in America,* an "academic fundamentalism" that tolerates only certain kinds of ideas in the academy, certainly not religious ones.[19] Once this is acknowledged and once the inevitability of the value laden and normative character of scholarly pursuits is made clear then, according to this argument, the university should be open to all sorts of perspectives, including religious and theological ones. This is what I term the "everything is really theology in disguise, so theology should be included in the academy" argument. Here, theologians are still identified with religious communities and commitments but should now be welcomed into an academy that is self-critical and truly open to multiple contending cultural voices.

A third way of approaching the situation argues *against* the claims that religious commitments and academic commitments are necessarily in tension. This perspective rejects the notion that the university is at heart secular or antireligious and seeks to articulate ways in which, on the one hand, religious and theological visions might contribute to the work of higher education and, on the other, how critical reflection can contribute to religious vitality. There are, to reduce the arguments to caricature, Catholic and Protestant versions of this argument. The Catholic has emphasized, as it has for centuries, the supportive relation of reason and faith in the service of God, and the Protestant view, emphasizing the radical transcendence that calls all human enterprises into question, has linked critical reason to religious commitment. Here the anti-intellectualism of much religion and the antireligious sentiments of much of the academy are both rejected. Theology, in this view, is not only permitted in the university but might well hold a valued position as the site of integration and fuller critical reflection on both religious traditions and the larger societal good the university seeks to serve. For the most part, theologians continue to be assumed to be members of and representatives for particular religious traditions, with this not being seen as a problem but a strength.[20]

A fourth and, for our purposes, final option that is being articulated takes more seriously, I think, the shifts indicated by cultural theory.[21] It should be stated that holders of especially the immediately preceding position can and sometimes do see themselves as also embracing, at least in part, this option. According to this position, the university is not a neutral site but one that does embody all sorts of values and commitments, including commitments to open inquiry, critical reflection, and public argumentation. These are indeed not impartial values. They have emerged within human history (including from within human religious history) and represent certain cultural values and options over others. In contrast to those who would argue that the recognition of the nonneutral character of the university mandates the admission of all voices as equal, this view suggests another conclusion. Only those who are willing to enter the sphere of public argumentation in which they make their case in conversation with their fellows are welcome. Such canons of public argumentation are the result of ongoing historical negotiation and hence open to contestation and transformation. Moreover, as various cultural theorists have suggested, there are diverse and conflicting versions of these canons and there are counter or alternative values that contend for ascendancy. But their historical and cultural character does not, in the context of the university, make them illegitimate. As Jonathan Z. Smith has stated, "the anthropology of the last century, the study of religions in the academy, has contributed to making more difficult a naïve, ethnocentric formulation of the 'rules of reason,' but this does not require that such 'rules' be denied, or suggest that we should slacken in our attempts to formulate them."[22]

The attempt to formulate the historicized rules of reason and to live within them in the academy requires several commitments. It means that scholars must continually cultivate a self-critical and self-reflective attitude toward their own assumptions, methodologies, and conclusions. If reverence toward the religious objects of our academic investigation is, as Bruce Lincoln has declared, not a scholarly virtue, then neither is an uncritical stance toward our own procedures and contingent values.[23] To acknowledge the historicized and culturalized character of our "rules of reason" requires that we are always willing to question and revise them in light of changing information and circumstances, including the recognition that, across the disciplines of academic inquiry, wide ranges of data, experience, and perspectives have historically been denied access to the academy. Furthermore, while reverence may not be the ideal academic stance towards objects of inquiry, neither is contempt; self-critical reflexivity entails the willingness not only to criticize but also to be challenged by that which we seek to study.

To commit oneself to work within the university requires, thus, a delicate balancing act. On the one hand, scholars can only study, interpret, and proffer explanations for what falls within the range of human knowing. This entails, I think, something like the naturalizing and culturalizing of the human phenomena we study; it involves, in particular, the treatment of religious beliefs, practices, and institutions as part of human culture and history that can and must be studied using the multiple approaches applicable to all other human realities. On the other hand, such an approach should not determine ahead of time what interpretive strategies or explanatory paradigms are legitimate or illuminating of the myriad data that confront the scholar. In a context that prizes open and critical inquiry, many approaches are required and all claims that are willing to be tested according to the canons of such inquiry deserve a hearing.

These commitments—to self-critical reflexivity on the part of scholars, to treating religions as human phenomena like other human phenomena, and to arguing for our interpretations in the public context—allow many interpretations and explanations to enter the academic fray. They rule no position in or out because of its origins but only according to whether it is willing to be tested according to reigning academic criteria. Thus, as David Griffin has put it, "pedigree would be ignored in favor of performance."[24] Or as Richard Rorty has recently noted, the origin of an idea is not determinative of its acceptability. Ideas and visions and values emerging in religious communities are neither ruled out of court nor given a privileged status.[25]

This position also suggests that, just as the origin of an interpretation or explanation is less important than how it holds up in the court of academic argumentation, so too the religious identity or nonidentity of the scholar becomes a moot issue. Scholars all have perspectives embued with values and cultural commitments. The question again is not whether we have them or can bracket them but whether they become part of the data for self-critical analysis and whether they undermine our commitments to critical and open inquiry.

What does all of this suggest for theology and for theologians whose primary professional identity is as scholars within the academy? As a way of closing, I will list, though not unpack, several ideas:

1. The subject matter of academic theology is the identification, critical analysis, and construction of religious beliefs and practices understood as cultural phenomena.
2. A theologian is differentiated from other scholars of religion by subject matter, not religious affiliation or lack thereof. This means, therefore, that being an academic theologian neither rules out nor requires that the theologian belong to, share the beliefs of, or participate in the practices of the community she or he studies. Identity and motivation are not what differentiate a theologian from other academics who study religions.
3. Academic theology is not a separate or competing discipline positioned over against religious studies but is a subset of the wider field of the academic study of religions.
4. As scholars in a subdiscipline of the field of religious studies, theologians can, as other scholars do, make interpretations, explanations, and normative proposals, but they, also like other scholars, must argue for them according to the canons of the university.
5. The primary audience of the academic theologian is his or her students and academic colleagues. An academic theologian can, as do other scholars, have secondary audiences, such as the larger society or indeed religious communities. Just as political scientists or economists or space scientists may hope and intend that their research will have wider impact, so too might religious studies scholars, including academic theologians. But, as it is important for scientists and other scholars to resist the commodification of knowledge and the reduction of

research to market interests, while simultaneously providing knowledge for the wider community, so too must religious studies scholars seek to contribute to the broadening of knowledge without reducing their scholarly efforts to the interests of particular subcommunities.

6. The primary purpose for carrying out the work of academic theology is, thus, not the preservation of a religious tradition, the induction of students into a way of life, or caregiving to religious communities. Nor is it the destruction of these communities. The primary purpose is that of the university generally, to quote a few notables: "widening the conversation of mankind" (Geertz), "deepening understanding" (Karen McCarthy Brown), "reducing puzzlement" (Margery Wolf), and "making intelligible all human phenomena" (Jonathan Z. Smith). Such purposes may indeed serve religious communities, or may seriously undermine their viability, but those are secondary results, not primary purposes. Moreover, to the point of this essay, they are purposes to which academic theologians, no less than other scholars, might commit themselves.

The study of religions is not what it was in the nineteenth century. Its varied subdisciplines have engaged in both historical examination and theoretical analysis that have led to the radical revisioning about what constitutes the field, what methods are applicable, what terms make sense, and even what constitutes the object of our inquiry. Few today would cavalierly claim for religious studies an essential character that has defined it in all times and places and that determines its parameters today. This essay suggests that theology, too, is a historical and cultural phenomenon, that it lacks an invariant character or essence, and that its practitioners are engaged, no less than other religious studies scholars, in a radical reworking of its tasks. To fail to recognize this is to engage in ideologically driven rhetoric, not scholarship—at least not scholarship with very good footnotes.[26]

NOTES

1. Ray L. Hart, "Religious and Theological Studies in American Higher Education: A Pilot Study," *Journal of the American Academy of Religion* 59, no. 4 (1991): 732.

2. Russell T. McCutcheon, *Manufacturing Religion: The Discourse of Sui Generis Religion and the Politics of Nostalgia* (New York: Oxford University Press, 1997).

3. Hart, "Religious and Theological Studies in American Higher Education: A Pilot Study," 732.

4. Mark C. Taylor, "Introduction" in *Critical Terms for Religious Studies*, ed. Mark C. Taylor (Chicago: University of Chicago Press, 1998), 13.

5. Jonathan Z. Smith, "The Devil in Mr. Jones" in *The Insider/Outsider Problem in the Study of Religion: A Reader*, ed. Russell T. McCutcheon (London: Cassell, 1999), 370.

6. Van A. Harvey, *The Historian and the Believer: The Morality of Historical Knowledge and Christian Belief*, 3rd ed. (Urbana/Chicago: University of Illinois Press, 1996), 38.

7. Jonathan Z. Smith, "The Devil in Mr. Jones," 371.

8. Donald Wiebe, "Does Understanding Religion Require Religious Understanding?" in *The Insider/Outsider Problem in the Study of Religion: A Reader*, ed. Russell T. McCutcheon (London: Cassell, 1999), 299. See also Wiebe, *The Politics of Religious Studies* (New York: St. Martin's Press, 1998) for his argument for religious studies as "scientific" vs. theology as a faith practice.

9. Martin S. Jaffee, "Fessing Up in Theory: On Professing and Confessing in the Religious Studies Classroom" in *The Insider/Outsider Problem in the Study of Religion: A Reader*, ed. Russell T. McCutcheon (London: Cassell, 1999), 284.

10. Bruce Lincoln, "Theses on Method" in *The Insider/Outsider Problem in the Study of Religion: A Reader*, ed. Russell T. McCutcheon (London: Cassell, 1999), 397.

11. Ibid., 398.

12. See John Milbank, *Theology and Social Theory: Beyond Secular Reason* (Oxford: Basil Blackwell), 1990, and Robert N. Bellah, "Religious Studies as 'New Religion'" in *Understanding the New Religions*, ed. Jacob Needlemann and George Baker (New York: Seabury Press, 1978), 106–112, for the argument that religious studies is an expression of secular ideology.

13. José Casanova, *Public Religion in the Modern World* (Chicago: University of Chicago Press, 1994).

14. Linell E. Cady, "Loosening the Category that Binds: Modern 'Religion' and the Promise of Cultural Studies" in *Converging on Culture: Theologians Dialogue with Cultural Analysis and Criticism*, ed. Delwin Brown, Sheila Greeve Davaney, and Kathryn Tanner (New York: Oxford University Press, 2001).

15. David Chidester, *Savage Systems: Colonialism and Comparative Religion in Southern Africa* (Charlottesville: Universtiy of Virginia Press, 1996).

16. Arie L. Molendijk, "Transforming Theology: the Institutionalization of the Science of Religion in the Netherlands" in *Religion in the Making: The Emergence of the Sciences of Religion*, ed. Arie L. Molendijk and Peter Pels (Leiden: Brill, 1998), 70, 75. See also Richard King, *Orientalism and Religion: Postcolonial Theory, India and 'The Mystic East'* (New York: Routledge, 1999), especially chapter 2, for both a review of the western and Christian shaping of the notion of religion and a nuanced analysis of the current issues and options.

17. There is another option sometimes cited in which theology becomes the encompassing rubric and religious studies is a subset of theology. Since such a position holds little credence in the American situation, I have not noted it. See Richard King, *Orientalism and Religion*, and Francis Schüssler Fiorenza, "Theological and Religious Studies: The Contest of the Faculties" in *Shifting Boundaries: Contextual Approaches to the Structure of Theological Education*, ed. Barbara G. Wheeler and Edward Farley (Louisville, Kentucky: Westminster/John Knox Press, 1991), 119–149, for both analyses and criticisms of this paradigm.

18. Francis Schüssler Fiorenza's position in "Theological and Religious Studies: The Contest of the Faculties" can be read as a slightly transformed version of this position. In this essay, Fiorenza suggests the difference between the two disciplines is that religious studies deals with multiple traditions and theology works within singular traditions.

19. Page Smith, *Killing the Spirit: Higher Education in America* (New York: Penguin Books, 1990) 5–6, 107.

20. See Peter C. Hodgson, *God's Wisdom: Toward a Theology of Education* (Louisville, Kentucky: Westminster John Knox Press, 1999).

21. This fourth option most clearly articulates my own position. See also Davaney, "Theology and the Turn to Cultural Analysis" in *Converging on Culture: Theologians Dialogue with Cultural Analysis and Criticism*, ed. Delwin Brown, Sheila Greeve Davaney, and Kathryn Tanner (New York: Oxford University Press, 2001), and Davaney, *Pragmatic Historicism: A Theology for the Twenty-First Century* (Albany: State University of New York Press, 2000).

22. Jonathan Z. Smith, "The Devil in Mr. Jones," 373.

23. Bruce Lincoln, "Theses on Method," 396. Lincoln's own new book is an excellent example of just such disciplinary critical reflection. See *Theorizing Myth: Narrative, Ideology and Scholarship* (Chicago: University of Chicago Press, 1999).

24. David Ray Griffin, "Professing Theology in the State University," in *Theology and the University: Essays in Honor of John B. Cobb, Jr.*, ed. David Ray Griffin and Joseph C. Hough, Jr. (Albany: State University of New York Press, 1991), 30.

25. Richard Rorty, "Religious Faith, Intellectual Responsibility, and Romance," in *Pragmatism, Neo-Pragmatism, and Religion: Conversation with Richard Rorty*, ed. Charley D. Harwick and Donald A. Crosby (New York: Peter Lang, 1997).

26. See Lincoln, *Theorizing Myth: Narrative, Ideology and Scholarship*, especially the Epilogue.

11

Religious Studies and the Alienation of Theology

DARRELL J. FASCHING

IS THEOLOGY A DISCIPLINE
WITHOUT A FUTURE IN THE ACADEMY?
THE CHALLENGE OF "SECULAR ORTHODOXY"
IN RELIGIOUS STUDIES

Ninian Smart seems to speak for many in a recent *CSSR Bulletin* devoted to the issue of theology and religious studies.[1] According to Smart: "Religious Studies, as conceived and developed during the 1960's and beyond, is the multidisciplinary or polymethodic study of religions and analogous institutionalized ideologies (such as East German Marxism, varying nationalisms, and so on)." Theology, by contrast, he says, "typically connects to denominational roots in a community."[2] Religious studies is secular, impartial, and empathic; theology is religious, partisan, and apologetic. Theologies and theologians are data which religious studies scholars sometimes study, alongside of texts, rituals, archeological artifacts, etc. Religious studies, Smart asserts, is empirical, descriptive, explanatory, and methodologically agnostic while theology is "essentially preaching" no matter how sophisticated it gets. It is the difference, we are told, between "descriptive studies and value judgments" and anyone who can't tell the difference is "unprofessional."[3] In contrast, engaging in religious studies, he tells us, is like holding up a mirror to the religions of the world, it reflects them but makes no judgments, leaving that to each individual beholder.

Smart does entertain the notion that in the "modern world" there might be something like a "pluralist theology department" exploring diverse theological worldviews with a view to judging their coherence and truth values, but this would not itself be theology but rather a "multiform philosophy of religion." Indeed, Smart goes so far as to warn theologians not to try to sneak into religious studies under the guise of philosophy of religion: "If you think theology is a reputable discipline, remember you cannot call it cross-cultural philosophy of religion or Worldview Reflection."[4] In contrast to these restrictions that Smart places on theology, he views religious studies as "non-finite" in nature. Its subject matter is inherently open-ended, including things like "nationalisms" and "Marxism." Religious studies "needs to go beyond religion as conventionally and traditionally understood."[5]

It is odd and somewhat arbitrary that Smart views theology in essentialist terms and religious studies in existentialist terms. Theology is what it is and must never try to become anything else, while religious studies is seen as open-ended and self-transcending, going beyond conventional understandings. Unlike religious studies, theology has only a past but no future (except to repeat its past). It is a curious worldview offered us by the master of "worldview analysis." In the absence of any reasons why we should accept these antithetical characterizations, one has to judge Smart's distinctions to be ideological and arbitrary.

Every discipline, I would argue, is defined by a history of questions that lead to answers that raise yet further questions. In this fashion, the horizons of every discipline continue to be transformed in often new and surprising ways. This is as true of physics as it is of theology. Moreover, as Smart argues, institutional contexts play an important role in defining intellectual activity. In the move from the monasteries and church schools to the universities, theology learned to serve two masters. It became a form of inquiry responsive not only to church authority but also to the Aristotelian philosophical canons of rationality. The emergence of scholastic theology in the first universities of medieval Europe was an important moment in the emergence of the autonomy of academic disciplines.

Today all disciplines are guided only by their own internal canons of rationality. Traditional theology, however, typically still serves two masters. Nevertheless, with the differentiation and autonomy of disciplines as the defining feature of the modern university, the stage has been set for the further transformation of theology itself. We are now witnessing the emergence of academic theology as distinct from church (confessional and apologetic) theology. It would be a great irony if the theological guilds that were integral to the founding of the university tradition (along with those of medicine and law) would be the only academic communities of inquiry to be excluded from the university, not by the logic of their own requirements but by the new secular orthodoxy of those, like Ninian Smart, who refuse to allow theology to undergo the evolution permitted to other disciplines.

Does Religious Studies Have a Future Without Theology? Religious Studies, Theology, and the Sacred

If the secular orthodox have their way, theology will be studied as a datum in religious studies but the doing of constructive theology will be forbidden as a violation of the line between "being religious" and "studying religion." This view is driven by a social science model of religious studies as a "value-free" activity. Smart concludes that theology is basically "preaching" because it is not social science. According to Smart, "Christian Theology might be a humanities discipline, but it is not a social science and no one so far as I know recognizes it as such."[6]

While Smart grudgingly admits that the humanities do have a place in religious studies and the university, curiously, he seems to view them as marginal at best, perhaps because, like preaching, they sometimes express themselves normatively. However, unlike preaching, the humanities operate by public norms of rationality specific to their areas of inquiry in ways analogous to other disciplines in the university. To marginalize the humanities is both common and very dangerous. A university in which the humanities in their normative modes of reflection are viewed as marginal is a university educating a generation of technological barbarians—those whose knowledge of scientific facts and technological skills are for sale to the highest bidder without qualms, since all normative views are purely "subjective."

The terms in which Ninian Smart puts the issue between religious studies and theology predetermines his conclusion, and does so in quite an arbitrary way. The issue is not whether church theology belongs in religious studies (other than as a datum of study) but whether there can be an academic mode of theologizing. His essentialist definition of theology precludes this possibility. I believe, however, that the inner contradictions in Smart's own position show that there not only can be, there must be, an academic mode of doing theology if religious studies is to maintain its integrity as an objective scholarly area of study.

In order to make that case, we need to look at the core problem in Smart's definition of religious studies. Ninian Smart has trouble limiting the study of religion to "religions" and includes nationalisms and Marxisms among its data because the real focus of our energies as scholars in this interdisciplinary area of study is not religion but "the sacred." Sociologist and theologian Jacques Ellul helps us get things into correct perspective when he argues that "the sacred is not one of the categories of religion. Religion, rather, is one possible rendition of the sacred."[7] Ellul, standing in the French sociological tradition that goes back to Durkheim, is simply stating what is obvious to sociologists and anthropologists: namely, that every society is legitimated by some sense of the sacred. This sense of the sacred pervades every aspect of culture, not just "religion" in its obvious institutional forms. Indeed, in most times and places in history, religion and culture have been indistinguishable. It is the differentiation of institutional and intellectual life in complex cultures, especially in modern "secular" cultures, that misleads us into thinking of religion as one institutional function alongside of many others in society. At some level, Smart half-consciously recognizes that "religion" is not the key category on which we ought to focus and so he makes the awkward suggestion that some "non-religious" phenomena ought to be included in religious studies. But such a suggestion surely indicates that there is something wrong with his fundamental categories. If Smart replaced "religion" with "the sacred" as the core concept of our discipline, recognizing that "religion" as an institutional phenomenon is only "one possible rendition of the sacred," the awkward bridging of religion and nonreligion in his work would disappear.

"Religion" must be defined in terms of the sacred and not vice versa. What we are really studying is the diverse ways in which a sense of the sacred is manifested and responded to in various cultural activities (in science, politics, economics, art, religions, etc.) and how that affects belief and action in every sphere of human activity People hold as sacred that which matters most to them. And what matters most typically centers on issues of life and death—issues of human destiny. Moreover, it is not just biological life that is at stake in these concerns but a "way of life." People around the globe universally hold their diverse ways of life sacred. Viewing some ways of life as religious and some as not, in the way that Smart does, distorts our ability to see this. And that distortion then makes religious studies scholars apologize for including "nonreligious" phenomena in the study of religion. The felt need to include such phenomena is an implicit recognition that another, more inclusive frame of reference is called for.

Our situation as scholars of the sacred is complicated by the fact that there is no neutral place to stand from which to evaluate these diverse sacred ways of life. For wherever we stand, we humanities scholars and social scientists are also part of a culture and/or subculture (an academic one) that considers its way of life sacred. Understanding this goes a long way toward understanding the reactions of someone like Ninian Smart to the intrusion of church theology into the modern academy, an academy whose sacred order was constructed precisely by excluding and/or privatizing "religion."

Smart is intent on protecting the sacred way of life in which he participates, as well he should be. But here is the paradox: he cannot do this without engaging in something like theological reflection. Smart says that theology is tied to a denominational community whereas religious studies is tied to the larger public. But this is not quite true. Certainly, statistically, the public (at least in the United States and almost everywhere outside of Europe) is overwhelmingly religious. Thus Smart's claim of legitimation by appeal to the larger public is not an empirical claim but a normative claim. It is, in his terms, a "value judgement" on what "public" *ought* to mean or which public *ought* to carry normative weight. If the truth be told, what Smart is really arguing is that the sacred way of life of the academy is tied not to the larger public but to that public shaped by the Enlightenment tradition. He is speaking of that elite portion of the public who has not only undergone education in the modern university but undergone conversion to its sense of what is sacred.

It should not surprise us then that Smart equates public and secular, for that is exactly the equation that was constructed by the Enlightenment privatization of religion. Nor should it surprise us that this particular public should be viewed by him as normative, because that is how the sacred affects human thought and behavior. Smart is himself a denominational thinker engaged in value judgments which he (quite wrongly) would label as "unprofessional" if engaged in by others. He is wrong to consider it "unprofessional" because such judgments are unavoidable. We do not need to avoid such judgments to be "professional" but we do need a way to make such judgments conscious, explicit, and accountable by the public canons of rationality that are continually refined self-critically within our traditions of scholarship. And that is why we need an academic theology, one which is more than just a "multiform philosophy of religion" in the modernist sense but very much a philosophical theology that has parallels with premodern theology, even as its pluralistic focus and academic context will give it a postmodernist orientation.

Just as religious studies is about more than "religions," so theology is about more than "God." If religious studies must be reconceived in terms of the study of "the sacred," manifest in a sacred way of life, theology must be reconceived in terms of "the holy," manifest as an experienced "inner" demand for self-transcendence that calls for an alternative way of life. "Theos" or "God" is only one name for such experiences (Buddhism, for example, offers significant alternatives). Theology is the task of critical normative reflection on the sacred dimensions of life. It is most accurate to call such activity philosophical theology rather than just philosophy, because all philosophy that engages in critique (whether in the sciences or humanities) is engaged in a critique of what is held as sacred. And all critique of the sacred, I would argue, is rooted in some experience of the holy. The early Buddhist questioning of the sacred order of caste society in the name of emptiness, and its construction of the sangha as a community of equals open to all strangers (even the outcaste), is an example.

In putting the issue this way, I realize I am using the terms "sacred" and "holy" in an unusual way—as antonyms rather than synonyms. What I have in mind in using these terms in this way can be illustrated not only by Theravada Buddhism but by the example of Socrates's critique of Athenian society. Socrates was arrested and put on trial for his life on two charges, impiety toward the gods and corrupting youth. His crime was asking people whether what they called the good really was the good. It was a crime of corrupting youth because he taught them to question the sacredness of the Athenian way of life and so led them astray. It was a crime of impiety toward the gods because what people called the good was a way of life legitimated by an appeal to divine origins. His enemies accused Socrates of being an atheist. But Socrates himself argued that, on the contrary, he was compelled to question the Athenian way of life by some mysterious God (apparently a stranger to the Athenian pantheon) who had sent him as a "gadfly" to the city of Athens. Thus Socrates's protest against the sacred order of Athenian society was itself rooted in an alternative type of religious experience. An experience he described as an inward motion of "the soul" toward a wholly other reality—an "Unseen Measure" which called all other measures of the public good into question.

For Socrates, the act of doubt and of questioning was apparently rooted in a form of religious experience, an openness to transcendence, to an infinite unseen measure that demanded of him a continual questioning. Our answers are always finite, but there are always more questions than answers, this is what keeps us open to the infinite. To follow the questions is to "go beyond" (the literal meaning of "transcendence") the answers and transcend the sacred worldview they presuppose. Socrates's crime was that he surrendered to the questions, which led him, in turn, to transcend the Athenian sacred way of life in order to propose an alternative way. The Athenians were not entirely wrong to be concerned. That which is sacred is virtually by definition "beyond questioning." The sacred is typically surrounded by a taboo that forbids all questions. Socratic questioning is inherently subversive and desacralizing, that is, secularizing activity. As with Buddhism, it produces the paradox of a form of religious expression that seems irreligious.

To identify this alternate category of religious experiences, that demands not conformity to sacred order but individual and communal self-transcendence, I am following Jacques Ellul's suggestion that the terms "sacred" and "holy" be used as antonyms. As the Hebrew term for "holy" (*qadosh*) suggests, to be holy is to be "set apart." When we are seized by doubt and by wonder, we are set apart from the sacred order of things. We find ourselves alienated from our sacred way of life and able to see it as if through the eyes of a stranger. Seeing from this perspective enables us to put all things in question. From this point of view, the inner demand for rationality (i.e., that our doubts and questions be pursued and answered) in every field of human inquiry is itself a form of religious experience (in the broadened sense of "religious" that this essay advocates)—an opening of the self to the infinite. For we do not initiate such experiences of doubt and wonder, they come upon us. We are seized by them, the way Siddhartha was when he felt compelled to leave the security of the palace grounds only to encounter the old man, the sick man, the dead man, and even more doubts and questions.

Such experiences demand from us the integrity to follow the questions wherever they lead.[8] Just as the sacred cannot be confined to "religions" neither can the holy. We ignore the inner demand for integrity at our own peril, whether we are doing physics, sociology, or theology. And it is this ongoing demand for integrity in every field of inquiry that gives each discipline a "self-transcending" history of open-ended development beyond the horizon of its originating questions. What we call the "autonomy" of modern academic disciplines is not really rooted in "self-rule" or self-possession (as the Greek roots of the term "autonomy" suggest), but rather in a surrender to the inner demand for self-transcendence, i.e., to follow the questions wherever they lead, even if they force us beyond our pet theories. The demand for integrity in our inquiries is a symptom of being seized by the holy—or to put it another way, of being seized by the infinite. This is what makes not only religious studies but also all academic disciplines non-finite and open-ended.

If such experiences were not an opening up to the infinite, we would not experience the gap between "what is" and "what might be," and between "what is" and "what ought to be." To make this claim does not, at this point, require making any metaphysical claims about "the Infinite." But it does require an ontological claim, namely, that our humanity is constituted by our openness to infinite possibilities that carry us beyond the horizon of possibilities culturally defined by the sacred order of our particular time and place. To be human is to be capable of migrating into new worlds in time, space, and imagination. Our openness to the infinite requires of us an openness to other worlds (both actual and possible). In this sense, the claims of the holy as a type of human experience demand from us a hospitality to strangers and their strange worlds. Theology, academically conceived, requires engagement with the plurality of human experiences of the sacred and the holy.

Academic theology is philosophical reflection upon and critique of the sacred in the name of the holy, beginning with our own sacred way of life as the first step. For without such critique, the ethnocentric bias of our sacred world limits the horizon of our insights. As a consequence, our analyses of other sacred ways of life will simply be a reflection of our own "denominational" prejudices—as Smart's dismissal of theology from the academy well illustrates. The irony is that the very model of objectivity that demands that we privatize normative judgements is what makes it impossible for Smart to be objective. If religious studies is purely descriptive, and normative reflection is privatized, as it is in Smart's modernist paradigm, then personal bias escapes public accountability and objectivity is undermined. Academic theology assumes that we all (whether "secular" orthodox or "religious" orthodox) begin our reflections from within a sacred world and holds us accountable. Academic theology is essential to our ability to function as scholars of religion in a way that does justice to the manifestations of the sacred and the holy in all their diversity. Therefore, I would maintain that there is no future for religious studies as an "objective" discipline without the inclusion of academic theology. Ninian Smart is right to suggest that confessional and apologetic theology, Christian or otherwise, is not an academic discipline as understood in the contemporary university, but he is wrong to suggest that theology cannot be academic.

THEOLOGY WITHIN THE CONTEXT OF RELIGIOUS STUDIES: FROM CHURCH THEOLOGY TO THEOLOGY OF CULTURE

Paul Tillich is the pivotal and pioneering figure for the emergence of academic theology. Tillich spent most of his life as an apologetic church theologian. However, that is not how he began his career nor how he ended it. At the beginning of his career, in his first published paper ("On the Idea of a Theology of Culture," which appeared in 1920), Tillich outlined a new direction for theology to be done within the framework of the modern university rather than the church.[9] It was a proposal for a theology of religions and cultures rather than a church theology. Over the next forty-five years, Tillich's energies were primarily consumed in doing apologetic theology on behalf of his own Christian tradition, culminating in his *Systematic Theology*. And yet, in the last paper he delivered just before he died in 1965, "On the Significance of the History of Religions for the Systematic Theologian,"[10] he returned to his original theme of developing a theology of the history of religions and cultures, as if he had gotten sidetracked in the intervening forty-five years and suddenly remembered what he had started out to do.

The question that preoccupied Tillich in his first published paper was the function of theology in a modern secularized, scientific culture, and the place of theology among the faculties of the modern university. Tillich's approach to religion and culture is especially relevant here for two reasons. First, he recognized that the study of religion was first and foremost the study of what people held sacred and that therefore religion could not be narrowly defined in opposition to other cultural activities. On the contrary, he sees religion and culture as two sides of the same coin. Second, he recognized that the academic study of religion changed the way in which one would have to do theology, so that the Christian theologian (and his or her parallels in other traditions) would have to learn to wear two hats—only one of which was appropriate for that part of his life spent in the academy. That is, academic theology could not be "Christian theology" in any traditional sense.

RELIGION AND CULTURE

Tillich's views in his 1920 essay reflect the sea change in human self-understanding that occurred during the nineteenth century. With the emergence of modern critical historiography and ethnography (giving rise to sociology and anthropology), human beings came to realize that they lived not directly in nature but rather in language and story—that is to say, in culture. For the first time in the history of civilizations, human beings thought of themselves as living not in a divinely constructed natural order but a humanly constructed social order. Consequently, natural theology would have to be replaced by theology of culture. Every culture, Tillich argued, is driven by its religious "substance," which is the human need for meaning expressed and embodied in its religious, that is, its "ultimate concerns" (i.e., what matters most or is held "sacred"). The way in which such meaning is expressed is shaped by the symbolic forms available in that culture.

Neither substance (i.e., meaning) nor form should be confused with the content of culture. The religious dimension is revealed not by the content in itself (whether it is scientific, political, economic, or artistic activity, etc.), but rather by the meaning attributed to the content through symbolic forms of expression (the narratives and ritual actions that convey the power and importance of these activities). This relationship between religion as the drive for meaning and culture as the expressed patterns or forms of meaning is summed up in Tillich's formula that "religion is the substance of culture and culture is the form of religion."

This way of approaching the question of the relationship of religion and culture therefore does not see religion so much as a separate sphere within culture but rather as a depth dimension that underlies all cultural activities, attributing to them a sense of sacred meaning, value, and purpose—whether that culture assumes a "religious" or a "secular" guise. At the same time, at the level of surface structure, religion as an institutional function of society plays an important but restricted role in the social order. This is because in a modern society every sphere of human activity is differentiated from every other and each has its own autonomy (whether we are speaking of the differentiation of disciplines in the university or the differentiation of institutional functions in society). That these activities should fall directly under the authority of the church (or any other single institution) would be alien and unacceptable. And yet the religious dimension remains pervasive, since each differentiated realm, whether intellectual or institutional, is a human activity rooted in an unconditional drive toward meaning, the religious substance of all cultural activities. Insofar as each is faithful to this religious dimension or drive for meaning, its "autonomy" may become "theonomous," that is, self-transcending. Religious substance, says Tillich, has the power to transform cultural form in every sphere of human activity.

THE PARTICULARITY OF THE THEOLOGIAN
AND THE PROBLEM OF NORMS

In the "modern university," it is no longer acceptable for a theologian on a university faculty to define his or her role confessionally. Nor is it acceptable for academic theology to be the intellectual arm of a church that dictates the normative order of society. This would threaten the autonomy characteristic of modern intellectual disciplines—the freedom to evolve their own self-definition in terms of the data, questions, and publicly verifiable criteria of judgment.

Thus Tillich argues that only when theology is understood as a "normative branch of knowledge concerned with religion" can it find its place in the secular university.[11] The theologian of culture then is not a church theologian. He is not bound by a confessional stance but is rather "a free agent," open to exploring the import of religious and cultural phenomenon in all their diversity. "As a theologian of culture, he has no interest in ecclesiastical continuity and this of course puts him . . . in danger of becoming a fashionable religious prophet."[12] As a human being, he needs to responsibly assume a concrete standpoint. That is, none of us exist in a religious and cultural vacuum. Each of us is shaped by some sense of the sacred and, therefore, every theologian must give account for his or her own particularity and how that shapes his or her perceptions of other sacred worlds.

Intellectual and ethical integrity demand that the concrete standpoint of the theologian be explicit and acknowledged in his or her work rather than implicit and unacknowledged. Thus a theologian of culture may also be a church theologian, but he will keep the two roles in a precarious dialectical balance. This, I would argue, is a task that every scholar of religious studies, not just theologians, must engage in. And to do that requires theological reflection on the part of each.

Our postmodern situation is forcing us to acknowledge that there is no neutral, universal public realm of discourse, and that "secular" discourse is just one more narrative tradition of sacred discourse alongside many others. There is no neutral language of explanation. Rather, each narrative world will have to stretch its vocabulary to understand and include the stranger and his or her world.

The theologian of culture, operating as an interdisciplinary scholar within the secular university, sets about this task in a manner that sets him or her apart from the confessional theologian. Theology is "brought . . . down from heaven to earth."[13] Theology of culture defines its subject matter not as "God" or "revelation," or even "dogma," but rather as the study and critique of human religious experience (i.e., of the sacred) in all its diversity. Tillich viewed the task of the theologian of culture as one of identifying and critiquing the religious dimension implicit in all culture, including secular culture. This critique draws upon a typology of possible relations between religious meaning and culture to which we have already made some allusions—namely, the typology of heteronomy, autonomy, and theonomy.

Heteronomy (i.e., rule by another) is the temptation to identify ultimate or sacred meaning with some particular institution, which then is experienced as having the authority to impose a normative order on self and society as if from the outside. Autonomy (i.e., self rule) rebels against authority imposed from the outside, seeing it as arbitrary and authoritarian, but makes the mistake of substituting its own vision of order, which is an equally arbitrary expression, making itself a law unto itself. Between these extremes there is always the possibility of "theonomous culture," which occurs whenever there is a surrender to the dynamic drive toward ultimacy that is at work in every sphere of human activity. Heteronomy and autonomy tend toward the opposite extremes of totalitarianism and anarchism. Theonomy, by contrast, represents a middle way born out of the inner dynamic of the drive toward ultimacy, which brings every finite form under the criticism of the experience of the infinite embodied in our doubts and questions. Theonomy is what happens, for example, in every scientific and every scholarly discipline whenever academics avoid dogmatic adherence to past theories (heteronomy), on the one hand, and arbitrary allegiance to their own pet theories (autonomy), on the other, and instead follow the questions wherever they lead. In this sense, what we call the autonomy of academic disciplines in the modern university is, at its best, "theonomy."

Theonomy is not about God (Theos) as a dogmatic category but about the experienced demand for self-transcendence—both individual and communal. Theonomy, in this context, must be understood to refer to all authentic experiences of self-transcendence, whether construed in theistic or nontheistic terms. It is the question put to every answer, the utopian inner drive for meaning and understanding that can break through any given form and transform any and every sphere of cultural activity. Thus, the ethical task of theology of culture is not to impose some arbitrary dogmatic heteronomous religious vision on culture, but to release the inner drive toward self-transcendence already at work in every sphere of culture.

Given that the data for critical reflection is the sacred dimension manifested in *all* realms of human activity, theology becomes, in the Socratic tradition, a "theological questioning of all cultural values."[14] Thus, although theology is relativized as a discipline, it retains a kind of universal relevance to all disciplines, and all realms of human experience and interest. This questioning of all cultural values presupposes the identification of theonomous or culturally self-transcending norms for the critique of cultures, wherever the sacred has been called into question, in order to remain open to the infinite (for example, Socrates's questioning of the good, Abraham's questioning of God in the name of justice, the Buddha's encouraging his followers to question all authority, even his own, etc).

ON THE IMPORTANCE OF BEING ALIENATED: ACADEMIC THEOLOGY, PHENOMENOLOGY, AND POSTMODERNISM

For Ninian Smart, what separates religious studies from theology is the phenomenological attitude of empathic and imaginative participation in the religious worldviews of diverse peoples. It is the ability to be both objective and sympathetic, "bracketing" one's own viewpoint in order to see the world through the eyes of the other.[15] Despite Smart's essentialist bias towards theology, there is no reason in principle why an academic theology could not operate out of a phenomenological attitude. And yet we must not underestimate how difficult such a task may be.

FROM TILLICH TO ELIADE

Tillich offers us a good example of the difficulty, for he never fully developed the theological model he proposed in 1920. When he returned to reflect on that model just before his death in 1965, he still could not free himself from his apologetic orientation. He spoke of his own theological stance as being "on the boundary"—between Christianity and secular culture, between Christianity and other religions, etc. But what the phenomenological attitude calls for is passing beyond the boundary and seeing the world through the eyes of the stranger. It requires the "bracketing" of one's own views and empathic participation in the worldviews of others. Tillich never succeeded in making this step.

His 1965 essay on "The Significance of the History of Religions for the Systematic Theologian" grew out of a seminar he had conducted in cooperation with Mircea Eliade the previous year. Despite proposing an academic theology of the history of religions, Tillich still offered a tentative Christological center to the history of religions that he outlined in that essay.[16] Tillich never quite became the free agent he envisioned at the beginning of his career. The reason, I think, is that for Tillich even the theologian of culture needed to speak from a concrete religious standpoint so as to avoid the irresponsible illusion that he or she could speak from some neutral vantage point. Tillich's dilemma was how to speak from a concrete standpoint (for instance, as a Christian) and still be open to other experiences of transcendence.

That openness, however, was exactly what Eliade advocated with his own phenomenological approach. Eliade described history of religions as bracketing one's own views in order to enter sympathetically into the diverse sacred worlds of cultures around the globe. Indeed, in his book *The Quest*, published in 1969,[17] Eliade suggested that such a phenomenological approach can lead to new normative insights. He argued that the comparative study of religions is the hermenutic key to the emergence of a new humanism, a humanism demanded by the pluralism of an emerging world civilization. His humanistic vision had what we might now see as a decidedly post-European and post-Christian orientation to it, an orientation that in its own way opens a door to postmodernism. Postmodernism is characterized, as Jean-Francois Lyotard suggests, by the collapse of totalistic metanarratives and an openness to narrative diversity.[18] I use "postmodern" here to suggest "a style of thought which is suspicious of classical [primarily Euro-centric] notions of truth, reason, identity and objectivity, of the idea of universal progress or emancipation, of single frameworks, grand narratives or ultimate grounds of explanation."[19] It is a style of thought that is decentered, ungrounded, playful, eclectic, and pluralistic.

Eliade's thought shared many of these characteristics. He called on Western scholars to grasp the relativity of their own cognitive positions, de-center their perspective, and see the world through non-European and non-Christian eyes. His hermeneutics of diverse sacred worlds, he argued, would generate a humanism that transcended Western culture to grasp the depth and breadth of the possibilities of the human in cross-cultural perspective, especially through attention to the religious experiences of Asia and of the primal religions. "Contrary to the natural sciences and to a sociology that strives to follow their model, hermeneutics ranges itself among the living sources of a culture. For, in short, every culture is constituted by a series of interpretations and revalorization of its 'myths' or its specific ideologies."[20] Therefore, culture is, itself, a form of "creative hermeneutics." We become, to a large degree, what we interpret ourselves to be in the face of ever new historical situations. The history of humanity ". . . from Paleolithic to present times is destined to occupy the center of humanist education, whatever the local or national interpretations. The history of religions can play an essential role in this effort toward a *planétisation* of culture."[21]

Both Tillich and Eliade, each in their own way, were moving toward the boundary between modern and postmodern consciousness. If modernity was defined by the hegemony of European and Christian culture, Eliade envisioned a time when religious studies and theology would be post-European, post-Christian, and hence postmodern. And yet Tillich could not entirely free himself from his Christocentrism, and Eliade would be suspect in the view of many postmodernists who would see him as replacing Christocentrism with an understanding of the "sacred" that was itself too monolithic or logocentric for all his praise of diversity. And both find a depth dimension in culture, where typically postmodernists find only superficiality.

FROM ALIENATION TO POSTMODERN THEOLOGY

Perhaps Ninian Smart is right after all. Perhaps theology can only be confessional and apologetic. As one who is a Christian yet committed to doing academic theology, I, too, face this challenge. And yet, as I have argued, it is not a challenge that is peculiar to Christians, or even to theology. As Tillich insisted, no theologian of culture can escape his or her own religious and cultural history. Nor can anyone else. Every scholar in the social sciences and humanities is a "participant observer" in the human condition being studied. There is no neutral vantage point from which to begin. As Alasdair MacIntyre and Stanley Hauerwas have both argued, no scholar lives in a storyless world, not even the Enlightenment modernist who pretends to. One must acknowledge one's particularity and find a way to stretch his or her own narrative worlds to make a place for the stranger.

I believe the way out of the dilemma created by the particularity of one's standpoint lies in the experience of alienation, of being a stranger even to oneself. I used to think that the experience of alienation was a problem in need of resolution. I have come to see it, however, as a promising opportunity, for when we have become strangers to ourselves, we experience a new vulnerability and (if we don't panic and retreat into some sacred and unquestionable world) a new openness to the other—other persons, other ideas, other cultures, and other ways of life.

The best way to describe the style of academic theology I am proposing is to suggest that it is a "decentered" or "alienated theology." Alienated theology is the opposite of apologetic theology. Apologetic theology seeks to defend the "truth" and "superiority" of one's own tradition against the "false," "inferior," and "alien" views of other traditions, much the way Ninian Smart defends his modernist understanding of religious studies vis-à-vis theology. Alienated theology, by contrast, is theology done "as if" one were a stranger to one's own narrative tradition, seeing and critiquing one's own tradition from the vantage point of the other's narrative tradition. It is my conviction that alienated theology is the appropriate mode for academic theology in an emerging postmodern world civilization.

There are two ways to enter world history, according to John Dunne—you can be dragged in by way of world war, or you can walk in by way of mutual understanding. By the first path, global civilization emerges as a totalitarian project of dominance that risks escalating into a nuclear apocalypse. By the second path, we prevent the first, creating global civilization through an expansion of our understanding of what it means to be human. This occurs when we *pass over* into another's religion and culture and *come back* with new insight into our own.[22]

"Passing over" short-circuits apocalyptic confrontation and inaugurates utopian new beginnings—new beginnings for the "postmodern" world of the coming millennium. Passing over enables a postmodern alienated theology, in which the bracketing of our own views occurs not just out of empathy but as part of a quest for insight and normative wisdom.

The alienation required to do academic theology converges with the phenomenological attitude required by religious studies (for what is "bracketing" but a form of estrangement from oneself to enter the world of the stranger?). It also converges (and this is important for me as a Christian) with the requirement of hospitality to the stranger that is central to the biblical tradition. In the biblical tradition, God, like the stranger, is the one whose ways and thoughts are not ours (Isaiah 55:8–9). To welcome the stranger is equivalent to welcoming God (Genesis 18:1–5), or the Messiah (Matt 25:35), or, at the very least, an angel of God (Hebrews 13:2). It is this convergence of alienation and the phenomenological attitude with the biblical tradition of hospitality that allows me to engage in academic theology without either privileging, or breaking faith with, my Christian commitments.

POSTMODERN THEOLOGY AND THE HUMANITIES

The danger of modern secular civilization, according to Eliade, is spiritual impoverishment—the smothering of the sacred beneath a veneer of secularity, creating an inability to understand the variety of sacred worlds that have shaped, and continue to shape, our humanity. This inability cuts modern individuals off from a sense of participation in life as a meaningful drama. And yet, he suggests, the sacred lies hidden in every secular culture just waiting to be awakened. That is the spiritual task of the academic study of religion, as Eliade envisioned it. "A considerable enrichment of consciousness," he tells us, "results from the hermeneutical effort of deciphering the meaning of myths, symbols, and other traditional religious structures; in a certain sense, one can even speak of the inner transformation of the researcher and, hopefully of the sympathetic reader. What is called the phenomenology and history of religions can be considered among the very few humanistic disciplines that are at the same time propeaedeutic and spiritual techniques."[23] In suggesting such a program for religious studies, Eliade has violated the sacred boundary between public and private forged by Enlightenment modernism. He has violated the boundary between the study of religions (as descriptive) and academic theology (as normative), between studying religion and being religious. Contrary to Ninian Smart, these are not inappropriate moves; they are a matter of integrity. To be so, however, they must be done self-consciously in a way that makes each scholar (not just the theologian) accountable. If all human activity is shaped by the sacred and the holy, then all scholarly activity has a religious dimension. It cannot be avoided, so it must be accounted for by being explicit so that it can be both critiqued and defended.

Eliade was right to see the secular study of religion (like all other forms of science and scholarship that follow the questions wherever they lead) as a religious activity, but his definition of religion as "the sacred" in opposition to the "profane"—which equated "profane" with "secular"—made it difficult for him to see the task of religious studies in the manner I have been proposing. For, drawing on Tillich and following the lead of not only Jacques Ellul but also Gabriel Vahanian,[24] I have been proposing that the holy and the secular are dialectically related and complementary, standing in opposition to the nondialectical dualism of the sacred/profane. Therefore, the task of the study of religion lies not in awakening the sacred hidden beneath the profane so as to overcome the secular, but rather in discovering that the study of religion as a secular activity is itself a manifestation of another kind of religious experience—the experience of the holy. Paradoxically, the secular gives us access to multiple sacred worlds when we accept the theonomous imperative of self-transcendence to follow the questions wherever they lead. It is only through secular, social scientific, historical consciousness, made possible by faithfulness to this imperative, that we have access to the multiple religious worlds of human meaning that Eliade would have us explore humanistically.

To engage in religious studies, including theology of culture, within the context of the humanities requires that I desacralize all sacred traditions, beginning with my own, through a surrender to the critical questions of the scholar who seeks to understand. The purpose of these questions is not to profane these traditions but to secularize them. Secularizing the sacred narrative traditions of the stranger makes it possible for me to enter into these strange worlds, these other worlds, and see reality through the eyes of the stranger in order to come back with new insight into my own sacred worlds, the worlds of my own religion and (academic) culture. Doing so opens me to what is holy in each.

As long as these traditions are considered sacred and beyond question, they can only be approached by their own initiates. But the wisdom to be learned from the religious experiences of human beings is too valuable to be held captive by the traditions in which they originate. To desacralize these narrative traditions, therefore, is not to desecrate them but to treat them as holy. A holy text is one that welcomes the stranger and the stranger's questions. A holy text and its meanings cannot be owned or possessed by any one person or community any more than the experience of the holy itself. Once they are desacralized, the narrative worlds of the stranger become narrative worlds open to strangers—open to anyone who is human.

The phenomenological attitude (i.e., seeking to understand the meaning of human action from the actor's point of view) that is central to religious studies simply makes explicit what is unique to the intentionality of the humanities in general. For, contrary to the impression left by Ninian Smart, when that attitude does appear in the social sciences, it is borrowed from the humanities. From such a point of view, it is never sufficient to study the social and psychological factors that led Shakespeare to write his plays, for example. As helpful as such "scientific" approaches may be for establishing a hermeneutic context, one must still come to grips, finally, with the unique insights and meanings embodied in Shakespeare's plays themselves. And so it is with all great narratives in the study of religions and cultures.

Religious studies is not focused on "the religious" as opposed to the "non-religious," but rather on the patterns of the sacred and the holy that inform all human/cultural activities. The quest of the humanities is the quest for insight into what it means to be human. The humanities embody two of the most important characteristics of what I would call a secular holiness: (1) surrender to the questions wherever they lead, and (2) openness (hospitality) to strangers from diverse times and places who have a story to tell. In their commitment to understanding our humanity in all its diversity, the humanities go beyond analysis and description to engage in prescription, that is, to engage in ethics. In the humanities, especially in philosophy and theology (as academic disciplines), we attempt to describe not only what "Is" but say what "Ought" to be. The humanities have a normative responsibility—a responsibility not only to understand sympathetically but also to both evaluate critically and be audacious in their defense of our common humanity in its openness to self-transcendence.

Through the humanities, we attempt to distill from such human experiences, in every religion and culture, the wisdom to live more humanely. Academic theology as I have been proposing it reflects such an understanding, an understanding of theology not as a confessional discipline but a professional discipline. Its task is not confessing the truth as seen through one narrative tradition but rather professing the wisdom that can be discerned through a comparative study of the great narrative traditions in their normative moments of self-transcendence. It seeks the wisdom that comes from a wrestling with the stranger. In this context, the story of Siddhartha is as much my story as is the story of Jacob/Israel or Jesus or Arjuna or Socrates, no matter which narrative tradition I personally identify as "my own."

NOTES

1. Ninian Smart, "Religious Studies and Theology" in *The Council of Societies for the Study of Religion Bulletin* 25, no. 3 (September 1997): 66–68.

2. Ibid., 66.

3. Ibid., 68.

4. Ibid., 67f.

5. Ibid., 68.

6. Ibid., 68.

7. Jacques Ellul, *The New Demons* (New York: Seabury Press, 1973 & 1975), 48.

8. In saying this, I have in mind Augustine's *Confessions*, where he says that a key turning point in his life was reading Cicero's *Hortensius*, which set him on fire with the desire to seek wisdom. This experience, he said, made him resolve never to cling to any partisan

answers but rather to follow the questions wherever they led him (Book 3:4). Later in the *Confessions*, he identifies this passion for wisdom with Christ as the wisdom of God (Book 11:9). Thus faith begins, for Augustine, with a surrender to doubt—a surrender that opens him to the infinite wisdom of God through a quest for insight. Interestingly, it is through reading the pagan author Cicero, not the Bible, that this openness to self-transcendence and divine wisdom first occurs. For Augustine, faith is setting out on a life journey without knowing where he is going, trusting his surrender to doubt, his passion for wisdom to lead the way.

9. Paul Tillich, "On the Idea of a Theology of Culture" in *What is Religion?* trans. James Luther Adams (New York: Harper & Row, 1969).

10. Paul Tillich, in *The Future of Religion*, ed. Jerald C Brauer (New York: Harper & Row, 1966).

11. Paul Tillich, *What is Religion?* 180.

12. Ibid., 178.

13. Ibid., 157.

14. Ibid., 165.

15. Ninian Smart, "Religious Studies and Theology," 67.

16. Tillich, *The Future of Religion*, 87. See "Negation in Mahayana Buddhism and in Tillich: A Buddhist View of the Significance of the History of Religions for the Systematic Theologian" by Masao Abe in *Negation and Theology*, ed. Robert P. Scharlemann (Charlottesville: University Press of Virginia, 1992), 86–99. Abe criticizes Tillich on just this point.

17. Mircea Eliade, *The Quest* (Chicago: University of Chicago Press, 1969).

18. Jean-Francois Lyotard, *The Postmodern Condition: A Report on Knowledge* (Minneapolis: University of Minnesota Press, 1979, 1984).

19. Terry Eagleton, *The Illusions of Postmodernism* (Oxford: Blackwell Publishers, 1996). vii.

20. Mircea Eliade, *The Quest*, 61.

21. Ibid., 69.

22. John Dunne, *The Way of All the Earth* (New York: Macmillan, 1972).

23. Mircea Eliade, *The Quest*, Preface.

24. Gabriel Vahanian, *God and Utopia* (New York: Seabury Press, 1977).

12

The Place of Academic Theology in the Study of Religion from the Perspective of Liberal Education

Paula M. Cooey

Theology, defined specifically as academic theology, belongs as a legitimate area of expertise in the study of religion.[1] Academic theologians, like historians, comparatists, philosophers, and social scientists of religion, should hold a rightful and honorable place as teachers and scholars in the discipline. Like other scholars of religion, academic theologians advance knowledge of religion. As intentional critics and makers of religious symbol systems and as critics of the wider cultures within which such systems flourish, academic theologians make a distinctive, valuable contribution to teaching and to scholarship—in nonsectarian liberal education environments, as well as in seminaries and divinity schools. In this essay, I seek ultimately to represent the contribution of academic theology to institutions of liberal education in particular.

First, however, some more general remarks are in order. Contention over whether academic theology properly belongs to the study of religion arises out of long-standing disputes over whether the study of religion constitutes a distinct discipline, the precise nature of religious studies as a multidisciplinary field or distinct discipline, and the meanings of the concepts "religion" and "academic theology." While addressing these wider disputes is both necessary and useful to the continued growth and flourishing of the discipline, it is unlikely that scholars will reach consensus on this issue once and for all. To quote Stuart Nuland, speaking to a different set of issues, "In the United States and democratic countries in general, the importance of airing different viewpoints rests not in the probability that a stable consensus will ever be reached but in recognition that it will not."[2] Lack of consensus notwithstanding, for any progress in discussion to occur, it is important to begin by examining the central concepts of the dispute.

Context of the Dispute

The dispute over what properly constitutes the study of religion takes place within a wider context of disarray throughout the academy. Since the 1960s, student activists and faculty alike have challenged the theoretical conception of the academic disciplines as having discrete essential characteristics that clearly distinguish them from one another. Within the disciplines, faculty have criticized traditional methodologies and pedagogies and sought constructive alternatives in both arenas. These shifts have produced and continue to produce a democratization in access to the classroom, in faculty hiring, and in conceptualizing what counts as knowledge.

At the same time, economic and political factors have worked against this democratizing tendency. Soaring tuition costs, tight labor markets, scarce resources for poorly endowed schools and state institutions, tenuring-in of faculties, overproduction of doctoral students, dissolution of entire academic departments, and misuse of the electronic classroom have internally beset institutions of higher education. These difficulties, coupled with external factors such as well-grounded public fear for economic security, successful discrediting of the political left during the Reagan years, ongoing political backlash to affirmative action, and repeated attacks on higher education by neoconservatives and the religious Right, have eroded public confidence in higher learning. The idea of liberal education as not only valid without reference to a specific vocation, but necessary to the life of the mind and to civic life, has all but disappeared. Against this backdrop, academic departments depend for their future existence not only on students' registering for their courses, but also on how well their faculties, particularly their chairs, can justify their disciplines both practically and theoretically. This is no less true for the study of religion.

Within the study of religion, this disarray has intensified what was already long-standing, ongoing, internal conflict over what properly constitutes the discipline. What are the purposes of studying religion? Precisely what kind of knowledge does the study of religion produce—description, explanation, critique, constructive knowledge, or all of the above? Should the study of religion presuppose a single model for advancing knowledge, and, if so, should the model be social scientific or humanistic? Is there a specific method unique to the study of religion or does the study of religion necessarily entail appropriation of methods associated with other academic disciplines? What role, if any, might theological studies[3] have to play? Answers to these questions depend heavily on one's epistemological assumptions and one's theoretical conception of religion.

Epistemology and the Concept of Religion

Much of the debate surrounding the study of religion, as in the case of other academic disciplines, erupts due to epistemological disputes.[4] Twentieth-century poststructuralist epistemologies challenge the very notion of a stable subject who can know without reference to the subject's perspective, interests, and values, and, further, without reference to the wider historical, material context of the knowing relationship. The deconstruction of both the knowing subject and the known object renders knowledge perspectival, contingent, relative, and subject to suspicion in regard to the subject's interests, values, and social location. Such a view additionally renders transparent the human role in the construction or production of culture, of human claims to knowledge, and of human subjectivity itself. In short, in terms of substance, practically everything about human society or culture could have been done differently.[5] In this respect, the academic disciplines and the knowledge they produce reflect human fabrication and human politics. These features put the lie to claims of knowledge solely as pure description and full explanation, in other words, to objectivity or absolute truth.[6]

That knowledge is conditioned by the knower and her or his location does not mean it is no longer knowledge; however, it does require constant critical revision of the methods, theories, and contents of knowledge, as well as cognizance of the historical location of the knower. That the traditional disciplines are themselves artifacts does not mean necessarily that they should cease to exist, but justification for their continued existence does require more than a territorial carving of ostensibly unique methods, theories, and contents.

Within this epistemological framework, religion is first and foremost a category with a history. Religion was historically defined in terms of substance, for example, religion as grounded in a feeling of absolute dependence upon the "Whence" of our existence.[7] Some scholars have more recently defined religion in terms of function as well as substance, in order to avoid insupportable ahistorical and essentialist claims. I would define religion functionally, for example, as a reciprocating artifact of human culture, that is, a product of human imagination that in turn shapes imagination.[8] As such, religion, as I understand it, refers to highly fluid, historically conditioned symbol systems that structure and on occasion destabilize human individual and communal life, identity, and practice through ritual, narrative, and social institution.[9]

That religious adherents attribute extracultural or supernatural origin, power, and reality to the central symbols governing religious systems introduces a substantive element into an otherwise functional definition and makes religion all the more fascinating to study. The attribution of transcendence further distinguishes religious symbol systems from other symbolic systems interacting on human life studied by other disciplines. Attributions of transcendence notwithstanding, religious identity, life, and value are accordingly thoroughly embedded in the cultures in which they are located.[10] In this inextricable entanglement with culture lies the necessity for a multidisciplinary approach within the study of religion, though such an approach does not preclude attributing disciplinary status. Furthermore, such attributions of transcendence, as well as all other features of religious life and practice, may be approached from a number of different scholarly perspectives, including those of both insiders and outsiders to the tradition, provided that the student approaches religious phenomena critically and analytically.

The study of religion, similarly to that of literature, philosophy, history, communication, and anthropology, among others, will be inherently multidisciplinary, and the justification for its continued existence political as well as rational. So, for example, just as literature departments include critics, authors, poets, historians, theorists, linguists, social scientifically oriented interpreters, and teachers of composition—in other words, those who make literature, those who criticize it, those who reflect on its making, and those who study the artifacts for their own sake— so the study of religion will include, among others, social scientists of religion, historians of religion, critics of religion from both within and without the actual religious traditions being criticized, and those who actively seek to deconstruct and intentionally reconstruct the religious symbol systems. Thus, the multidisciplinary character of the study of religion requires that scholars necessarily develop different areas of expertise from one another, areas that may complement or may conflict. Conflicts should be particularly useful to generating fresh theories of religion and methods for studying it.

One studies religion to understand it historically, comparatively, and normatively as a central feature in human life, just as one studies history, literature, philosophy, the arts, politics, and the social and natural sciences. One teaches religion so that others might understand it, perhaps with the conviction that gaining such an understanding enhances both individual and civic life, particularly in a secular, religiously plural democracy. Whether one is personally religious or antireligious is not directly relevant to the study of religion, though it might be interesting to study what kinds of people are engaged by the study of religion and why.

The knowledge produced by the study of religion has been and will continue to be only relatively descriptive, provisionally explanatory, critically evaluative, and constructive. (I use the term "constructive" here and throughout this essay in a technical sense as an intervention in the systems themselves, a modifying or making of these systems that can be either intentional or unintentional.) Insofar as scholars fail to acknowledge the elements of critical evaluation and construction, often unintentional, going on in the production of knowledge of religion, they fail to address religious life and practice adequately. This failure occurs both in regard to those scholars who seek theories of and approaches to religion by positing a religious essence and with respect to those scholars who reductionistically describe and explain religious phenomena in terms of other features of society.[11]

As in the case of categories defining other academic disciplines, religion as a category is used rhetorically by scholars and nonscholars alike to authorize and de-authorize various practices and institutions. So, for example, defining religion positively with respect to sacred texts privileges the historical traditions while de-authorizing oral traditions, rendering invisible much of popular religion. Likewise, defining religion without reference to the practices and institutional systems developed by women authorizes the elevation of men, whether or not the tradition studied actually warrants the elevation. Conversely, defining religion negatively as ideological superstructure intended by a political elite to dull the minds of the masses de-authorizes the entire category in relation to politics and economics.[12] There is thus a profound sense in which scholars themselves, in defining the discipline and approaching its objects, have created the category religion and superimposed it as an interpretive lens so that the definition of the concept reacts on the phenomena it selects, creating a new reality—a sort of self-fulfilling prophecy, if you will.[13] In other words, scholarship itself, as a discursive practice, is a constitutive act, an unintentional act of construction, though not one without limits. Any given scholar's work is itself a symbolic structuring or re-presenting, and thus a modification rather than solely a documentation of a tradition.

To assume then that knowledge of religion is solely descriptive and explanatory, even when qualified as relative and provisional, is to assume a modernist epistemology that is ultimately insupportable. Rather than being simply descriptive and explanatory, knowledge of religion is in itself construal. Like the religious phenomena it interprets, knowledge of religion is a cultural artifact that is historically conditioned, relative, and subject to constant critique. The ongoing revision, refinement, and invention of theories and methods of approach involved in critique further requires not only evaluations of the adequacy of theory and methodology, but also normative judgments of what is better or worse reflective thinking. Such evaluations may also legitimately entail additional provisional proposals of alternative construals of the symbolic frameworks of the systems themselves, that is, acts of intentional construction. Academic theology has a distinctive contribution to make to the study of religion, particularly at this intersection of theory with critique and intentional reconstruction, for the academic theologian, unlike other scholars of religion, intervenes directly in religious symbol systems, constructing and deconstructing traditions with particular reference to their central symbols.

ACADEMIC THEOLOGY AND THE ADVANCE OF KNOWLEDGE

Academic theology finds its intellectual roots in Immanuel Kant's concept of philosophical theology. In the preface to *Religion Within the Limits of Reason Alone*, Kant coined the phrase that he proposed as a science directly related to biblical theology. He defined the concerns of biblical theologians as the care of the soul (what we might designate as spiritual or religious instruction), the establishment of right teaching (therefore involving censorship), and, if biblical theologians were scholars as well as clergy, the prevention of theological interference in the cultivation of the other sciences (thus implicitly involving self-limitation and self-critique). The philosophical theologian might well draw upon some of the same materials as the biblical theologian; nevertheless, the distinguishing purpose of philosophical theology was to be critical rather than doctrinal, and the chief criterion of accountability to be human reason rather than ecclesiastic or biblical authority. The philosophical theologian thus had the responsibility, among others, for rendering the care of the soul, right doctrine, and theological self-critique accountable to reason, ideally without fear of censorship.

Exploring biblical and dogmatic theological assumptions within limits set by reason meant for Kant focusing especially on theological assumptions about the relation between human nature and religion. However, Kant recommended further that academic instruction in biblical theology be concluded each term with a series of lectures on what he called "a purely philosophical theory of religion," thereby extending the task of the philosophical theologian to include a constructively theoretical role. As an instance of theorizing, Kant submitted the second section or "book" of *Religion within the Limits*, his treatment of good and evil as conflicting principles governing human nature—in other words, a constructive, theological anthropology—in 1792. This critical analysis was denied permission for publication by the state's theological censors on the grounds that it controverted biblical teaching, evidence itself in support of the need for staking out philosophical theology as distinguished from biblical theology. Nevertheless, the volume in its entirety was finally published in 1793, though the controversy over Kant's rights as a scholar (as distinguished from a cleric) to publish the work continued beyond its publication.[14]

Some two hundred years later, Western culture has lost much of the antiauthoritarian, antiestablishment, democratizing power associated with reason. Reason, now defined far more narrowly and without reference to its moral and political functions, in contrast to Kant's richer, more profound conceptualization, has itself taken on a censorial and, on occasion, authoritarian function. Reason in the Western present, not unlike revelation in the Western past, has become a domain of elite interpreters, now primarily academicians, whose knowledge is so specialized and esoteric as to become unintelligible to intelligent lay people. Defined even more narrowly in a positivistic, scientific context as technological ratiocination (again in striking contrast to Kant's view) and abstracted from any historical context, the exercise of reason has often masked authoritarian ideological concerns, so that one wisely comes to regard appeals to reason with suspicion and to view authority vested in reason and its products as troubling and problematic.

At the same time, honesty requires admitting that healthy suspicion and skepticism regarding reason depend themselves at least partly on the ability to analyze critically and to articulate publicly to one another, in short, upon the ability to reason about the limits of reason. Critical reason in this sense, historicized and politicized, is not only potentially available to almost everyone; it is indispensable to historical agency, however socially constructed, just as it is necessary to change for the better—both individual and social betterment. Though Kant's own assumptions regarding reason are now as subject to questioning as those he challenged, his point was, among other objectives, to legitimate questioning as a supreme value in its own right, as empowering activity. In delineating philosophical theology as a legitimate, scholarly approach both to religion in general and to theological studies more particularly, Kant proposed nothing less than an area of study devoted to questioning the presuppositions of religious life and thought for purposes of both critique and intentional construction.[15]

"Philosophical theology" may continue to be a useful way to describe analysis and critique of systematic and dogmatic theology in regard to their underlying presuppositions concerning the relation between religious phenomena and behavior, on the one hand, and what it means to be human within religious and other cultural traditions, on the other hand. However, theologians so engaged, particularly those in institutions of liberal education, have extended both the domain and the methodology of their critical and theoretical work. These shifts, coupled with the professionalization of the discipline of philosophy, now render the designation "philosophical" too narrow and hence misleading and "academic" the preferred alternative.

What shifts in domain and methodology does "academic theology" designate, and what kind of knowledge does it produce? In regard to domain, critical analysis performed by academic theologians extends to include the underlying assumptions involved in theories of religion proposed by scholars of religion across all fields within the discipline, including that of academic theology itself. In regard to methodology, this analysis relies not only on theological training and background coupled with philosophical reasoning, but also on social theory and social scientific and humanistic approaches or methods.[16] While these extensions do not distinguish academic theology from other scholarly endeavor in the study of religion as such, they are marshaled for a distinctively different task—intentional cultural construction. The academic legitimacy of this endeavor generates the most stringent disagreement among scholars of religion, an issue to which I shall shortly return.[17]

With respect to intentional theological construction, Kant's understanding of philosophical theology included the formulation of theories of religion and religious life. Paralleling Kant's own constructive work on human nature, good and evil, and the significance of God to moral action and religious life, academic theologians have proposed constructive conceptions of human subjectivity, human-divine relations, and theological and religious ethics. Like Kant, they draw upon some of the same resources as scholars in theological studies representing specific traditions, usually but not always Christianity, though without reference to the dogmatic or doctrinal constraints of a specific religious tradition. Here, however, as in the case of critique, academic theologians have turned increasingly to the social sciences, the visual and literary arts, and the law and jurisprudence for methodological and substantive resources for their constructive efforts.[18]

Academic theology nevertheless remains theology and is not simply theory in some abstracted sense. It is theology precisely because it reflects an approach to culture in general and to religious symbol systems in particular centered by concerns with the governing symbols or conceptual limit setters that drive religious symbol systems—like God, Goddess, Brahman, Nirvana, Sunyata, and Tao—and the values such symbols generate and anchor. What distinguishes academic theologians from other theologians and from other scholars of religion in Western culture in particular is that they make and unmake the central concept, "God."[19] In so doing, they are not only critical of religious symbol systems, but also critical of the wider cultures within which these systems occur. So, for example, feminist theologians reject exclusively masculine imagery and language for God within Christian traditions and propose reconceptualizing God in more inclusive language; they further draw upon God, now reconstructed, as an authority by which to challenge sexist values characteristic of both specifically Christian traditions and the wider secular culture within which these traditions stand.[20] The knowledge such theologians have contributed to the study of religion includes, among other things, the knowledge of the role played by concepts of deity in the formation of religious subjectivity, in the development of particular values of particular religious systems, and upon the values of a wider, surrounding secular culture. Nevertheless, such deliberate constructive endeavor focused on the central symbols and their associated ethos fuels the central dispute among scholars of religion over the place of academic theology in the study of religion.

The Conflict Surrounding Academic Theology

What I understand to be the central objection to including academic theology in religious studies emphasizes that all theologians and their counterparts from non-theistic traditions are part of the very religious symbol systems studied by non-theological scholars of religion. This would hold true even for those academic theologians who claim no personal affiliation to a particular system. Irrespective of personal commitments, theologians in general bear the responsibility for conceptually maintaining theistic religious symbol systems. Indeed, academic theologians claim additional, direct responsibility as intellectual creators, insofar as they consciously intend to deconstruct and reconstruct the central symbol of the system, namely, God. Thus, academic theologians in particular presume to be the architects and poets of the system itself. From this perspective, precisely by virtue of its necessary intervention *in* the construction of theistic religious symbol systems, theology has no role to play in the study *of* such systems.

This is tantamount to saying that poets and fiction writers should be excluded from teaching English, composers from teaching music, and clinicians from teaching psychology. In short, it reduces all humanistic and social scientific studies to some form of historical studies. It presumes that students have nothing to learn from the makers of a system about such systems in general, a point the opponents to including theology have yet to establish. Such a view is further based on the erroneous assumption that because nontheological scholars of religion do not *intend* to intervene in the systems they study, they are not actually intervening through their study of them. As I have already pointed out, this assumption is simply methodologically and epistemologically self-deceptive.

This dispute further arises in part from those who fail to distinguish theological construction sufficiently from spiritual instruction or elaboration of orthodox teaching.[21] While such instruction and elaboration are noble endeavors in their own educational contexts, theology in general has for some time now far exceeded these boundaries, and academic theology in particular, rooted in Kant's notion of philosophical theology, should not be confused with other forms of theology representing confessional and sectarian interests, however legitimate these other interests may also be.

Extending the domain and range of resources and methods of approach notwithstanding, the constructive efforts of academic theologians nevertheless continue to resemble in important respects those of many of their peers in the discipline of philosophy. Yet, as far as I know, no one is suggesting that philosophical construction, for example, John Rawls's work on justice or Martha Nussbaum's work on pleasure, be discounted as scholarship, or excluded as course material from the classroom. Just as philosophers intentionally construct theories of human moral life and practice, of justice, of aesthetics, of nature, and of language, academic theologians develop theological anthropologies, cosmologies, and ethics. (Note that in both cases, scholars are critically constructing a transempirical realm.) Just as philosophers individually represent various philosophical schools of thought, theologians are trained in one or more religious traditions, the resources of which they may draw upon in their own work. Both philosophers and academic theologians are expected to know, to teach, and to address in their scholarship positions with which they disagree with fairness; both are expected to be self-critical in their work. In the context of liberal education, neither should be seeking converts to the particular intellectual traditions they represent. Though both will hold in common some degree of training in philosophical thought and reasoning, academic theologians differ from their philosophical counterparts by virtue of the emphasis on theological content in their backgrounds. This difference in content most distinguishes academic theologians from their philosophical counterparts.

Academic theologians do indeed share this content to a great degree with doctrinal and biblical theologians, though most doctrinal and biblical theologians would eschew intentional construction. At the same time, academic theologians by virtue of being critics and construers of culture, stand in contrast with doctrinal and biblical theologians in that their task does not depend on representing a particular religious faith as an adherent. They also stand in contrast to those scholars who confine the study of religion to description, explanation, or critique, excluding constructive endeavor. Nevertheless, like historians, comparatists, and social scientists of religion, academic theologians may be religious, antireligious, or indifferent to religion in terms of their own personal beliefs. The point is that, whatever their particular perspectives, academic theologians will focus critically on the authority with which humans invest belief and experience and on the theoretical assumptions they hold regarding what constitutes experiencing human selves, the worlds they populate, and the deities or other transcendent realities with which they stand in relation, seek to worship, or insist on denying—with the explicit aim of intentionally altering the symbol systems themselves.

CONTRIBUTIONS TO LIBERAL EDUCATION

Irrespective of our different specific fields of scholarly expertise, we as scholars of religion share the common vocation or task of teaching. While for some of us this takes place in a research-oriented environment, most of us do not engage in teaching graduate studies. Even when we teach in research institutions, our first obligation is most often to teach undergraduates (though, regrettably, producing graduate students merits higher status in the pecking order of higher education). Teaching undergraduates differs markedly from teaching graduate students in both pedagogical values and goals. Graduate students in many respects essentially apprentice themselves to a mentor in their chosen, relatively narrow field of expertise, or learn a set of specialized skills. By contrast, undergraduates acquire breadth of knowledge and, hopefully, at least a beginning ability to think analytically and critically—contents and skills assumed by the graduate student. (I am aware that this is not always a safe assumption.) The purpose for graduate education is to master a field of expertise in order to join a particular profession—business, education, engineering, institutional religion, law, or medicine. By contrast, liberal education prepares undergraduates primarily for a lifetime of learning regardless of a chosen career, for an intellectually enriched personal and civic life, and (irrespective of the dominant values of a consumer- and career-oriented society) only indirectly for a particular vocation or profession. Within this context of teaching undergraduates, academic theology as a field within the study of religion benefits liberal education in a number of ways.

To illustrate some of these benefits, I shall draw upon my own courses taught in a small, private, nonsectarian undergraduate institution.[22] My Ph.D. is secular; my field of expertise is academic theology, which specifically focuses on Christian thought, with special attention to the intersection of theology and theory, where theory includes theory of religion, feminist theory, social theory, aesthetic theory, and legal theory. I also possess a generalist's knowledge of contemporary reflective thought in Jewish, Muslim, and Buddhist traditions.

Most of the students who take these courses and those taught by my colleagues in the department of religion will not go on to major or minor in religion, though quite a number come back for a second course, and we normally carry a combined total of about thirty-six majors and minors any given year. Moreover, many of our courses fulfill requirements in other programs, notably, International Affairs, Women's Studies, the Humanist Teacher Program, and Ethnological Studies. In addition to the requirements of their chosen majors and minors, the students must fulfill the requirements of what we call the "common curriculum." These students, though largely from some kind of Christian background, come increasingly from secular, Muslim, Hindu, Jewish, and New Age traditions. I shall address two contributions of academic theology to liberal education through the common curriculum (and by inference to affiliated programs), as well as to the disciplinary major and minor.

Academic theology benefits liberal education in general as a species of cultural studies. Academic theologians have traditionally analyzed and challenged religious, and more specifically theological, regulation of gender, class, ethnicity, and political power in courses in women's studies and religion, in ethnic minority studies, and in post-colonial studies. As a species of cultural studies, academic theology not only benefits liberal education, it also contributes directly to the curriculum for majors and minors in religion by connecting reflective thought to religious life as manifested in narrative, ritual, and practice.

I teach, for example, a lower-division comparative course called Contemporary Religious Thought that can be taken to fulfill the common curriculum requirement for understanding values, as well as to fulfill a distribution requirement in the major. The course focuses on the role played by religion in the construction of human identity and the worlds of value in which humans find themselves. It explores foundational narratives for Jewish, Christian, Muslim, and Buddhist traditions as these are appropriated through ritual and practice and reflectively challenged and reconstructed in the present. The last three weeks of the semester are devoted to student presentation of projects in oral and written form on the significance of religion in contemporary life. These projects confront issues such as: religious pluralism in a secular democracy and First Amendment freedoms; the significance of religion for contemporary U.S. politics; religion and racism; religion and the militias; emerging religious traditions; international religious movements; and the role of religion in international conflict. As a course focused on values and as a study in constructive as well as critical religious thought, that is, a study that requires of students that they engage in construction as well as critique, this course exemplifies what I have sought to define as distinctively academic theology. As such, the course requires that students think critically and constructively about religious meaning and value in ways that consider explicitly their own possible responsibilities and choices as "co-makers of culture," in relation to the culture in which they live—goals at the very heart of liberal education.

The chief benefit to my mind, however, both to liberal education and to the disciplinary curriculum, accrues from teaching the content of my field—the reflective thought of one or more religious traditions. The content of what I teach, whether Augustine's theology and Buddhist sutras from the past, or liberation theologies, feminist theory, and comparative environmentalist thought of the present, draws on and builds on religious legacies to contemporary culture. By its very nature, the content forces questions of meaning and value. As students study formative writings and subsequent reflection upon them in Western or Eastern religious history, they exercise the skills definitive of critical thinking.

I teach, for example, an upper-division course titled Problems in Religious Thought that currently focuses on the problem of suffering and can be taken to fulfill not only the major or minor, but also a common curriculum requirement in Western culture. The reading requirements include a mix of Jewish, Christian, and secular thought, among them the book of *Job*, Elie Wiesel's *Night*, Camus' *The Plague*, Kushner's *When Bad Things Happen to Good People*, the gospel according to *Mark*, and Sands' *Escape from Paradise*. Students who take the course write critical analyses of all readings that must lead to and conclude with a question suitable for class discussion. These analyses include evaluation of the texts on rational grounds and in relation to the students' own intellectual positions. These writing assignments thus focus on understanding content, analyzing it, and evaluating it, as these exercises lead to ever deeper questions brought forward for group discussion. While this course could be taught quite differently, depending on the field or discipline of the professor, only an academic theologian brings the theological background to bear on the topic—a topic that, bereft of theological content, would be impoverished, to say the least.

I have also taught this same course by focusing it on the concept of religion as itself an intellectual problem. In this version of the course, I drew upon both theoretical writings and theological ones. Again, this course could have been taught with the same focus, but altogether differently; however, without the theological content (for example, Schleiermacher and Barth), it would be misleading in relation to the historical development of the concept of religion and more difficult to understand just why the concept is itself problematic. In short, in either version of this course and with respect both to the discipline of religion in particular and to the values of liberal education in general, the theological content, taught critically and without the intention of religious or spiritual instruction, has merit in its own right.

CONCLUSION

Ongoing dispute over what properly constitutes the study of religion can be productive if it leads to creative self-critique and clarification, even if it does not lead to consensus. Certainly this dispute has forced to me to reflect on and clarify the significance of academic theology as my own field of expertise, its relation to the study of religion within which it stands, and the nature of religious studies as a whole. Such disputes, however, have limited value when abstracted from the political context in which they occur. At a time when higher education is in crisis, prolonged discussions may even serve ultimately to distract from equally pressing issues facing faculty in the study of religion and in the other academic disciplines as well. Within the study of religion, we should be concerned with the appalling ignorance of religion and its special significance for both local and global life among doctors, lawyers, judges, journalists, politicians, policy developers, diplomats, and other government officials. As we have seen from the events surrounding the Branch Davidians at Mt. Carmel in Waco, Texas, such ignorance can be devastating.[23] Moreover, scholars of religion should be joining with their colleagues from the other disciplines and emerging fields to challenge at every turn efforts to reduce higher education to a commodity and to vocational training, even as we struggle to make it more accessible to more people in a time of dwindling institutional resources. In addition to disputing the place of theology, if any, in the study of religion, we need to be conducting serious discussions about the erosion of affirmative action as a strategy for recruiting students and faculty, the future of doctoral studies, the future of tenure, the significance of electronic media for pedagogy and curriculum, institutional responsibility to the different public arenas higher education serves, and public responsibility to higher education.

NOTES

1. Whether other areas of theological studies, for example, biblical studies, properly belong to the study of religion as an academic discipline is beyond the scope of this essay. I do think that arguments can be made to validate their inclusion.

2. See Sherwin Nuland, *How We Die: Reflections on Life's Final Chapter* (New York: A. A. Knopf, 1994), 156.

3. Here I include biblical studies, theology (philosophical, systematic, and practical), religious or theological ethics, and church history.

4. For a comparative analysis of parallel contentions within the discipline of economics, see Linell E. Cady, "The Public Intellectual and Effective Critique," *The Council of Societies for the Study of Religion Bulletin* 27, no. 2 (1998): 36–38.

5. See Peter L. Berger and Thomas Luckmann, *The Social Construction of Reality: A Treatise in the Sociology of Knowledge* (New York: Anchor Books, 1967). Though one could move quickly to philosophical idealism here, it does not necessarily follow from this way of viewing things that nothing is real or that all is arbitrary or that no judgments can be made regarding truth, falsity, goodness, or evil, or that the possibilities for doing things differently are unlimited by material conditions. If one assumes that nature requires that humans make cultures in order to survive as a species, then one can avoid reduction either to thoroughgoing idealism or to crude realism. But this is an issue beyond the scope of this discussion. See Cooey, *Religious Imagination and the Body: A Feminist Analysis* (New York: Oxford University Press, 1994). For an excellent critique of the limits of postmodernism, see Terry Eagleton, *The Illusions of Postmodernism* (Oxford: Blackwell, 1996).

6. For the implications of this epistemological position for the natural sciences, see, for example, Sandra Harding, *The Science Question in Feminism* (Ithaca: Cornell University Press, 1986). For a highly polemical disputation of this view, see Paul R. Gross and Norman Levitt, *Higher Superstition: The Academic Left and Its Quarrels with Science* (Baltimore: Johns Hopkins University Press, 1998).

7. Friedrich Schleiermacher, "The Definition of Dogmatics," in *The Christian Faith*, vol. 1, trans. H. R. Mackintosh and J. S. Stewart, with intro. by Richard R. Niebuhr (New York: Harper & Row, 1963), 3–93.

8. See Elaine Scarry, *The Body in Pain: The Making and Unmaking of the World* (New York: Oxford University Press, 1985).

9. This is my own slightly modified version of Clifford Geertz's definition. See Geertz, "Religion as Cultural System," in *The Interpretation of Cultures: Selected Essays*, (New York: Basic Books, 1973), 87–125.

10. See Wayne Proudfoot, *Religious Experience* (Berkeley: University of California Press, 1985).

11. Essentialists insist that religion be studied on its own terms without reference to other approaches to cultural phenomena; they usually define religion with reference to a single essential feature, hence ironically performing an internal reduction. In contrast, self-proclaimed reductionists reduce religion to other historical, nonreligious elements of culture, e.g., economic, political, social, or psychological forces. For a classic example of the former, see *The Idea of the Holy* (London: Oxford University Press, 1969). For examples of the latter, see Sigmund Freud, *The Future of an Illusion* (Garden City, New York: Anchor Books, 1961).

12. See Russell McCutcheon, "A Default of Critical Intelligence?: The Scholar of Religion as Public Intellectual," *Journal of the American Academy of Religion*, 65, no. 2 (1997): 443–68, and *Manufacturing Religion: The Discourse on "Sui Generis" Religion and the Politics of Nostalgia* (New York: Oxford University Press, 1997).

13. Gerald K. Larson pointed this out with particular reference to the historical production of "Hinduism" in "Discourse about 'Religion' in Colonial and Postcolonial India" (paper presented to the Critical Theory Group at the national meeting of the American Academy of Religion, Kansas City, Missouri, November 1992). For more recent developments, see Gauri Vishwanathan, *Outside the Fold: Conversion, Modernity, and Belief* (Princeton: Princeton University Press, 1998).

14. Immanuel Kant, *Religion within the Limits of Reason Alone*, trans. with intro. by Thomas M. Greene and Hoyt H. Hudson, with further intro. by John R. Silber (New York: Harper & Row, 1960), 7–10.

15. There are, of course, other ways to think and to effect change as well. I think, however, that at bottom, reason consists of questioning or wondering, and that wondering is necessary, though not sufficient, not only to critique, but also to most forms of transformation.

16. Early exemplars of these shifts include the incorporation of social theory and sociology of religion by H. Richard Niebuhr and Gordon D. Kaufman, as well as the incorporation of the visual arts by Richard R. Niebuhr. See respectively, *The Responsible Self: An Essay on Christian Moral Philosophy* (New York: Harper and Row, 1963); *An Essay on Theological Method* (New York: Oxford University Press, 1995); and *Streams of Grace: Studies of Jonathan Edwards, Samuel Taylor Coleridge, and William James* (Kyoto: Doshisha University Press, 1983).

17. See Cady, "The Public Intellectual and Effective Critique."

18. While some may see this wide a sweep as the deterioration, even dissolution, of theology, I see it as a necessary move if religious traditions themselves are to survive (the desirability of their survival also being disputable, of course). See, for examples, Milner S. Ball, *The Word and the Law* (Chicago: University of Chicago Press, 1993), and Paula M. Cooey, *Family, Freedom & Faith: Building Community Today* (Louisville: Westminster John Knox, 1996).

19. It is important to keep in mind that there are counterparts to academic theologians who do the same kind work in the context of polytheistic, Goddess-centered, and nontheistic traditions.

20. See Rosemary Radford Ruether, *Sexism and God-Talk: Toward a Feminist Theology* (Boston: Beacon Press, 1983), and Sallie McFague, *Models of God: Theology for an Ecological, Nuclear Age* (Philadelphia: Fortress Press, 1987).

21. McCutcheon's work generally neglects this distinction.

22. Since writing this article, I have changed institutions. I taught for eighteen years at Trinity University in San Antonio, Texas. I now teach at Macalester College in Saint Paul, Minnesota. Though my circumstances and courses have changed somewhat, the two institutions and my work remain in many respects the same, certainly regarding the focus of this volume.

23. James Tabor and Eugene V. Gallagher, *Why Waco?* (Berkeley: University of California Press, 1995).

13

The Epistemic Publicity
of Academic Black Theology

Frederick L. Ware

The relation of theology to religious studies is addressed by black theologians within the context of their debate on the need for Black Theology to be epistemically public, that is to say, intelligible and relevant to a large public audience.[1] The problem of relating theology and religious studies pales in importance compared to other issues discussed by black theologians. The earliest debates in Black Theology revolved around such issues as the meaning of liberation, the use of violence in the struggle for liberation, the desirability and place of racial reconciliation in black liberation, the nature and relation of black religion (or more precisely, black sources) to Black Theology as the latter's proper subject matter, and the validity of belief in a black God in solidarity with oppressed blacks in the face of black suffering apparently to the contrary.[2] The early debates have since been augmented by recent conversations that seek to expand the notion of liberation to redress classism, sexism, homophobia, ecological devastation, and inaction on the part of church and clergy in liberation movements.[3] In spite of the truncated debate on the relation of theology to religious studies in academic Black Theology, I turn to this debate and discuss, from a university context, how academic Black Theology may become public theology.

THE ISSUE OF PUBLIC THEOLOGY
IN ACADEMIC BLACK THEOLOGY

Is God a White Racist?, by William R. Jones, is a highly sophisticated and thought-provoking contribution to academic Black Theology. Jones attempts to show that leading black theologians, namely James Cone, Albert Cleage, Joseph Washington, Major Jones, and J. Deotis Roberts, lack sufficient foundations for their theological programs. According to Jones, these leading theologians' black liberation theism, that is, the belief that God is in solidarity with and thus working to liberate oppressed black people, is untenable in the absence of empirical evidence that demonstrates unambiguously God's solidarity with oppressed blacks.

James Cone's comment about Jones's book is most revealing. Cone says the book:

> . . . remains as a challenge to Black theological proposals and will continue to require the serious attention of Black theologians. We cannot remain satisfied with an easy internal solution, because what we say about God and suffering should be publicly defensible outside the confessional contexts from which they emerge. If we do not test the credibility of our theological judgments in a public arena, without resource to confessional narrowness, then we should not complain if what we say about God is ignored by those outside of our confession of faith. It is because Christians claim to have a universal message that they are required to speak its truth in a language publicly accessible to all.[4]

To Jones's demand for evidence justifying belief in black liberation theism, Cone cites the ministry, death, and resurrection of Jesus Christ as the definitive proof of God's solidarity with the oppressed, and therefore with black people, because they have experienced oppression.[5] However, he recognizes the implications of Jones's claims that academic Black Theology, as practiced by himself and the vast majority of black theologians, is irrelevant to an intelligent public.

Cone explains the difference between himself and Jones on the issue of sufficient evidence in terms of their respective approaches to Black Theology.[6] Cone contends that Jones approaches Black Theology from the perspective of the philosophy of religion with no absolute commitment to Christian faith or to the Black Church. Cone sees his approach in great contrast to that of Jones. He claims to approach Black Theology with an absolute commitment both to Christian faith and the Black Church. He sees himself as operating, and doing so legitimately, within a circle of faith. J. Deotis Roberts also contends that Black Theology must be done within a circle of faith. For Roberts, theology involves faith in God; commitment to a way of believing; taking seriously the Bible, tradition, and the total revelation of God as Christians understand these concepts, not as the philosopher of religion understands them.[7]

Underlying the difference between Cone and Roberts, on the one hand, and Jones, on the other, is the conventional distinction between theology and religious studies. The conventional way of relating theology and religious studies puts the two in a relationship characterized by conflict and tension. For example,

> According to the conventional formulation, "religious studies" names an inclusive program or department that explores and teaches religion according to the canons of university scholarship. Given these canons, no single religious faith can claim primacy or priority and religion itself must be interpreted without special pleading and under universal scholarly criteria. Theology, on the other hand, presupposes a specific religious community as its setting. . . . In addition, the educa-

tional institution accommodating theology is almost exclusively the professional
school for clergy education. Furthermore, according to the conventional viewpoint, the grounds of validity and verification in theology are not publicly accessible but esoteric, private, and authoritarian.[8]

This description of the relation of theology to religious studies is, without question, played out in the debate between Cone and Jones. As a philosopher of religion, Jones is committed to the study of religion according to the canons of university scholarship. He acknowledges that the Black Church informs his
experience but he does not allow it to control his thinking.[9] Confident in the
validity of university canons of rationality, he is not reluctant to charge Cone and
other black theologians with unsound judgment and multiple errors in logic.[10] As
a theologian committed to the Black Church, Cone is similarly confident that his
analysis of black Christian faith is truthful and contributes to the liberation of
oppressed black people, despite the supposed logical contradictions that he says
Jones finds in his work with the aid of white Western philosophy.[11] The stalemate
between Cone and Jones, and the failure of both to explore and settle upon an
amicable relation between theology and religious studies, suggests that academic
Black Theology is trapped at a critical juncture. Beyond this juncture may lie more
relevant and public theologies.

The Place of Academic Black Theology
in Religious Studies

Gayraud Wilmore situates academic Black Theology within the field of religious
studies. However, his conception of religious studies does not follow convention.
In a conventional sense, religious studies is the study of religions according to
canons of university scholarship with no religion enjoying primacy or privilege.
Wilmore uses "religious studies" as a covering term for various studies of African
American religious life. He does not accommodate academic Black Theology to
these studies. Instead, he views these studies as conforming to the liberationist orientation of academic Black Theology.

Wilmore defines African American religious studies as "the investigation,
analysis, and ordering of a wide variety of data to the religions of persons of
African descent for the purpose of authenticating and enriching personal faith and
preparing both clergy and laity for a ministry in the Black Church and community, understood in terms of competent and faithful leadership in worship, nurture,
education, and corporate action on behalf of God's mission of liberation for all
people."[12] As he sees it, religious studies is interdisciplinary, faith oriented, and
politically active.[13] He acknowledges that the analysis of data on African American
religion requires the work of several disciplines.[14] He includes academic Black
Theology among those disciplines. It is obvious from Wilmore's statement of the

goals of religious studies as the enrichment of personal faith and training for church leaders that he centers religious studies in and makes them a tool for black churches. According to Wilmore, the desired end of religious studies is for African American churches and communities to become politically active, faithfully executing "a ministry of social transformation and liberation from the dehumanizing forces of institutional racism, economic injustice, and political oppression."[15]

Wilmore's conception of religious studies and the relation of theology to it does not cohere with the interest of a significant number of African American scholars seeking to demonstrate the relevance and contributions of their academic specialties to a public which includes and is larger than the totality of African American churches. In a 1991 "Report on the Profession" published in the *Journal of the American Academy of Religion*, 52 percent and 58 percent of faculty surveyed at two historically and predominately African American seminaries reject a rigid distinction and dialectical tension between theology and religious studies, preferring instead to identify their studies as existing primarily within the broader field and context of religious studies.[16] These scholars are opposed to the notion of religious studies being skewed towards and regulated by theology. It is the opinion of these scholars that academic Black Theology has for too long dominated the study of African American religion. One surveyed faculty member is reported to have said:

> At seminary, there should be no distinction as I feel strongly that both theology and religion should be taught as intellectual disciplines and not for dogmatic purposes. This approach enables ministers to become more tolerant of other religions. This would also promote ecumenicity and ecclesiastical broad-mindedness in approaching human problems.[17]

Working in the seminary setting, these scholars do acknowledge their responsibility to educate church leaders. However, it seems that their professional work context, that is, teaching in a seminary, does not determine their understanding of what religious studies is. Neither the idea of Black Theology within a religious studies/university context nor Black Theology's becoming public theology, as I am defining it in this paper, is contrary or offensive to their sensibilities.

AN ALTERNATIVE MODEL OF ACADEMIC BLACK THEOLOGY IN RELIGIOUS STUDIES

What would be an adequate model for African American theology and its relationship to religious studies in the university? I shall attempt to answer this question in the statement and explanation of the following five theses. The theses render clarity to what religious studies is and African American theology's place within it.

Thesis 1. The term "religion" is a malleable category for the description and study of a pervasive and almost universal phenomenon in human societies.

"Religion" is a term that is used often without hesitation. When asked, most persons have a ready answer for what religion is. But when pressed with intense questioning, few persons can offer a definition of religion that meets the satisfaction of all inquirers. This situation obtains not because of personal ineptitude but rather because "religion" is a term that has several and sometimes conflicting meanings. For some persons, religion means the Transcendent—things set apart and forbidden, that which concerns humans ultimately, a world or reality beyond normal spatio-temporal relations or a world inhabited by gods, spirits, and so forth. For some persons, religion means the beliefs, philosophy (theology or wisdom tradition), myths, symbols, rituals, ethics, and the institutions peculiar to a community of persons. For some persons, religion means, on the one hand, deviant beliefs and practices of individuals or, on the other hand, the quality and intensity of individuals' appropriation of the formal, institutional religion of their society. So, religion is seen as deeply held convictions that put individuals in either opposition to or greater conformity with prevalent forms of belief in their society or community. For some persons, religion means those aspects of society and culture (such as art, science, literature, medicine, politics, morality, and so forth) that are influenced by, exemplify elements of, or serve as avenues for the expression of faith. In some respects, all of their views are right. Because religion is so pervasive, no one extension of the term captures fully what religion is. In order to grasp mentally something so large as religion, multiple meanings and perspectives are required.

As a malleable category, religion defies reduction to any kind of unique property or essence. This does not mean that there are no tendencies or patterns within a religion. Clearly, there are. However, no tendency or set of tendencies in one religion is typical of all other religions. Also, no religion is capable of an absolute reduction to the tendency or set of tendencies identified in it. The proper study of a religion may legitimately follow several paths of inquiry.

Like other religions, African American religion is incapable of reduction to any kind of unique property or essence. Consistent with what I just said, this denial of reductionism in African American religion does not involve a denial of observable tendencies and patterns in African American religion. Religion is a pervasive phenomenon among African Americans, like all other humans. African Americans express themselves religiously in many ways. Indeed, "African American religious life has never been confined solely to the Christian tradition. It has found expression in Islam, Judaism, Hinduism, Vodun, New Thought, and many other religious modalities, some created *de novo*."[18]

A considerable problem emerges when this diversity of expression is denied and, even worse, when various tendencies within a particular religion are denied. Wilmore acknowledges forthrightly that there are various tendencies in African American religion. Yet he selects the tendency towards radicalism, that is, the quest for liberation, as the most significant and defining quality of African American religion.[19] Using radicalism also as the defining quality of African American religion, James Cone labels all forms of Christianity as demonic and heretical if they lack a priority and focus on liberation.[20] Wilmore's and Cone's narrow conception of African American religion in terms of radicalism results in African American religion's own alienation from its other tendencies, not to mention its alienation from other religions that exhibit different concerns.

Thesis 2. The field of religious studies has its own integrity apart from those religions or aspects of religion that it studies.

Wilmore's definition of religious studies asserts, in effect, the necessary role of religious studies in the enhancement and maintenance of a religion. Wilmore's insistence denies more than just the right of religion scholars to pursue their academic interests as they will. He overlooks the obvious fact that the institutional maintenance of a religion does not require academic study. Religions are not constituted by academic study. In other words, religions are not created nor do they fall on the basis of academic study. This independence of religions from academic study does more than emphasize the capacity of religions to chart their own course. The independence of religions from academic study implies that religious studies has some degree of independence from the religions studied. These religions obviously supply the data for study but they need not and do not determine the methods and ends of academic study.

Thesis 3. The study of religion does not depend upon or require of its researchers, teachers, or students any specific religious belief or affiliation, political commitment, race, culture, or gender.[21]

Does the social context of the inquirer influence the study of religion? Yes. Is there a privileged context that guarantees that some inquirers will be right and others wrong? I think not. In some cases, socially constructed differences do make a difference. In other cases, it makes no difference.

Along with the increasing numbers of African Americans taking up the study of African American religion, there has been a definite change in how the religion of African Americans is perceived. Few white scholars, especially during the period prior to the black consciousness movement of the 1960s, elevated the religion of African Americans above the practice of superstition and emotionalism. As members of African American religious communities, African American scholars sought to correct misconceptions about African American religion. Who can deny that some of the most positive and insightful studies of African American religion have come from African Americans themselves? Further, some of the most significant scholarship in African American religious studies has come from African Americans who are actively involved in the life and affairs of their churches and communities.[22]

It is permissible for persons to undertake academic study for deeply held personal convictions and vested interests. Personal commitments and interests often serve as motivation for study. A person may be motivated to understand or defend the stories, practices, and symbols of his or her declared or favored religion. A sense of identification with the religious community being studied or a sense of having something at stake other than professional advancement or the evaluation of student performance does seem to drive and sustain many persons' interest in the study of religion.

The personal or subjective dimension of religious studies, however, does not guarantee better insight, brilliant study, or correct analysis. Blackness is not necessarily an advantage and whiteness a disadvantage in the study of African American religion. The scholarship of African Americans, such as E. Franklin Frazier and Joseph Washington, differs little from the disparaging studies of earlier white scholars who viewed the religion of African Americans as superstition, emotionalism, folk religion, and aberrations of white Protestant Christianity. Wilmore does acknowledge that white scholars, such as David Wills, Richard Newman, Randall Burkett, and Mary Sawyer, have made positive contributions to the study of African American religion and culture.[23] He praises and cites Theo Witvliet as proof that "a white theologian who has the correct instincts, inspiration, and information can do black theology as critically and constructively as those who claim African descent."[24]

Thesis 4. The sources or data of a religion are not normative in the study of that religion.

A serious problem arises when the data of a religion is regarded as normative for the study of that religion: the inquirer excludes other disciplines, perspectives, and insights that, if used, would result in a more thorough critical assessment of a religion than if he limited himself to that religion's own norms. This problem exists in the study of African American religion.

The temptation for African American scholars to make the data of African American religion (i.e., black sources) foundational is great and not so easily resisted. African Americans have always been "signified," that is, trapped within the larger American framework of interpretation over which they possessed little or no control in the production of the languages used to describe them.[25] African Americans are a people of Western civilization. Yet, they "possess an African ancestry and have an effective history and religious tradition that is larger than the West."[26] African religions and traditions, as well as African American generated sources, constitute a critical source and proper point of departure for a restatement of African American identity. The discovery, retrieval, and use of black sources are crucial for overcoming erroneous and oppressive signification. The most profound illustration of the potential of black sources to correct stereotypes and distortions of history is the 1991 discovery of an eighteenth-century African burial ground in downtown Manhattan.[27] Though only partially unearthed, the burial ground contained hundreds of human remains and countless artifacts. The discovery of the burial ground dispelled three long-standing myths: (1) that Africans played no major part in the creation of colonial cities, (2) that slavery was not widespread in the North, and (3) that African culture did not flourish among slaves.

While the temptation to make black sources normative is great and difficult for many African American theologians to resist, the potential political import of these sources does not justify their placement at the center of any and every analysis that involves African Americans. The fourth thesis obliges theologians to begin their analysis of African American religion with data drawn from African American religion, but not for the purpose of establishing the data itself as the norms of study. Acceptance of the data alone as normative seriously mutes the critical and objective study of African American religion. Norms are subject to negotiation and revision. If norms are based on, or are identical to, the data, negotiation over the norms of theological study is extremely difficult because an argument against and rejection of such data-based norms is tantamount to disparagement of the data itself.

Thesis 5. African American theology is an integral component in the study of religion.

Presupposed by this thesis is the claim that no form of racial apologetics is needed to justify the study of African American theology. No attacks need to be made on any so-called white Western theology that excludes and is antithetical to the black experience in order to legitimate the study of African American theology. The abandonment of a rhetoric of racial antagonism does not mean that racial oppression does not exist or is any less a problem. However, it does mean that no special pleading is needed to situate African American life within the broader scope and multiple dimensions of human life, if in fact religion is a malleable category that has several extensions and warrants study from various perspectives and disciplines. It also means that African American religion does not exist in a cultural vacuum. African American religion is part of the landscape of religion in America, an arena of dynamic interaction where it has influenced, as well as received influences from, various events and aspects of American life.

My thought on the place of African American theology in the academic study of religion follows that of Charles H. Long. His intention is to develop a methodological perspective that treats aspects of African American religion that are overlooked by what he sees as the two most dominate and narrow approaches to the study and interpretation of African American religion. These two dominate approaches to the study of African American religion are sociological and theological/apologetic.[28] Examples of the sociological studies that he has in mind are W.E.B. DuBois's *The Negro Church* (1903), Carter G. Woodson's *The History of the Negro Church* (1921), Benjamin E. Mays and Joseph W. Nicholson's *The Negro Church* (1933), Arthur H. Fauset's *Black Gods of the Metropolis* (1944), C. Eric Lincoln's *The Black Muslims in America* (1961), E. Franklin Frazier's *The Negro Church in America* (1962), Howard Brotz's *The Black Jews of Harlem* (1970), and E.U. Essien-Udom's *Black Nationalism* (1962).[29] In his opinion, these studies have not "come to terms with the specifically religious elements in the religion of black Americans."[30] In other words, these studies deal mostly with the history, organization, experiences, and political ideologies of African American communities. Rarely do they identify and examine the images and meanings of religious significance to these communities. The theological studies that Long has in mind are Joseph Washington's *Black Religion* (1964), Albert Cleage's *The Black Messiah* (1968), James Cone's *Black Theology and Black Power* (1969), and subsequent interpretive works on black religion.[31] According to him, these theological studies are aimed at defending and legitimating the existence of a religious tradition, namely black religion, that differs significantly from the mainstream of American religion. Using Washington's book to illustrate the limitation of theological/apologetic works, he points out that these kinds of studies are severely restricted by their inability "to deal with religion outside of the normative framework of Christian theology."[32] In contrast to the theological/apologetic and sociological approaches, he contends that the history of religions approach does not obligate scholars to restrict their studies to or defend Christianity, or any other religion, for that matter.[33] Instead, it is an approach that allows the identification and exploration of religious images, symbols, and meanings of significance to various African American communities, whether Christian, non-Christian, or secular.

Long, so far as I know, does not claim that a history of religions approach is the only legitimate alternative to sociological and theological/apologetic studies. I think that he would be open to approaches from other human science disciplines. He seems to be advocating a kind of maturation in academic theology and religious studies as well. He does not want academic theology to be limited only to serving the interests of religious communities. Furthermore, he argues for the inclusion of academic theology, that is, critical and normative studies of religion, in the field of religious studies. According to Long, religious studies too often operate under an illusion of objectivity.[34] So-called neutral descriptive studies of religion must be complemented with studies of how religions function positively or negatively in the lives of individuals and society.

For Long, the history of religions approach is characterized by an acknowledgment of universalism in existing academic disciplines. No arguments for the uniqueness of African American religion or its neglect by white scholars, which may well be true, is necessary to warrant the study of Black Theology. Long endorses the study of African American religion because the nature of his academic discipline, the history of religions, permits just that—the study of religions. Long therefore contends that the history of religions contains a universalism that provides an opening for the study of the authentic religious expressions of all peoples.[35] As a study of the religious beliefs of African Americans, Black Theology is automatically a part of the study of religion. As a study in the field of religion, the study of Black Theology has a legitimate place in the human sciences of the university.

CONCLUSION

These five theses together make possible a plurality of perspectives for the study of African American religion. Multiple possibilities for African American theology emerge when there is a simultaneous recognition of the various tendencies, concerns, and aspects of African American religion but no regard for any of them as some kind of essence or dominant theme. If African American religion has no one essence or dominant theme, then it stands to reason that African American theology may use multiple categories and methods and pursue several paths of inquiry. In addition to expanding research opportunities, African American theology is open for scholarly participation from interested persons of all backgrounds. As I see it, academic Black Theology within the university context of religious studies proceeds along several paths. To one degree or another, they all contribute to the presentation of Black Theology to the various audiences that comprise the intelligent public.[36]

NOTES

1. Theology that is public involves (1) the use of faith, theological language, and other religious resources in the resolution of societal and cultural problems; (2) interaction with, scrutinizing, and interpreting the actual beliefs and practices of a religious community; (3) the use of prevalent standards of truth, rationality, and argument; (4) dialogue and collaboration with persons outside the theologian's circle of faith, academic specialty, and social class; and (5) in addition to traditional means of publishing academic study, the use of popular media such as television, radio, newspaper, church learning institutes, fiction, poetry, and so forth for disseminating knowledge. Each meaning of public theology finds expression and emphasis in the field of Black Theology. This essay emphasizes only the publicness of Black Theology in terms of its openness to multiple interpretations of African American religion and culture, critical use of prevalent standards of rationality in the university, and conducting black theological research within a climate of interdisciplinary and interracial dialogue and cooperation.

2. James H. Cone, "An Interpretation of the Debate among Black Theologians," Epilogue to *Black Theology: A Documentary History, 1966–1979*, ed. James H. Cone and Gayraud S. Wilmore (Maryknoll: Orbis Books, 1979), 612.

3. James H. Cone, General Introduction to *Black Theology: A Documentary History, Volume 2: 1980–1992*, ed. James H. Cone and Gayraud S. Wilmore (Maryknoll: Orbis Books, 1993), 2–3.

4. Cone, "An Interpretation of the Debate among Black Theologians," 621–622.

5. Ibid., 621; idem, *God of the Oppressed* (San Francisco: Harper & Row, 1975), 191–192.

6. Cone, "An Interpretation of the Debate among Black Theologians," 620–621.

7. J. Deotis Roberts, *Black Theology Today: Liberation and Contextualization* (New York: Edwin Mellon Press, 1983), 50.

8. Edward Farley, *The Fragility of Knowledge: Theological Education in the Church and the University* (Philadelphia: Fortress Press, 1988), 57. His own position is that this conventional way of relating theology and religious studies is detrimental and that each field of inquiry must incorporate elements from the other. I have quoted him here only because of the lucid description he gives of the conventional relation of theology and religious studies.

9. William R. Jones, *Is God a White Racist?: A Preamble to Black Theology* (Garden City, NY: Doubleday, Anchor Press, 1973), xiv–xv.

10. Ibid., xiii.

11. James H. Cone, *Speaking the Truth: Ecumenism, Liberation, and Black Theology* (Grand Rapids, Michigan: Eerdmans, 1986), 14–15.

12. Gayraud S. Wilmore, *African American Religious Studies: An Interdisciplinary Anthology*, ed. Gayraud S. Wilmore (Durham: Duke University Press, 1989), xii-xiii.

13. Ibid., xx.

14. Ibid., xix.

15. Ibid.

16. Ray L. Hart, "Religious and Theological Studies in American Education: A Pilot Study," *Journal of the American Academy of Religion* 59, no. 4 (1991): 740.

17. Ibid., 740 n. 32.

18. Larry G. Murphy, "Religion in the African American Community," in *Encyclopedia of African American Religions*, ed. Larry G. Murphy, J. Gordon Melton, and Gary L. Ward (New York: Garland, 1993), xxxii.

19. Gayraud S. Wilmore, "A Revolution Unfulfilled but not Invalidated," in *A Black Theology of Liberation*, (Philadelphia: Lippincott, 1970; Maryknoll: Orbis Books, 1990), 147.

20. Cone, *God of the Oppressed*, 36, 83.

21. Sam Gill, "The Academic Study of Religion," *Journal of the American Academy of Religion* 62, no. 4 (1994): 965. Gill claims that this proposition is basic to the academic study of religion.

22. Thomas R. Frazier, "Changing Perspectives in the Study of Afro-American Religion," *Journal of the Interdenominational Theological Center* 6, no. 3 (Fall 1978): 62.

23. Gayraud S. Wilmore, "Doing the Truth: Some Criteria for Researching African-American Religious History," in *African American Religion: Research Problems and Resources for the 1990s*, ed. Victor N. Smythe and Howard Dodson (New York: Schomburg Center for Research in Black Culture, New York Public Library, 1992), 135.

24. Gayraud S. Wilmore, Foreword to Theo Witvliet's *The Way of the Black Messiah: The Hermeneutical Challenge of Black Theology as a Theology of Liberation* (Oak Park: Meyer-Stone, 1987), ix.

25. Charles H. Long, *Significations: Signs, Symbols, and Images in the Interpretation of Religion* (Philadelphia: Fortress Press, 1986), 7–8.

26. Preston N. Williams, "An African American Perspective on the Nature and Criteria of Theological Scholarship," *Theological Education* 32, no. 3 (1995): 72.

27. Spencer Harrington, "Bones and Bureaucrats," *Archaeology* 46, no. 2 (1993): 28–38.

28. Long, *Significations*, 173.

29. Ibid., 183 n. 1.

30. Ibid., 173.

31. Ibid.

32. Ibid., 174.

33. Ibid.

34. Charles H. Long, "A Common Ancestor: Theology and Religious Studies," in *Religious Studies, Theological Studies, and the University-Divinity School*, ed. Joseph Kitagawa (Atlanta: Scholars Press, 1992), 149.

35. Long, *Significations*, 8.

36. See my *Methodologies of Black Theology* (Cleveland: Pilgrim Press, 2002). In this analysis, I identify and critique three methodological perspectives used in the academic study, interpretation, and construction of Black Theology in the United States from 1969 to 1999. These perspectives are painstakingly detailed with respect to how they are alike and differ on what are the tasks, content, sources, norm, method, and goal of Black Theology. Each perspective has its own unique approach and capabilities for making Black Theology intellectually and publicly accessible.

14

Theology and Cultural Contest in the University

Kathryn Tanner

No one questions the rightful place of Christian theology in American universities so long as its location is a university-affiliated divinity school devoted primarily to professional training of intellectually responsible religious leaders. Theology in that case is as appropriate to the university as a divinity school is (and the latter, at least as a matter of fact, has an established institutional location in many of the best U.S. universities). But theology's inclusion in the humanities curriculum of secular universities is another matter.

Academic theology of that sort is under attack from both its church and academic audiences. The usual worry of recent times from the academic side is methodological in nature. Because of its prior commitment to Christianity, theology is thought to lack objectivity and to disdain the disinterested search for the truth. Theology fails, it is argued, to meet scholarly standards of critical inquiry, operating instead with sources and norms that Christians alone find plausible and refuse to put seriously into question. Yet the more that theology has tried to meet such criticisms by becoming a rather typical academic guild, the more the churches find their own needs and concerns neglected. Theology becomes very much like a regular humanistic discipline, with the consequence that issues of importance to the churches tend to drop out of consideration. Theologians concerned about bridging the gap between academic theology and the churches—say, by stressing the way academic theology can provide an intellectually responsible training in the faith—fail to explain why secular universities should commit themselves to the task. Without the idea of the United States as a Christian commonwealth, such training seems unnecessary to the well-educated and socially responsible citizenry it has traditionally been one job of the university to promote.

In this paper, I will first sketch how this impasse between concerns for church and academy figures in some prominent proposals about theology's inclusion in the university—the proposals of Gordon Kaufman and Schubert Ogden on the one hand, and George Lindbeck on the other.[1] I will then try to move beyond the impasse by transferring to the field of theological education a lesson to be learned from the drift of recent discussion in academic theology itself.

That discussion has seen a shift from methodological to more substantive questions in the effort to legitimize theology as an intellectual inquiry. Briefly, with the onset of a postmodern humility about pretensions to universality and dis-interestedness, theology seems less suspect in its methods; what theology is accused of has been so spread around that significant differences among fields become mere matters of degree, and methodological fault becomes not the defining fea-ture of one field but an internal risk for any. The legitimacy of theology on the wider intellectual scene shifts then from the question of whether theology can meet some scholarly minimum in its procedures to the substantive question of whether theology has anything important to say about the world and our place in it. What, if anything, is the positive contribution of theology, as one outlook among others from its own point of view, to a search for the true and the right on particular issues of concern in the twentieth century? What, in short, could a Christian perspective on life have going for it? How might a contemporary Chris-tian theology promote (or not) a more adequate understanding of the world or a more just way of living?

Compared to the rampant methodological preoccupations of academic the-ologians in the U.S. some scant fifteen or twenty years ago (say, the struggles of theologians to wrestle with the de-legitimizing effects of positivism and reduc-tionism in the natural and social sciences), these are clearly the new questions that now, in the early twenty-first century, prompt the most discussion. Might the place of theology in the secular university be reconceived according to this more topi-cal and less methodological focus? And what interest might the churches find in an academic theology so conceived?

THE IMPASSE

Let me sketch some ways not taken in order to set my own proposal in relief. The first way is common among theologians most interested in arguing for theology's place in a humanistic curriculum. The general strategy is to make theology and the academic study of religion—or humanistic studies generally—seem alike. Towards that end the nature of theology and/or those other disciplines is reconceived. Additionally (sometimes alternatively), the type of theological inquiry appropriate in a university context is rather severely limited.

In the case of Ogden and Kaufman, other disciplines are reconceived in that theology or the religious questions it addresses are extended to every intellec-tual or cultural field. Whether they recognize the fact or not, religious questions (Ogden) or faith stances in answer to such questions (Kaufman) enter into all the disciplines and thereby the relevance to university education of a discipline that explicitly considers the adequacy of such answers (theology) is firmly established. All university disciplines, in short, are implicitly religious (Ogden) or explicitly theological in nature (Kaufman).

At the same time that religion or theology is found everywhere, the sort of theology admissible in the university is restricted. Thus, in Ogden's case this theology seems solely critical, rather than constructive, in that its concerns are limited to the assessment of theological proposals already on the ground. Theology's job as a discipline of the humanities, in other words, is not to produce a religious stance but to evaluate it. As something like a humanistic discipline, theology is thereby eviscerated of part of its normative focus: those who do theology, in the sense of actively proposing what it is that Christianity should stand for in contemporary times, become the object of study rather than participants in academic theology. One can study what theologians say or put one's own theological sensibilities into a subjunctive mode as perspectives that students might temporarily imagine themselves occupying, but the assertion of a judgment concerning what it is proper for Christians to say and do in response to the challenges of contemporary life is off-limits in the university.

Even where, as in Kaufman's case, the theology admissible in university settings is explicitly constructive—developing, for example, frames of orientation on the basis of a sense of trust in and loyalty to what gives life its ultimate meaning (what Kaufman means by 'faith')—the theology appropriate to the university is not what one would ordinarily think of as a specifically Christian theology. While Christian theology usually privileges a particular set of texts (e.g., the Bible) and practices (e.g., the liturgy) as sources and norms of insight, the only theology appropriate in a university context is a far broader effort. For Ogden, such a theology must include the critical assessment of *all* religions by means of general philosophical methods. For Kaufman, it must blur into a range of studies exploring matters of ultimate concern throughout human culture so as to be pluralistic from the very start.[2] Proposals of even a specifically Christian (or Buddhist or Marxist) faith ought to emerge, Kaufman argues, only in conversation with other faiths of a traditionally religious or secular sort. Christian theology in the university is then a species of a wider theological enterprise indistinguishable from the academic study of religion (when that is given the normative cast of a critical field–inclusive field, judging meaningfulness and truth), and is never appropriate per se, apart from its inclusion in that wider effort.

While the need to rethink the tasks of both the university and academic theology is beyond question, this sort of reconceptualization does not seem to do much to resolve the problems from the side of either church or academy. Thus, the attribution of essentially religious concerns to all academic fields is unlikely— to say the least—to go over well in present-day secular universities. An equally cool reception would meet Kaufman's effort to make theology into some sort of Ur-discipline unifying the search for knowledge in modern research institutions. Both efforts are likely to appear to secular/atheistic academics as an imperialistic grab to inflate the importance of religion, while the latter effort in particular seems suspiciously like an outdated return to the nineteenth-century dream of a unified science, with theology replacing philosophy as its organizing center.

One might think that these reconceptualizations of theology to bring it in line with other humanistic disciplines of the academy would appease academic objections. However, they primarily aim to meet a strict methodological bar that no longer exists. Disqualifying Christian theology for its particularism in Ogden's case, for example, seems a strangely blanket judgment given suspicions in the contemporary academy about the existence anywhere of genuinely universal standards of meaningfulness and truth. Kaufman's worries about the authoritarian character of any theology short of the radically pluralistic one he commends sound quaint in an academic climate that now recognizes the tradition-bound, culturally determined, and interested character of even the 'hard' sciences.[3] It is, moreover, this very effort to meet a strict methodological bar that no longer exists which threatens to widen the gap between theology admissible in the university and that dedicated to service of the churches.

The other way not taken is that commonly endorsed by theologians whose primary concern is to readjust the balance in academic theology towards church concerns. Thus, for its chief advocate, George Lindbeck, the first task of academic theology is to socialize students into a Christian way of life, through the rigorous academic study of Christian traditions of thought and action. Christian theology in an academic setting is therefore part and parcel of the process of Christian identity formation. Such an activity is permissible in a university setting because, again on a methodological level, the way judgments are made in theology about proper Christian action and belief is purportedly continuous with the way religion is studied in established university disciplines such as anthropology, sociology, or cultural history: there too nonreductive but critical redescriptions are often offered of religious ways of life.

Such a proposal has its troubles, however, in formulating any strong justification for the place of theology in religious studies departments—university-affiliated divinity schools are usually the primary targets for discussion. It is unclear, first of all, why the interdisciplinary and interreligious character of most religious studies departments should be important for theology's primary task of inculcation. Study with that interdisciplinary and interreligious focus seems at best to be relevant to later stages of Christian reflection, when, for example, Lindbeck says, advanced students begin to try to construe the contemporary world in terms of the particular religion, Christianity, in which they have previously been socialized. At worst, the religiously pluralistic and interdisciplinary character of religious studies departments seems a distraction from academic theology's main task—students never learn enough about their particular religious tradition, in a sufficiently concentrated way, to make it their own.

If it is therefore not clear from a church interest in inculcating Christians into the faith why theology should be part of the humanistic curriculum of the university, it is also unclear from the university side. Apart from the possible mandate for professional schools to train a religious leadership, why should a secular university be interested in an intellectually responsible form of Christian socialization? Lindbeck offers only the feeble suggestion here that sending intellectually responsible Christians out into the world serves the university's interest by influencing the character of religion outside the academy and therefore the cultural environment in which the university exists.[4]

Finally, the blurring of normative theological judgments—judgments about what is authentically Christian—with the descriptive claims of sociocultural humanistic disciplines seems ultimately unhelpful: there is more to the former than the latter and it is just the question of the legitimacy and importance of that 'more' in a secular university context that is never adequately addressed. Especially with the resurgence, within the very disciplines that are to shore up the legitimacy of theology, of a postmodern respect for the divergent and the deviant, it has become evident that judgments of Christian authenticity are not decided by historical or cultural forms of analyses themselves. As has become increasingly apparent in the academic study of religion in recent years, the course of Christian thought and life, past and present, is far too messy and diverse for any easy transition on that basis to normative judgments about properly Christian beliefs and actions—at least beyond the most vapid of supposed rules or boundaries distinguishing what is appropriately Christian.[5]

Without some academically respectable affirmation of the normative posture of the academic disciplines, this normative 'more' in theological judgment remains suspect, again threatening a divorce between academic and constructive theology by pushing the latter out of humanistic study. The academy must be somehow about the critical extension of normative traditions of life and thought like Christianity, if Christian theology, in all its usual constructive senses, is to have a rightful place there. Something then like Kaufman's position, but without the overarching, bridge-discipline claims for theology, is again called for, therefore, from this more church-oriented side of the coin. Something like it will be incorporated into my own position, to which I now turn.

A PROPOSAL

If we follow the above analysis of the impasse between concerns for academy and church in academic theology, we need to resolve two sets of issues. First, we need a reconceptualization of the university disciplines that would help establish a place for theology in all its constructive aspects, a reconceptualization that could be justified apart from appeal to religious or theological concerns, which have dropped out of the secular university's mandate. Second, we need to make clear how a constructive theology, which includes in its purview the active proposal of appropriately Christian belief and action at least in part on typical particularistic grounds (e.g., by way of biblical interpretation and the assessment of trends in the life of the churches), can find the interreligious and interdisciplinary character of the university essential to its tasks.

On the first point, it is important to be aware of the mixed mission of universities in the United States.[6] That mission is at least as eclectic as its famous German models, particularly in Berlin, where a concern to serve society as a whole through the formation of an educated leadership class eventually joined forces with an overriding interest in pure research. In the United States, disciplinary specialization fragmented the nineteenth-century German ideal of the university as a place for the formation of a unified science, and it is this vision of specialized research that now seems its *raison d'être*. The leading U.S. universities are primarily research institutions purportedly seeking knowledge for its own sake (despite the heavy dependence of university funding on the interests of the military-industrial complex) and serving the wider society only indirectly through pursuit of primarily scholarly ends. Wider social concerns, a sense of social responsibility—the idea, in short, that the university is there to produce an educated citizenry capable of making good decisions about the running of their lives together—remain part of the university ideal, however. Tapping into that neglected side of the university's historical mission might be a way of developing the normative aspect of university disciplines as a whole and so make constructive theology less anomalous. But, aside from an interest in pleading theology's case, are there any more general intellectual or cultural trends pushing in that direction?

The modern research institution reflects a view of knowledge that is at once both abstractive and universalizing.[7] Behind the idea of disciplinary specialization seems to be the sense that things are best understood in isolation and stripped of influences from their broader contexts. The ability to think this abstractly funds, in turn, a confidence in generalization from particular instances: one can universalize abstract cases since they do not seem bound to anything local or historically particular, since they seem fundamentally unconditioned by time and place or by special interests and limited perspectives. The resulting confidence about generalization across particular differences—confidence that such differences will not affect the validity of abstract laws and structures—works against any perceived need for interdisciplinarity. Universal generalizations are made by each intellectual discipline while the whole of them remains a mere confederation, absent the need for consultation and correction by others.

The academic and cultural trends of the last half of the twentieth century run directly contrary, however, to these concerns for abstraction and universalization. Global capitalism, the media reach, an ecological sensibility in biology, systems analysis in the social sciences, the stress in the physical sciences on the complex statistical interplay of multiple forces, interdependent processes, and complex configurations of possible events, all suggest an expansive cognitive model attentive to contextual relationality rather than abstract analysis. A university that integrates rather than simply aggregates disciplines seems called for, then.[8] Disciplines that isolate attention on de-contextualized bits of the world of human experience cannot hold off for long consideration of the concrete fullness of that experience, but are forced by the intellectual climate of the times to put their own concerns back into the larger picture.[9]

Hope of a return to the integration of knowledge by way of general principles—the nineteenth-century hope for the university as a site of a unified general science according to universal principles—is blocked, however, by equally prominent intellectual trends emphasizing the historical particularity and interested character of all claims to knowledge, even and perhaps especially those that claim a universality of insight. With the chastening of universal pretensions comes a renewed stress on the practical character of rational judgment, since all claims now gain a topical and situation-specific focus. A critical stance on knowledge claims requires one to know who makes the claim, in what context, and for what purpose. Premature generalization from isolated cases is defeated by growing suspicions that procedures and conclusions appropriate for any one subject matter, or perspective on it, may be so only up to a point, in limited circumstances, or from a restricted or warped angle of vision in need of subsequent expansion or revision. Interdisciplinarity in such an intellectual climate would have to mean, then, an engagement across differences in discipline-defining subject matters and angles of vision, with any unifying principles, agreement about investigatory processes across disciplines, or consensus in conclusions remaining open questions for resolution only in the course of such engagement.

The focus for interdisciplinary discussion could itself, moreover, be broadly construed as practical in a way that would hook up with the idea of the university as a socially responsible institution. The same intellectual and cultural trends I have been talking about stress the difference that human beings and their outlooks make to physical and biological processes (the Heisenberg Principle; ecological science). The purely disinterested stance of a contemplative reason thereby falls before an understanding of the way humans are active participants, and therefore fully integrated into, physical and natural processes. Knowledge claims, moreover, are never pure descriptions but reflect interests in maintaining or altering the social structures in which their purveyors participate. This attention to the social implications of even the most scholarly points of view feeds into the heightened sense, after the Enlightenment at least, that human beings are responsible for their own social circumstances: society as a whole becomes a possible object for intellectually responsible decision making.

If something like this is the contemporary cultural climate, what better time for the university to regain a sense of its mission to serve society as a whole through the formation of a citizenry educated to make good decisions about the character of their lives together? Presumably that training would come in systematically unprincipled interdisciplinary exchanges among academics who bring to the discussion of issues of contemporary moment (what initially at least seem to be) irreducibly different concerns and angles on the phenomena of human life.[10] The university would become the site for a socially significant cultural contest among old and new, familiar and foreign, rediscovered and newly constructed, visions of the world and our place in it. In a search for truth humbled by the recognition of constant change and limitations of perspective, this cultural contest would require the widest possible purview, including in its reach the sort of ever-expanding range of positions that only the best critical scholarship makes readily available and that only a university dedicated to comprehensive knowledge can set easily in conversation with one another. Without presupposing or expecting much in the way of universal principles in method or conclusions, this would be a cultural contest that proceeds instead with special attention to the way general outlooks of a scientific, religious, or otherwise humanistic nature address and are shaped by contextually specific perspectives and topics. All might be a resource ultimately for a consideration of today's problems, in the university and outside it by the students it has educated.[11]

If theology were included in the mix of this new sort of interdisciplinary exchange in the university, it might easily do so as a constructive theology, formulating for today a Christian outlook on the world and our place in it with special attention to the most pressing problems and challenges of contemporary life.[12] Such creative extension of a Christian outlook would be matched by the creative extension of outlooks and fields by scholars in the other scientific or humanistic enterprises of the university (including scholars with interests in other religions). From this point of view, a scientific advance becomes as much a creative extension of a particular outlook on life as a new treatment of Christ's atoning work is, and each has its own possible social significance or ramifications for the way we are to live in the world, to be considered together in the wider debate that defines university life as a whole.

In this way of looking at things, the positive mandate for constructive theology's inclusion in the cultural contest of the university need not involve the definition of that contest itself as theological or crypto-religious in nature. Theology's inclusion would be justified instead by the importance of its particular contribution to the mix. In part, that importance might be based upon Christianity's historical and present-day influence as a cultural force, but such an argument is not essential. Inclusion need not, in other words, be based on any principle of representation proportionate to actual sociocultural influence. The primary justification for inclusion is the ability to produce an interestingly different angle on life. No one would dispute, for example, the importance of considering Buddhist views of suffering, should that be the topic for university-wide cultural contest; Buddhism's statistical underrepresentation in the United States at least is of no matter. The same would go for Christianity (and this means in effect that, in university curricula, Christianity could be put on a level playing field with other religions on intellectual grounds).

If making an interestingly different contribution to the mix is the primary requirement for theology's inclusion, then there is no prima facie reason for excluding a theology that retains the importance of particularistic sources and norms in its constructive work. Indeed, such a requirement encourages the inclusion of theology of that sort, since it is just those particularistic sources and norms—e.g., the Christian Scriptures—that account for the distinctiveness of theological proposals. Worries about the legitimacy in a university context of proposals based on such sources and norms are deflected in my account of cultural contest. In the wider cultural contest of university life, the focus is not so much on where proposals came from or how they were generated, but on the conclusions themselves and what they have going for them.

Of course, theological proposals would not have anything going for them if they were inseparable from sources and norms that lack all intellectual credibility, meaning by that now that they are inappropriate to the subject matter and the angle taken on it by a particular field of study. The bases of theological judgment cannot be exempted, then, from critical scrutiny in the cultural contest of university life. But bereft of easy appeals to universally applicable procedures, definitive determination of such appropriateness is not very easy to make.

Moreover, even if the usual theological sources and norms remain suspect—which they undoubtedly are in the academy—it is far from clear that the theological proposals themselves are inseparable from them. Theologians on the basis in great part of distinctively Christian sources and norms purport to say something important about the nature of human flourishing. What is an authentically Christian outlook on life because it abides by those sources and norms is also supposed to be saying something of wider moment about our world and our place in it.[13] Claims of that force and scope cannot be of insular Christian concern, but are almost inevitably susceptible to challenge or support on other grounds (even if the theologians proposing them failed to consider any of those grounds). For example, a Christian view of justice might trade heavily on biblical accounts of the Jubilee Year, but surely such a proposal might be assessed, criticized, corrected, or possibly accepted as is, on grounds typical of other fields—say, on grounds of economic viability, or its compatibility with reigning models of equity in political science, or ability to improve on them from an unexpected angle, etc. Theological appeal to distinctively Christian sources and norms therefore need not deadlock argument on a wider university front.[14]

Why, however, would a Christian theologian, especially one making distinctively Christian sources and norms central to the constructive theological effort, want to engage in the cultural contest of university life? This is a species of the wider question, to which we now turn, of whether academic theology in the university might address any central concerns of the churches.

In part, one could say that the Christian churches and their theologians have always been in arguments like this with other religions and viewpoints of a scientific or philosophical nature about matters of human moment. My account of cultural contest in the university is simply a proposal to reenact there the sort of cultural contests that have always gone on in real life. European history, for example, is full of them: a Christian affirmation of free will versus Stoic fatalism or ancient astrological determinism; heavenly happiness versus an Aristotelian earthly one in the medieval period; religious versus secular accounts of state interests in the early modern period; original sin versus a naturalistic account of human failing in the Enlightenment (Pascal, say, against Voltaire); dogmatic certainties versus a nineteenth-century historical consciousness. None of these contests amounted to a simple either/or, but a complicated process of action and reaction, adjustment and refusal, which required serious attention by theologians to the conclusions of nontheological inquiry (even in cases where such conclusions were ultimately quite forcefully rejected).

In any historical period or locale, the subject matter with which theologians and others wrestle will see a great deal of overlap in just those matters that are thought at that time and place to be of wide human significance. Theologians to this extent always have a stake in addressing alternative perspectives to their own. Those perspectives are either attacks, confirmations, or salutary correctives to their own.

Something constructive, rather than something simply defensive or confrontational, is to be expected from such cultural contest the more theologians highlight, as they commonly do in the modern period especially, the human (and therefore the temporary and limited) character of their own (and everyone else's) proposals and of their own use of distinctively Christian sources and norms to construct them. One might argue, indeed, that Christians have always had the resources to be especially attentive to such fallibilism the more they recognized the transcendence of God.[15] That transcendence tells "against the presumption of any human voice to speak the ultimate word" and counsels those holding different viewpoints—Christians among them—to "the service of mutual limitation and creative conflict."[16] Putting their own presuppositions and proposals at risk in the cultural contest of university life would be one way for theologians to prove their fidelity to this aspect of a Christian outlook, too often neglected in the historical lapses of Christianity into dogmatism and fanaticism.

It might seem, however, that Christians would have only a secondary interest in the cultural contest of university life. Arguing with others about the true nature of the world and our place in it might seem, on my account, to be secondary to determining what it is that Christians should say about it. My proposal, in contrast to Kaufman's, suggests this because the distinctiveness of the Christian contribution to the mix of cultural contest appears to require theologians to have already formed judgments about what Christianity stands for prior to their entrance. Theologians are not required to make these judgments about Christianity on the *basis* of interdisciplinary contest; they are simply required to enter the fray of such contest after doing so.

Of course, the conclusions arrived at in other fields are usually a major influence on theological decision making about what Christians should do and believe. Theologians are aware that certain recommendations of Christian belief and action would conflict with the conclusions of, say, the physical sciences, and that might be one reason to reconsider them. But the entrance of theologians into a university-wide cultural contest presumes that they have already formed normative judgments about a Christian perspective on life and that that is their distinctive contribution to the debate. Every discipline or field has to bring something to the wider debate of a normative nature—not just "these are all the possible positions, or this is all the 'data' of relevance to my disciplinary purview." Otherwise, university-wide cultural contest would seem something like Kierkegaard's story of the seven in which no one can make a decision about anything because they are all waiting for somebody else to.[17] Or, more charitably perhaps, the decision-making processes of every discipline would be blurred into the one university-wide debate, from a nonexistent unified methodological viewpoint—that is, every discipline would have to be engaged in the same pluralistic inquiry, availing itself of the same set of materials donated by all the disciplines, in the very effort to draw any conclusions appropriate to it, from the perspective of its own field. There would be no 'contest' here, presuming as that does a real argument among substantive positions, drawn up by disciplines that retain their discipline-defining differences in procedures and objects of inquiry, no real argument from different points of view that have, initially at least, a fair bit of normative definition.[18]

It might seem then that my proposal brings us back to something like Lindbeck's position. Especially when the issues count for so much—when the very character of our lives together is at stake—Christians will want to get into the fray of working out the conflict of interpretations among Christians and non-Christians, science and faith, etc. But surely this is for advanced students who already have some sense of what Christianity stands for? In order to prevent a return to Lindbeck's position, we need to show how the more primary matter of forming judgments about properly Christian beliefs and attitudes is essentially involved with the sort of cultural contest I am proposing that universities enact.

Here a basic reconceptualization of the nature of theological construction is in order, one that brings theological self-understanding into line with what I believe theological construction has always actually been. One option here might be to extend a remark made earlier about the possible inclusion of other modes of inquiry within the sources and norms of properly theological inquiry. That is, specifically Christian sources and norms have never been sufficient for theological construction, and therefore something like the university-wide cultural contest I am proposing has always been part of theology itself as a constructive field. Thus, while it is not part of the discipline of economics to take into account Catholic bishops' statements about responsibilities for the poor, it is part of the discipline of theology to take into account the best of current economic theory when deciding what Christians should say about economic inequalities. One might again suspect, however, that this sort of similarity in procedure to university-wide cultural contest holds only for matters of secondary theological concern—i.e., when theologians turn their attention to the subject matters of other disciplines (e.g., economics)—and not when theologians are considering their own most proper subject matter—say, God and all things in their relation to God. The option I propose will, moreover, make this one seem unnecessarily restrictive: even if the sources and norms characteristic of other disciplines are not included in those appropriate to theological decision making (especially on basic issues concerning what Christians should say about God or Jesus), theological construction for the following reason still involves something like the cultural contest of university life.

The basic point here is that the construction of theological sense involves a *vis-à-vis* with other intellectual and cultural fields.[19] The very *meaning* of even the most fundamental theological claims is determined by what theologians do with the notions and affirmations of other intellectual and cultural areas. Theological sense is always constructed, in other words, through the alteration, through the new use, of notions and affirmations in circulation elsewhere. Typical for all construction of theological sense is the way, for example, in the early church a Christian affirmation of the humility of God in Christ has its sense determined by its very odd fit with, its subversive force within, the honor/shame code of Greco-Roman ethics. In order to establish, or understand, the meaning of Christian claims, one must be aware of the new spin being put on the intellectual currency of other fields. That new spin is just the meaning or point of what is being said theologically. Theology is fundamentally then a parasitic or consumptive field, establishing its distinctiveness from others in and through what it does with borrowed materials. As such a parasitic or essentially consumptive field, it repeats within itself the sort of cultural contest or tussle over matters of shared concern that constitutes university life as an integrated whole in my account. One cannot be a constructive theologian for the present day without familiarity with the currency of the other intellectual or cultural fields of the day, and it is through the assessment of how other theologians of the past and present have dealt with comparable material of their own times and places that one develops a sense for what needs to be done now. If this is the basic character of theological construction, then even the most narrowly defined, church-oriented academic theology ignores at its peril the wider cultural contexts of that construction which university disciplines discuss.

CONCLUSIONS

The virtues of my proposal are that it meets objections from both church and academy to the full inclusion of constructive theology in the university and that it does so without the need for any very radical reconceptualization of the university or constructive theology, to which either might take exception. Nothing about my proposal suggests, as other essays in this collection might, that constructive theology's only proper place is in the humanities curriculum of the university. My proposal does suggest, however, that the teaching of theology in institutions with other aims than the university *qua* university—say, denominational seminaries, freestanding or university-affiliated divinity schools—would do well to imitate in their curriculum the inter-religious and interdisciplinary character of the university that my proposal of cultural contest calls for. Even if the primary aim of the seminary or divinity school is an intellectually responsible inculcation or socialization into the Christian faith—through a knowledge of the Christian scriptures and the history of Christian thought and life and some direction concerning the creative extension of the faith for today—that aim could only be furthered, as my last remarks about the essentially parasitic or consumptive character of theology suggest, by the inclusion of disciplines or fields that make clear what theologians have borrowed for their own use in the past—and what they might now borrow in the present for the construction of distinctively Christian outlooks on life.

NOTES

1. See Schubert Ogden, "Theology and Religious Studies," and "Theology in the University," in his *On Theology* (San Francisco: Harper and Row, 1986), 102–33; Gordon Kaufman, "Critical Theology as a University Discipline," in his *God-Mystery-Diversity* (Minneapolis: Fortress Press, 1996), 204–215; and George Lindbeck, "University Divinity Schools: A Report on Ecclesiastically Independent Theological Education," in *Working Papers of the Rockefeller Foundation* (1976).

2. Kaufman, "Critical Theology," 211–13.

3. The classic text here is of course Thomas Kuhn, *The Structure of Scientific Revolutions* (Chicago: University of Chicago Press, 1970).

4. Lindbeck, "University Divinity Schools," 82.

5. For an extended argument to this effect, see Kathryn Tanner, *Theories of Culture: A New Agenda for Theology* (Minneapolis: Fortress Press, 1997), 72–79, 138–43.

6. See the helpful discussion of Joseph Hough, "The University and the Common Good," in *Theology and the University*, ed. David Griffin and Joseph Hough (Albany: State University of New York Press, 1991), 105–16.

7. For a much fuller account of the analysis offered in this and the next few paragraphs, see Stephen Toulmin, *The Return to Cosmology* (Berkeley: University of California Press, 1982), 228–74; *Cosmopolis* (New York: Free Press, 1990), 160–209; "The Historicization of Natural Science," in *Paradigm Change in Theology*, ed. Hans Kung and David Tracy (New York: Crossroad, 1989), 233–41; and Kathryn Tanner, *God and the Creation in Christian Theology* (Oxford: Basil Blackwell, 1988), 124–32.

8. Toulmin, *Return to Cosmology*, 228–34.

9. Toulmin, *Cosmopolis*, 201.

10. Such issues might include, for example, responses to global capitalism or environmental crisis. In the former case, one can easily imagine input from political and social scientists, of course, along with biologists, geologists, and anthropologists (who know something, say, about the impact of industrialization on land management and population),

theologians, ethicists, media specialists, and comparative literature professors (with some knowledge, say, of the effect of global cultural exchange on indigenous authors), and historians with a knowledge of earlier global economic systems (perhaps that of the Greco-Roman Empire after Alexander the Great, or forms of mercantilism and colonialism with the expansion of the West since the early modern period), etc.

11. Not all university disciplines—say, history or the "pure" sciences—would be required to make normative discussion of contemporary problems their focus. There is, however, by implication at least some social, moral, or practical significance to every intellectual outlook, and that significance would be brought out explicitly in university-wide interdisciplinary cultural contest.

12. But of course constructive theology of this sort is not the only sort of theology that might enter into the mix—e.g., historical theology could have its place too—for the same general reason that all other disciplines without an explicitly normative focus have their place. See the preceding note.

13. That is, a theological judgment about the properly Christian thing to say and do is usually also a judgment about what Christians should hold to be right action or true belief—for anyone, Christian or not. For example, loving one's neighbor is an appropriately Christian stance, but such a stance is also thought to be simply the right way to be and therefore concerns more than simply the character of Christian action.

14. For more on the character of public debate envisioned here, see Kathryn Tanner, "Public Theology and the Character of Public Debate," *Annual for the Society of Christian Ethics* (1996): 79–101

15. For a development of this point, see H. Richard Niebuhr, "Theology in the University," in his *Radical Monotheism and Western Culture* (New York: Harper Torchbooks, 1970), 93–99; Kaufman, "Critical Theology"; and Kathryn Tanner, *The Politics of God* (Minneapolis: Fortress Press, 1992), 35–74.

16. Niebuhr, "Theology in the University," 95, 97.

17. Søren Kierkegaard, *Works of Love* (New York: Harper Torchbooks, 1962), 120–2. My point here about a nonexistent methodological unification of the disciplines therefore takes into account Kaufman's denial that he is proposing a generic debate from nowhere in particular. For Kaufman, the different disciplines are to take, it seems, different perspectives on the same mix of data according to their particular commitments (e.g., to Christianity or Marxism or the worldview of the physical sciences).

18. My stress here on the normative character of proposals brought to the debate with other disciplines does not of course preclude the weakening of that normative character as the contest proceeds: one might very well be made unsure of one's position on the way to a reformulation.

19. For a more extended treatment of ideas in this paragraph, see Tanner, *Theories of Culture*, 110–19.

Bibliography

Allen, Charlotte. "Is Nothing Sacred? Casting out the Gods from Religious Studies." *Lingua Franca* 6 (1996): 30–40.

Allen, Charlotte. "Response to Bulletin 26, 4." *Council of Societies for the Study of Religion Bulletin* 27 (1998): 45–46.

Altizer, Thomas J. J. "Total Abyss and Theological Rebirth: The Crisis of University Theology." In *Theology and the University: Essays in Honor of John B. Cobb, Jr.* Edited by David R. Griffin and Joseph C. Hough, Jr., 169–184. Albany: State University of New York Press, 1991.

Anderson, Victor. *Pragmatic Theology: Negotiating the Intersections of an American Philosophy of Religion and Public Theology.* Albany: State University of New York Press, 1998.

Andrews, Allan A. "The Status of the Field: Normative, Humanistic and Social Scientific Approaches to the Academic Study of Religion." *Council of Societies for the Study of Religion Bulletin* 22 (1993): 101–105.

Apczynski, John, ed. *Theology and the University.* Lanham: University Press of America, 1990.

Asad, Talal. *Genealogies of Religion: Discipline and Reasons of Power in Christianity and Islam.* Baltimore: Johns Hopkins University Press, 1993.

Ashley, Benedict M. "The Discipline of Theology: Seminary and University." In *Does the Church Know How to Teach? An Ecumenical Inquiry.* Edited by Kendig Brubaker Cully, 261–288. New York: Macmillan, 1970.

Auld, A. Graeme. "Can a Biblical Theology also Be Academic or Ecumenical?" In *Text As Pretext: Essays in Honour of Robert Davidson.* Edited by Robert P. Carroll, 13–27. Sheffield, England: JSOT Press, 1992.

Baird, Robert D. *Category Formation and the History of Religions.* The Hague: Mouton, 1971.

Baird, Robert D., ed. *Methodological Issues in Religious Studies.* Chico, California: New Horizons Press, 1975.

Ballard, Paul H. "Practical Theology as an Academic Discipline." *Theology* 98 (1995): 112–122.

Beardslee, William A. "Theology and Rhetoric in the University." In *Theology and the University: Essays in Honor of John B. Cobb, Jr.* Edited by David R. Griffin and Joseph C. Hough, Jr., 185–200. Albany: State University of New York Press, 1991.

Bellah, Robert. "Between Religion and Social Science." In *The Culture of Unbelief.* Edited by Rocco Caporale and Antonio Grumelli, 271–293. Berkeley: University of California Press, 1971.

Bellah, Robert. "Religious Studies as 'New Religion.'" In *Understanding the New Religions.* Edited by Jacob Needleman and George Baker, 106–112. New York: Seabury Press, 1978.

Braun, Willi, and Russell T. McCutcheon, eds. *Guide to the Study of Religion.* London: Cassell, 2000.

Brown, Delwin. "Academic Theology and Religious Studies." *Council of Societies for the Study of Religion Bulletin* 26 (1997): 64–66.

Brown, Delwin. "Believing Traditions and the Task of the Academic Theologian." *Journal of the American Academy of Religion* 62 (1994): 1167–1179.

Brown, Delwin. *Boundaries of Our Habitations: Tradition and Theological Construction.* Albany: State University of New York Press, 1994.

Brown, Delwin. "Constructive Theology and the Academy." *Council of Societies for the Study of Religion Bulletin* 22 (1993): 7–9.

Brown, Delwin. "Public Theology, Academic Theology: Wentzel Van Huyssteen and the Nature of Theological Rationality." *American Journal of Theology and Philosophy,* 22 (2001): 88–101.

Brown, Delwin. "Refashioning Self and Other: Theology, Academy and the New Ethnography." In *Converging on Culture: Theologians in Dialogue with Cultural Analysis and Criticism.* Edited by Delwin Brown, Sheila Greeve Davaney, and Kathryn Tanner, 41–55. Oxford: Oxford University Press, 2001.

Brown, William Adams. *The Case for Theology in the University.* Chicago: University of Chicago Press, 1938.

Busse, Richard. "Editorial: Should Theology Be Taught in Departments of Religion?" *Council of Studies for the Study of Religion Bulletin* 22 (1993): 2.

Byrne, Peter. "The Study of Religion: Neutral, Scientific, or Neither." *Method and Theory in the Study of Religion* 9 (1997): 339–351.

Cady, Linell E. *Religion, Theology and American Public Life.* Albany: State University of New York Press, 1993.

Cady, Linell E. "Religious Studies and the Public University: A Case Study at Arizona State University." *Method and Theory in the Study of Religion* 7 (1995): 393–406.

Cady, Linell E. "The Public Intellectual and Effective Critique." *Council of Societies for the Study of Religion Bulletin* 27 (1998): 36–38.

Cady, Linell E. "The Social Location of the Theologian: Intellectual, Legal and Political Considerations." *Council of Societies for the Study of Religion Bulletin* 22 (1993): 3–7.

Cady, Linell E. "Loosening the Category that Binds: Modern 'Religion' and the Promise of Cultural Studies." In *Converging on Culture: Theologians in Dialogue with Cultural Analysis and Criticism.* Edited by Delwin Brown, Sheila Greeve Davaney, and Kathryn Tanner, 45–69. Oxford: Oxford University Press, 2001.

Cahill, P. Joseph. "Is Theology Necessary to Religious Studies?" *Religious Studies and Theology* 9 (1989): 27–34.

Cahill, P. Joseph. *Mended Speech: The Crisis of Religious Studies and Theology*. New York: Crossroad, 1982.

Cahill, P. Joseph. "Theological Studies, Where Are You?" *Journal of the American Academy of Religion* 52 (1984): 742–747.

Callahan, Daniel. *The Role of Theology in the University*. Milwaukee: Bruce Publishing, 1967.

Capps, Walter H. *Religious Studies: The Making of a Discipline*. Minneapolis: Fortress Press, 1995.

Capps, Walter H. "Religious Studies—Theological Studies: The St Louis Project." *Journal of the American Academy of Religion* 52 (1984): 721–730.

Cherry, Conrad. "Boundaries and Frontiers for the Study of Religion: The Heritage of the Age of the University." *Journal of the American Academy of Religion* 57 (1989): 807–827.

Cherry, Conrad. *Hurrying Toward Zion: Universities, Divinity Schools, and American Protestantism*. Bloomington: Indiana University Press, 1995.

Clark, W. Royce. "The Legal Status of Religious Studies Programs in Public Higher Education." In *Beyond the Classics? Essays in Religious Studies and Liberal Education*. Edited by Frank E. Reynolds and Sheryl L. Burkhalter, 109–139. Atlanta: Scholars Press, 1990.

Clarke, Paul A. B., and Andrew Linzey, eds. *Theology, the University and the Modern World*. London: Lester Crook Academic, 1988.

Coulson, John. *Theology and the University: An Ecumenical Investigation*. Baltimore: Helicon Press, 1964.

Cox, James L. "Religious Studies by the Religious: A Discussion of the Relationship Between Theology and the Science of Religion." *Journal for the Study of Religion* 7 (1994): 3–31,

Crites, Stephen D., and others. "Liberal Learning and the Religion Major. A Report of the American Academy of Religion Task Force on the Religion Major." *AAR Task Force* (1990): 1–22.

D'Costa, Gavin. "The End of 'Theology' and 'Religious Studies.'" *Theology* 99 (1996): 338–351.

Davis, Charles. "The Reconvergence of Theology and Religious Studies." *Studies in Religion/Sciences religieuses* 4 (1975): 205–221.

Davis, Charles. "Theology and Religious Studies." *Scottish Journal of Religious Studies* 2 (1981): 11–20.

Davis, Charles. "Wherein There is no Ecstasy" *Studies in Religion/Sciences religieuses* 13 (1984): 393–400.

Dawes, Gregory W. "Theology and Religious Studies in the University: 'Some Ambiguities' Revisited." *Religion* 26 (1996): 49–68.

Edsman, Carl Martin. "Theology or Religious Studies?" *Religion* 4 (1974): 59–74.

Eliade, Mircea. *The Quest: History and Meaning in Religion*. Chicago: University of Chicago Press, 1969.

Eliade, Mircea, and Joseph M. Kitagawa, eds. *The History of Religions: Essays in Methodology.* Chicago: University of Chicago Press, 1959.

Farley, Edward. *The Fragility of Knowledge: Theological Education in the Church and the University.* Philadelphia: Fortress Press, 1988.

Farley, Edward. "The Place of Theology in the Study of Religion." *Religious Studies and Theology* 5 (1985): 9–29.

Farley, Edward. *Theologia: The Fragmentation and Unity of Theological Education.* Philadelphia: Fortress Press, 1983.

Fiorenza, Francis S. "A Response to Donald Wiebe." *Council of Societies for the Study of Religion Bulletin* 23 (1994): 6–10.

Fiorenza, Francis S. "Theological and Religious Studies: The Contest of the Faculties." In *Shifting Boundaries: Contextual Approaches to the Structure of Theological Education.* Edited by Barbara G. Wheeler and Edward Farley, 119–149. Louisville, Kentucky: Westminster/John Knox Press, 1991.

Fiorenza, Francis S. "Theology in the University." *Council of Societies for the Study of Religion Bulletin* 22 (1993): 34–39.

Fitzgerald, Timothy. "A Critique of 'Religion' as a Cross-cultural Category." *Method and Theory in the Study of Religion* 9 (1997): 91–110.

Fitzgerald, Timothy. "The Ideology of Religious Studies." *Council of Societies for the Study of Religion Bulletin,* 28 (1999): 39–41.

Fitzgerald, Timothy. *The Ideology of Religious Studies.* Oxford: Oxford University Press, 2000.

Gamwell, Franklin I. "Should a University Include Theology?" *Criterion* 36 (1997): 18–27.

Geertz, Armin W., and Russell T. McCutcheon, eds. "Perspectives on Method and Theory in the Study of Religion: Adjunct Proceedings of the XVIIth Congress of the International Association for the History of Religions, Mexico City, 1995." *Method and Theory in the Study of Religion* 12 (2000): 3–338.

Gill, David W., ed. *Should God Get Tenure? Essays on Religion and Higher Education.* Grand Rapids, Michigan: Eerdmans, 1997.

Gill, Sam D. "No Place to Stand: Jonathan Z Smith as *Homo Ludens,* The Academic Study of Religion *Sub Specie Ludi.*" *Journal of the American Academy of Religion* 66 (1998): 283–312.

Gill, Sam D. "The Academic Study of Religion." *Journal of the American Academy of Religion* 62 (1994): 965–975.

Green, William Scott. "Something Strange, Yet Nothing New: Religion in the Secular Curriculum." *Soundings* 71 (1988): 271–278.

Griffin, David R. "Professing Theology in the State University." In *Theology and the University: Essays in Honor of John B. Cobb, Jr.* Edited by David R. Griffin and Joseph C. Hough, Jr., 3–34. Albany: State University of New York Press, 1991.

Griffin, David R., and Joseph C. Hough, Jr., eds. *Theology and the University: Essays in Honor of John B. Cobb, Jr.* Albany: State University of New York Press, 1991.

Gustafson, James. "The Study of Religion in Colleges and Universities: A Practical Commentary." In *The Study of Religion in Colleges and Universities*. Edited by Paul Ramsey and John F. Wilson, 330–346. Princeton: Princeton University Press, 1970.

Hann, Robert R. "Commitment, Theology, and the Dilemma of Religious Studies at the State University." *Horizons* 19 (1992): 263–276.

Hart, D. G. *The University Gets Religion: Religious Studies in American Higher Education*. Baltimore: Johns Hopkins University Press, 1999.

Hart, Ray, "Religious and Theological Studies in American Higher Education: A Pilot Study." *Journal of the American Academy of Religion* 59 (1991): 715–827.

Hartt, Julian Norris. *Theology and the Church in the University*. Philadelphia: Westminster Press, 1969.

Harvey, Van Austin. "On the Intellectual Marginality of American Theology." In *Religion and Twentieth-Century American Intellectual Life*. Edited by Michael J. Lacey, 172–192. Cambridge: Cambridge University Press, 1989.

Harvey, Van Austin. *The Historian and the Believer: The Morality of Historical Knowledge and Christian Belief*. New York: Macmillan Publishing, 1966.

Hauerwas, Stanley. "Christians in the Hands of Flaccid Secularists: Theology and 'Moral Inquiry' in the Modern University." In *Spirituality and Theology: Essays in Honor of Diogenes Allen*. Edited by Eric O. Springsted, 13–27. Louisville, Kentucky: Westminster/John Knox Press, 1998.

Honko, Lauri, ed. *Science of Religion: Studies in Methodology*. The Hague: Mouton, 1979.

Hough, Joseph C., Jr. "The Marginalization of Theology in the University." In *Religious Studies, Theological Studies, and the University-Divinity School*. Edited by Joseph Kitagawa, 37–68. Atlanta: Scholars Press, 1992.

Hough, Joseph C., Jr. "The University and the Common Good." In *Theology and the University: Essays in Honor of John B. Cobb, Jr.* Edited by David R. Griffin and Joseph C. Hough, Jr., 97–124. Albany: State University of New York Press, 1991.

Idinopulos, Thomas A., and Edward A. Yonan, eds. *Religion and Reductionism: Essays on Eliade, Segal, and the Challenge of the Social Sciences for the Study of Religion*. Leiden: E. J. Brill, 1994.

Isherwood, Lisa, and Dorothea McEwan. "An Introduction to Feminist Theology and the Case for its Study in an Academic Setting." *Feminist Theology* 2 (1993): 10–25.

Jaffe, Martin. "Fessing Up in Theory: On Professing and Confessing in the Religious Studies Classroom." *Method and Theory in the Study of Religion* 9 (1997): 325–337.

Jastrow, Morris. *The Study of Religion*. Chico, California: Scholars Press, 1981.

Jensen, Tim, and Mikael Rothstein, eds. *Secular Theories on Religion: Current Perspectives*. Copenhagen: Museum Tusculanum Press, 2000.

Juschka, Darlene M. "The Construction of Pedagogical Spaces: Religious Studies in the University." *Studies in Religion/Sciences religieuses* 28 (1999): 85–97.

Kant, Immanuel. *The Conflict of the Faculties*. Translated by Mary J. Gregor. New York: Abaris Books, 1979.

Kaufman, Gordon. "Critical Theology as a University Discipline." In *Theology and the University: Essays in Honor of John B. Cobb, Jr.* Edited by David R. Griffin and Joseph C. Hough, Jr., 35–50. Albany: State University of New York Press, 1991.

King, Richard. *Orientalism and Religion: Postcolonial Theory, India and "The Mystic East."* New York: Routledge, 1999.

King, Ursula, ed. *Turning Points in Religious Studies: Essays in Honour of Geoffrey Parrinder.* Edinburgh: T & T Clark, 1990.

Kitagawa, Joseph Mitsuo, ed. *Religious Studies, Theological Studies, and the University-Divinity School.* Atlanta: Scholars Press, 1992.

Klostermaier, Klaus K., and Larry W. Hurtado, eds. *Religious Studies: Issues, Prospects, and Proposals.* Atlanta: Scholars Press, 1991.

Kung, Hans, and David Tracy, eds. *Paradigm Change in Theology.* New York: Crossroad, 1989.

Lacey, Michael J., ed. *Religion and Twentieth-Century American Intellectual Life.* Cambridge: Cambridge University Press, 1989.

Lawson, E. Thomas. "The Illusions of Autonomy: Defining the History of Religions." *Annals of Scholarship* 6 (1989): 485–492.

Lease, Gary. "Pathologies in the Academic Study of Religion: North American Institutional Case Studies." *Method and Theory in the Study of Religion* 7 (1995): 295–414.

Lincoln, Bruce. *Theorizing Myth: Narrative, Ideology, and Scholarship.* Chicago: University of Chicago Press, 1999.

Lincoln, Bruce. "Theses on Method." *Method and Theory in the Study of Religion* 8 (1996): 225–227.

Lipner, Julius. "Theology and Religious Studies: Thoughts on a Crisis of Identity." *Theology* 86 (1983): 193–201.

Long, Charles H. "A Common Ancestor: Theology and Religious Studies." In *Religious Studies, Theological Studies, and the University-Divinity School.* Edited by Joseph Kitagawa, 137–150. Atlanta: Scholars Press, 1992.

Long, Charles H. *Significations: Signs, Symbols, and Images in the Interpretation of Religion.* Philadelphia: Fortress Press, 1986.

Long, Charles H. "The Study of Religion in the United States of America: Its Past and Its Future." *Religious Studies and Theology* 5 (1985): 30–44.

Lott, Eric J. *Vision, Tradition, Interpretation: Theology, Religion, and the Study of Religion.* Berlin: Mouton, 1988.

Main, Alan, ed. *But Where Shall Wisdom Be Found? A Volume of Essays Relating Theology and University.* Aberdeen: Aberdeen University Press, 1995.

Markham, Ian. "Teaching Theology in a Modern University." *Theology* 94 (1991): 260–269.

Marsden, George M. *The Outrageous Idea of Christian Scholarship.* Oxford: Oxford University Press, 1997.

Marsden, George M. *The Soul of the American University: From Protestant Establishment to Established Nonbelief.* Oxford: Oxford University Press, 1994.

Marsden, George M., and Bradley J. Longfield, eds. *The Secularization of the Academy*. Oxford: Oxford University Press, 1992.

Martin, Luther H., and Donald Wiebe. "On Declaring WAR: A Critical Comment on the Academic Study of Religion in the United States." *Method and Theory in the Study of Religion* 5 (1993): 47–52.

Marty, Martin. "Committing the Study of Religion in Public." *Journal of the American Academy of Religion* 57 (1989): 1–22.

Martin, Richard C., ed. *Approaches to Islam in Religious Studies*. Tucson: University of Arizona Press, 1985.

May, William. "Why Theology and Religious Studies Need Each Other." *Journal of the American Academy of Religion* 52 (1984): 748–757.

McCutcheon, Russell T. "A Default of Critical Intelligence? The Scholar of Religion as Public Intellectual." *Journal of the American Academy of Religion* 65 (1997): 443–468.

McCutcheon, Russell T. *Critics Not Caretakers: Redescribing the Public Study of Religion*. Albany: State University of New York Press, 2001.

McCutcheon, Russell T. *Manufacturing Religion: The Discourse on Sui Generis Religion and the Politics of Nostalgia*. Oxford: Oxford University Press, 1997.

McCutcheon, Russell T. "Methodology and Theory within the IAHR: A Survey." *Council of Societies for the Study of Religion Bulletin* 24 (1995): 53–59.

McCutcheon, Russell T. "Naming the Unnameable? Theological Language and the Academic Study of Religion." *Method and Theory in the Study of Religion* 2 (1990): 213–229.

McCutcheon, Russell T., ed. *The Insider/Outsider Problem in the Study of Religion: A Reader*. New York: Cassell, 1999.

McLean, Milton D., ed. *Religious Studies in Public Universities*. Carbondale: Southern Illinois University, 1967.

Michaelsen, Robert. "Constitutions, Courts and the Study of Religion." *Journal of the American Academy of Religion* 45 (1977): 291–308.

Miller, Richard, Laurie L. Patton, and Stephen H. Webb. "Rhetoric, Pedagogy, and Study of Religions." *Journal of the American Academy of Religion* 62 (1994): 819–850.

Minor, Robert N., and Robert D. Baird. "Teaching About Religion at the State University: Seriously and Strictly." *Council of Societies for the Study of Religion Bulletin* 14 (1983): 69–72.

Molendijk, Arie L., and Peter Pels, eds. *Religion in the Making: The Emergence of the Sciences of Religion*. Leiden: Brill, 1998.

Murphy, Tim, ed. "Taking the Bull by the Tail: Responses to the *Lingua Franca* Article." *Council of Societies for the Study of Religion Bulletin* 26 (1997): 78–85.

Neusner, Jacob. "The Theological Enemies of Religious Studies: Theology and Secularism in the Trivialization and Personalization of Religion and the West." *Religion* 18 (1988): 21–35.

Neusner, Jacob. "Teaching Jewish Studies 'Under Gentile Auspices' versus the Academic Study of Religion, including Judaism: Response to Zachary Braiterman." *Religious Education* 95 (2000): 95–104.

Neville, Robert. "Religious Studies and Theological Studies." *Journal of the American Academy of Religion* 61 (1993): 185–200.

Newman, Elizabeth. "Beyond Faith Versus Knowledge: Religious Commitment in the Academy." *Perspectives in Religious Studies* 23 (1996): 405–423.

Nielsen, Niels. "The Advancement of Religion Versus Teaching about Religion in the Public Schools." *Journal of Church and State* 26 (1984): 105–116.

Nord, Warren A. *Religion and American Education: Rethinking a National Dilemma.* Chapel Hill: University of North Carolina Press, 1995.

Norman, Ralph V., and Gerald James Larson, eds. "The Santa Barbara Colloquy: Religion within the Limits of Reason Alone." *Soundings* 71 (1988): 171–420.

O'Connell, Laurence J. "Religious Studies, Theology, and the Humanities Curriculum." *Journal of the American Academy of Religion* 52 (1984): 731–737.

O'Connell, Laurence J. "Religious Studies, Theology, and the Undergraduate Curriculum." *Council of Societies for the Study of Religion Bulletin* 15 (1984): 143–146.

O'Connor, June. "The Scholar of Religion as Public Intellectual: Expanding Critical Intelligence." *Journal of the American Academy of Religion* 66 (1998): 897–909.

Ogden, Schubert M. "Religious Studies and Theological Studies: What Is Involved in the Distinction between Them?" *Council of Societies for the Study of Religion Bulletin* 24 (1995): 3–4.

Ogden, Schubert M. "Theology and Religious Studies: Their Difference and the Difference it Makes." *Journal of the American Academy of Religion* 46 (1978): 3–17.

Ogden, Schubert M. "Theology in the University." *Journal of the American Academy of Religion Thematic Studies* 48 (1981): 3–13.

Ogden, Schubert M. "Theology in the University: The Question of Integrity." In *Theology and the University: Essays in Honor of John B. Cobb, Jr.* Edited by David R. Griffin and Joseph C. Hough, Jr., 67–80. Albany: State University of New York Press, 1991.

Ostovich, Steven T. "Theology in the Postmodern University: Reflections from Political Philosophy and Theology." In *Theology and the University.* Edited by John Apczynski, 179–192. Lanham, Maryland: University Press of America, 1990.

Pannenberg, Wolfhart. "The Task of Systematic Theology in the Contemporary University." In *Theology and the University: Essays in Honor of John B. Cobb, Jr.* Edited by David R. Griffin and Joseph C. Hough, Jr., 81–93. Albany: State University of New York Press, 1991.

Patton, Kimberly. "'Stumbling Along between the Immensities': Reflections on Teaching in the Study of Religion." *Journal of the American Academy of Religion* 65 (1997): 831–849.

Penner, Hans H. "Criticism and the Development of a Science of Religion." *Studies in Religion/Sciences religieuses* 15 (1986): 165–175.

Penner, Hans H. *Impasse and Resolution: A Critique of the Study of Religion.* New York: Peter Lang, 1989.

Penner, Hans H., and Edward Yonan. "Is a Science of Religion Possible?" *Journal of Religion* 52 (1972): 107–133.

Preus, James Samuel. *Explaining Religion: Criticism and Theory from Bodin to Freud.* New Haven: Yale University Press, 1987.

Pye, Michael, ed. *Marburg Revisited: Institutions and Strategies in the Study of Religion.* Marburg: Diagonal-Verlag, 1989.

Ramsey, Paul, and John F. Wilson, eds. *The Study of Religion in Colleges and Universities.* Princeton: Princeton University Press, 1970.

Readings, Bill. *The University in Ruins.* Cambridge: Harvard University Press, 1996.

Reynolds, Frank E., and Sheryl L. Burkhalter, eds. *Beyond the Classics? Essays in Religious Studies and Liberal Education.* Atlanta: Scholars Press, 1990.

Segal, Robert A. *Explaining and Interpreting Religion: Essays on the Issue.* New York: Peter Lang, 1992.

Segal, Robert A. "How Historical is the History of Religions?" *Method and Theory in the Study of Religion* 1 (1989): 2–19.

Segal, Robert A. "In Defense of Reductionism." *Journal of the American Academy of Religion* 51 (1983): 97–124.

Segal, Robert A. *Religion and the Social Sciences: Essays on the Confrontation.* Atlanta: Scholars Press, 1989.

Segal, Robert A., and Donald Wiebe. "Axioms and Dogmas in the Study of Religion." *Journal of the American Academy of Religion* 57 (1989): 591–605.

Sharma, Arvind. "On the Distinction Between Religious Studies and Theological Studies." *Council of Societies for the Study of Religion Bulletin* 26 (1997): 50–51.

Sharma, Arvind, ed. *The Sum of our Choices: Essays in Honour of Eric J. Sharpe.* Atlanta: Scholars Press, 1996

Sharpe, Eric J. *Comparative Religion: A History.* 2nd ed. La Salle, Illinois: Open Court, 1986.

Sharpe, Eric J. "Religious Studies, the Humanities, and the History of Ideas." *Soundings* 71 (1988): 245–258.

Sharpe, Eric J. "The Compatibility of Theological and Religious Studies: Historical, Theoretical, and Contemporary Perspectives." *Council of Societies for the Study of Religion Bulletin* 26 (1997): 52–60.

Shepard, Robert Stephen. *God's People in the Ivory Tower: Religion in the Early American University.* Brooklyn: Carlson, 1991.

Sloan, Douglas. *Faith and Knowledge: Mainline Protestantism and American Higher Education.* Louisville, Kentucky: Westminster/John Knox Press, 1994.

Smart, Ninian. "Concluding Reflections: Religious Studies in Global Perspective." In *Turning Points in Religious Studies: Essays in Honour of Geoffrey Parrinder.* Edited by Ursula King, 299–306. Edinburgh: T & T Clark, 1990.

Smart, Ninian. "Religious Studies and Theology." *Council of Societies for the Study of Religion Bulletin* 26 (1997): 66–68.

Smart, Ninian. "Some Thoughts on the Science of Religion." In *The Sum of our Choices: Essays in Honour of Eric J. Sharpe*. Edited by Arvind Sharma, 15–25. Atlanta: Scholars Press, 1996.

Smith, Jonathan Z. "Are Theological and Religious Studies Compatible?" *Council of Societies for the Study of Religion Bulletin* 26 (1997): 60–61.

Smith, Jonathan Z. "'Religion' and 'Religious Studies': No Difference At All." *Soundings* 71 (1988): 231–244.

Smith, Page. *Killing the Spirit: Higher Education in America*. New York: Viking, 1990.

Smith, Wilfred Cantwell. "Comparative Religion: Whither and Why." In *The History of Religions: Essays in Methodology*. Edited by Mircea Eliade and Joseph M. Kitagawa, 31–58. Chicago: University of Chicago Press, 1959.

Smith, Wilfred Cantwell. "The Academic Study of Religion: The Challenge of the World Parliament of Religions." *Religious Studies and Theology* 13–14 (1995): 5–11.

Smith, Wilfred Cantwell. "The Modern West in the History of Religion." *Journal of the American Academy of Religion* 52 (1984): 3–18.

Smith, Wilfred Cantwell. "Theology and the Academic Study of Religion." *Iliff Review* 44 (1987): 9–18.

Strenski, Ivan. "Our Very Own 'Contras': A Response to the 'St. Louis Project' Report." *Journal of the American Academy of Religion* 54 (1986): 323–335.

Strenski, Ivan. "Reduction without Tears." In *Religion and Reductionism: Essays on Eliade, Segal, and the Challenge of the Social Sciences for the Study of Religion*. Edited by Thomas A. Idinopulos and Edward A. Yonan, 95–107. Leiden: E. J. Brill, 1994.

Tanner, Kathryn. "Public Theology and the Character of Public Debate." *Annual of the Society of Christian Ethics* 1996, 79–101.

Tanner, Kathryn. *Theories of Culture: A New Agenda for Theology*. Minneapolis: Fortress Press, 1997.

Taves, Ann. *Fits, Trances and Visions: Experiencing Religion and Explaining Experience from Wesley to James*. Princeton: Princeton Univesity Press, 1999.

Thistlethwaite, Susan. "Settled Issues and Neglected Questions: How Is Religion To Be Studied?" *Journal of the American Academy of Religion* 62 (1994): 1037–1045.

Toulmin, Stephen. "Theology in the Context of the University." *Theological Education* 26 (1990): 51–56.

Vries, Jan de. *The Study of Religion: A Historical Approach*. Translated with an Introduction by Kees W. Bolle. New York: Harcourt, Brace & World, 1967.

Waardenburg, Jean Jacques. *Classical Approaches to the Study of Religion: Aims, Methods and Theories of Research*. The Hague: Mouton, 1974.

Waardenburg, Jean Jacques. *Reflections on the Study of Religion*. The Hague: Mouton, 1978.

Wach, Joachim. *The Comparative Study of Religions*. Edited with an Introduction by Joseph M. Kitagawa. New York: Columbia University Press, 1958.

Wainwright, William, ed. *God, Philosophy, and Academic Culture: A Discussion Between Scholars in the AAR and the APA*. Atlanta: Scholars Press, 1996.

Ward, Keith. "Theology in a University Context." *Scottish Journal of Theology* 24 (1971): 290–304.

Wasserstrom, Steven M. *Religion After Religion: Gershom Scholem, Mircea Eliade and Henry Corbin at Eranos.* Princeton: Princeton University Press, 1999.

Welch, Claude. *Religion in the Undergraduate Curriculum: An Analysis and Interpretation.* Washington: Association of American Colleges, 1972.

Whaling, Frank, ed. *Contemporary Approaches to the Study of Religion.* New York: Mouton, 1985.

Wheeler, Barbara G., and Edward Farley, eds. *Shifting Boundaries: Contextual Approaches to the Structure of Theological Education.* Louisville, Kentucky: Westminster/John Knox Press, 1991.

Wiebe, Donald. "A Religious Agenda Continued: A Review of the Presidential Addresses of the American Academy of Religion." *Method and Theory in the Study of Religion* 9 (1997): 353–375.

Wiebe, Donald. "Beyond the Sceptic and the Devotee: Reductionism in the Scientific Study of Religion." *Journal of the American Academy of Religion* 52 (1984): 157–165.

Wiebe, Donald. *Religion and Truth: Towards an Alternative Paradigm for the Study of Religion.* The Hague: Mouton Publishers, 1981.

Wiebe, Donald. "The 'Academic Naturalization' of Religious Studies: Intent or Pretence?" *Studies in Religion/Sciences religieuses* 15 (1986): 197–203.

Wiebe, Donald. "The Failure of Nerve in the Academic Study of Religion." *Studies in Religion/Sciences religieuses* 13 (1984): 401–422.

Wiebe, Donald. *The Irony of Theology and the Nature of Religious Thought.* Montreal: McGill-Queen's University Press, 1991.

Wiebe, Donald. *The Politics of Religious Studies: The Continuing Conflict with Theology in the Academy.* Basingstoke, England: Macmillan, 1999.

Wiebe, Donald. "Theology and the Academic Study of Religion in the United States." In *India and Beyond: Aspects of Literature, Meaning, Ritual and Thought.* Edited by Dick van der Meij, 651–675. New York: Columbia University Press, 1997.

Wiebe, Donald. "Toward Founding a Science of Religion." In *The Sum of our Choices: Essays in Honour of Eric J. Sharpe.* Edited by Arvind Sharma, 26–49. Atlanta: Scholars Press, 1996.

Wiebe, Donald. "Why the Academic Study of Religion? Motive and Method in the Study of Religion." *Religious Studies* 24 (1988): 403–413.

Wiebe, Paul G. "The Place of Theology within Religious Studies." In *The Academic Study of Religion.* Edited by Anne Carr, 17–25. Atlanta: Scholars Press, 1975.

Wiggins, James. "The Study of Religion in Higher Education: An Overview." *Religion and Public Education* 18 (1991): 201–211.

Wilson, John E. "Religious Studies and Theology." *American Theological Library Association: Summary of Proceedings* 48 (1994): 175–180.

Wolterstorff, Nicholas P. "The Travail of Theology in the Modern Academy." In *The Future of Theology: Essays in Honor of Jurgen Moltmann*. Edited by Miroslav Volf, Carmen Krieg, and Thomas Kucharz, 35–46. Grand Rapids, Michigan: Eerdmans, 1996.

This bibliography was compiled with the research assistance of Deborah Creamer, a doctoral candidate in the Joint Ph.D. Program at Iliff School of Theology and the University of Denver.

Contributors

DELWIN BROWN is the Harvey H. Potthoff Professor of Christian Theology at Iliff School of Theology. Prior to his appointment at Iliff, Brown taught at Arizona State University. His books include *To Set At Liberty: Christian Faith and Human Freedom*; *Boundaries of Our Habitations: Tradition and Theological Construction*, and *Converging on Culture: Theologians in Dialogue with Cultural Analysis and Criticism*, a volume coedited with Sheila Greeve Davaney and Kathryn Tanner.

LINELL E. CADY is Professor of Religious Studies at Arizona State University, where she has served as Chair of the Religious Studies Department and as Associate Dean and Interim Dean of the College of Liberal Arts and Sciences. Cady has published extensively on theological method, feminist theology, theology and cultural theory, and in particular on the study of religion as it relates to the public/private boundary in American culture. Her most extended discussion of this latter topic is *Religion, Theology, and American Public Life*.

CHRISTOPHER CHESNEK is a doctoral student in the Ph.D. program in Religious Studies at the University of California, Santa Barbara. He received his B.A. and M.A. degrees in Religious Studies from Arizona State University. His research interests include religion in America, the history of cultural contact between Native Americans and Euro-Americans, and method and theory in the academic study of religion.

PAULA M. COOEY is the Margaret W. Harmon Professor of Christianity and Culture at Macalester College. She received her Ph.D. in the Study of Religion from Harvard University. Prior to her recent move to Macalester College, she taught in the Department of Religion at Trinity University. Her most recent books are *Family, Freedom and Faith: Building Community Today* and *Religious Imagination and the Body: A Feminist Perspective*.

SHEILA GREEVE DAVANEY is Professor of Modern Theology at Iliff School of Theology. Her most recent book is *Pragmatic Historicism: A Theology for the Twenty-First*

225

Century. She is coeditor of *Converging on Culture: Theologians in Dialogue with Cultural Analysis and Criticism* (with Delwin Brown and Kathryn Tanner), *Horizons in Feminist Theology: Identity, Tradition, and Norms* (with Rebecca Chopp), and *Changing Conversations: Cultural Analysis and Religious Reflection* (with Dwight Hopkins).

DARRELL J. FASCHING holds a Ph.D. from Syracuse University and is currently Professor of Religious Studies at the University of South Florida in Tampa. He is the author of *The Thought of Jacques Ellul; Narrative Theology After Auschwitz: From Alienation to Ethics; The Ethical Challenge of Auschwitz and Hiroshima; The Coming of the Millennium*, and the coauthor (with Dell de Chant) of *Comparative Religious Ethics: A Narrative Approach.*

SAM GILL is Professor of Religious Studies at the University of Colorado, and owner/director of Bantaba World Dance and Music, a studio and school in Boulder. Gill has published numerous articles and essays and nine books, most recently *Storytracking: Texts, Stories, and Histories in Central Australia; Dictionary of Native American Mythology* (with Irene Sullivan); *Mother Earth: An American Story*, and *Native American Religious Action: A Performance Approach to Religion.*

WILLIAM D. HART is Associate Professor of Religion at the University of North Carolina, Greensboro. He received a B.A. in History and Politics from the University of Arizona, M.A. in Religious Studies from Arizona State University, and a Ph.D. in Religion from Princeton University. His research interests focus on religion, cultural theory, and critique. He has recently published *Edward Said and the Religious Effects of Culture.*

RICHARD C. MARTIN is Professor of History of Religions and Islamic Studies at Emory University. He has written several articles and books on Islamic thought, most recently *Defenders of Reason in Islam: Mu'tazilism from Medieval School to Modern Symbol* (with Mark Woodward), and he is coeditor (with John Witte, Jr.) of *Sharing the Book: Religious Perspectives on the Rights and Wrongs of Mission.* Martin is editor-in-chief of the forthcoming Macmillan Encyclopedia of Islam and the Muslim World.

RUSSELL T. MCCUTCHEON is Associate Professor and Chair of the Department of Religious Studies at the University of Alabama. He is the author of *Manufacturing Religion: The Discourse on Sui Generis Religion and the Politics of Nostalgia* and *Critics Not Caretakers: Redescribing the Public Study of Religion.* He edited *The Insider/Outsider Problem in the Study of Religion*, and coedited *Guide to the Study of Religion.* He also edits the *Bulletin of the Council of Societies for the Study of Religion.*

IVAN STRENSKI is the Holstein Family and Community Professor of Religious Studies at the University of California, Riverside. He is the author of numerous articles and six books. His recent books deal with the interrelations of Durkheimian thought and French religious traditions. These are *Durkheim and the Jews of France*, and, forthcoming, *Contesting Sacrifice: Religion, Nationalism and Social Thought in France,* and *"Theology" and the First Theory of Sacrifice*. He is North American editor of *Religion*.

KATHRYN TANNER is Professor of Theology at the Divinity School, University of Chicago. She is the author of *Theories of Culture: A New Agenda for Theology; God and Creation in Christian Theology; The Politics of God;* and *Jesus, Humanity and the Trinity: A Brief Systematic Theology*.

FREDERICK L. WARE earned a B.A. and M.A. in philosophy at the University of Memphis, and an M.Div. and Ph.D. at Vanderbilt University. Ware, a pastor in the Church of God in Christ, is Adjunct Assistant Professor of African American Studies at Memphis Theological Seminary and author of *Methodologies of Black Theology*. His research interests include Black Theology, philosophical theology, and religion and culture.

Index

Academic study of religion, 101–2; emphasis of religious studies, 32; as irreducibly religious, 48; liminal nature of, 46; religious dimensions of, 50. *See also* religious studies

Academic Theology, 28n.11, 38, 39–43, 127–28, 178–79; definition and characteristics of, 91–92, 106, 131, 138, 161; evaluation of, 41–43, 139n.3, 179–81; goals and contributions of, 135–36, 138, 150–52, 176; history of, 129–32; as an intellectual discipline, 120–21, 181–83; methodology of, 199; and religion, 42, 131, 133–34, 179, 202; and religious studies, 122; and the university, 40. *See also* theology

Academy, 135; as a cultural reality, 148, 174; and democratization, 173; and objectivity, 82; religious concerns of, 201; as a theological project, 91–92. *See also* university

African American scholars, 190. *See also* Black theology

Alienation, 167; and theology, 167–68

Allen, Charlotte, 1–2, 28n.8, 99

Alton, Bruce, 60–61

American Academy of Religion (AAR), 5, 71, 115, 149

Anthropological study of religion, 17–19, 97

Anthropology of credibility, 17, 26

Aquinas, Thomas, 41, 94, 130

Asad, Talal, 112

Augustine, 170n.8

Australia, aboriginal life, 84–90; and education, 85; and European influences, 86–87; and missionaries, 85–86; and ontology, 84; and scholars of, 86–91

Autonomy, 164

Barth, Karl, 33–36

Berger, Peter, 45–46

Black theology, 187–96; liberationist perspective, 189–90; as public, 187–89; relationship to religious studies, 189–96; and religious studies, 194–95. *See also* theology

Body, and the academy, 81; and history, 84; and learning, 88–89; and objectivity, 82; and ritual, 81; and scholarship, 90–91

Brown, Delwin, 28n.11, 32–33, 37–39

Brown, Karen McCarthy, 152

Buddhism, 35–36, 159–60; Tibetan, 113–14

Burkert, Walter, 16

Cady, Linell E., 146

Candide (Voltaire), 23–24

Capitalism, 204, 211n.10

Capps, Walter, 31, 82

Casanova, José, 146

Certeau, Michel de, 17

Chicago School, 100, 104, 108n.13

Chidester, David, 50, 118, 146

Church, relationship to university, 101; and theology, 122, 199, 202

Church and state, separation of, 57, 82, 98, 111–12, 128, 143

229